Successful Software Reengineering

Sal Valenti
University of Ancona, Italy

D1444831

IRM Press
Publisher of innovative scholarly and professional
information technology titles in the cyberage

Hershey • London • Melbourne • Singapore • Beijing

Acquisitions Editor: Mehdi Khosrow-Pour
Managing Editor: Jan Travers
Assistant Managing Editor: Amanda Appicello
Copy Editor: Amanda Appicello
Cover Design: Tedi Wingard
Printed at: Integrated Book Technology

Published in the United States of America by
      IRM Press
      1331 E. Chocolate Avenue
      Hershey PA 17033-1117
      Tel: 717-533-8845
      Fax: 717-533-8661
      E-mail: cust@idea-group.com
      Web site: http://www.irm-press.com

and in the United Kingdom by
      IRM Press
      3 Henrietta Street
      Covent Garden
      London WC2E 8LU
      Tel: 44 20 7240 0856
      Fax: 44 20 7379 3313
      Web site: http://www.eurospan.co.uk

Library of Congress Cataloguing-in-Publication Data

Successful software reengineering / [edited by] Sal Valenti.
      p. cm.
   Includes bibliographical references and index.
   ISBN 1-931777-12-8 (paper)
      1. Software reengineering. 2. Computer software--Development. I. Valenti, Sal, 1956-

QA76.758 .S83 2002
005.1--dc21   2002017311

eISBN: 1-931777-33-0

British Cataloguing-in-Publication Data
A Cataloguing-in-Publication record for this book is available from the British Library.

Other New Releases from IRM Press

Successful Software Reengineering

Table of Contents

Foreword

The reengineering of legacy systems is widely recognized as one of the most significant challenges to be faced by the software engineering community.

A legacy system is a technically obsolescent component of the infrastructure of a content management environment (Omnibus Lexicon Definition, http://www.fourthwavegroup.com/Publicx/1301w.htm). Legacy systems embody substantial corporate knowledge including requirements, design decisions and business rules. Databases, application programs and all of the other forms of hardware and software typically owned by companies, including mainframes, personal computers, terminals, networks and operating systems, constitute them.

Although the functionality delivered by a legacy system may be available from more modern technology, a migration to newer systems may be deterred by the possibility of service disruption during upgrading, or by the perceived difficulty in converting legacy content to new models and formats.

The need for reengineering legacy systems is thus implicitly contained in the definition given above, and is motivated by the desire to utilize more cost effective hardware or software platforms, to reduce the costs of maintenance (as the Y2K problem has taught) or to add significant new functionalities. The problem is widespread since it effects all kinds of organizations; failing to face it may hamper an organization's attempts to remain competitive if not threaten its very existence on the market. Finally, it is a problem that may persist over time, as there seems to be no good reason for being confident that systems currently under development will not be tomorrow's legacy systems.

Among the possible aspects that need to be taken into account while reengineering a legacy system, the software perspective represents the focal issue (and in fact reengineering is often treated as a synonym of software reengineering).

As with many new and evolving fields of research, the scientific community has yet to agree on a common taxonomy of terms with respect to software reengineering. In fact, although in 1992 the Joint Logistic Commanders Computer Resources Management group (JLC/CRM) authorized and sponsored a DoD policy workshop aimed to formally define a software reengineering terminology. As of today, there is not even an agreement upon the spelling of reengineering (the most common being "re-engineering" and "reengineering"). Therefore, it is important to provide some basic definitions of the domain, in order to gain a common understanding of the terms and the keywords that will be used throughout this volume.

Software Reengineering may be defined as "the examination and the alteration of an existing subject system to reconstitute it in a new form." On the other hand, it may also be defined as "the process of modifying the internal mechanisms of a system or program or the data structures of a system or program without changing its functionalities." Whichever definition is adopted, the primary goal of software reengineering is to attain new levels of efficiency of the existing assets, without recurring to the development of new systems. Therefore, an important aspect that needs to be further explored is to define the extent to which reengineering is helpful and to identify some metrics, if any, that can be used to decide whether the option of rebuilding from scratch should be followed.

Regardless, all of the researchers in the field seem to agree on the fact that the process of software reengineering encompasses a combination of sub-processes such as code-reengineering, restructuring, redocumentation, retargeting, reverse and forward engineering. Some of these sub-processes are aimed at program understanding, as for instance restructuring, redocumentation and reverse engineering. The others are geared towards evolution, as for instance, code reengineering, retargeting, forward engineering.

Thus software reengineering may imply, among many other tasks, restructuring "spaghetti-like" code (code-reengineering); transforming the system representation from one form to another at the same relative level of abstraction, while preserving the external functional behavior (restructuring); producing support documentation and reformatting the systems' source code listings (redocumentation); transporting and hosting or porting the existing system to a new configuration (retargeting); understanding, analyzing and abstracting the system to a new form at a higher abstraction level (reverse engineering), generating new source code from design information captured via previous reverse engineering activities (forward engineering).

These are just some of the topics that will be covered by the research contributions contained in this volume: a useful starting point for anyone interested in getting a deeper insight on software reengineering tools and techniques.

I would like to dedicate this book to my parents.

Sal Valenti
Università di Ancona, Italy,
September 18, 2001

Preface

Software Engineering, software development and software reuse are important issues to all organizations. Getting the most out of software packages by ensuring effective development, testing and use can save money and improve business practices. As the implications become more widespread, researchers, practitioners, academicians and information systems managers alike need to have access to the most up-to-date research and practice in software engineering and development. The chapters in this book address the timely topics of auditing software engineering processes, enterprise resource planning and software reuse and other relevant applications and technologies. From academics reporting research findings to developers reporting on best practices, the authors of these chapters are from diverse cultural and industry backgrounds and provide insights from their varied experiences.

Chapter 1 entitled, "Computer Aided Method Engineering" by Ajantha Dahanayake of Delft University of Technology (The Netherlands) discusses a conceptual model to specify the functionality of a support environment. The chapter first presents a review of basic concepts and approaches for deriving models for computer aided Software Engineering (CASE) environments. The chapter then offers an informal description of service component concepts used to derive a generic framework. Finally, the chapter outlines a configuration of service components to support computer aided method engineering (CAME).

Chapter 2 entitled, "Architecture and Implementation Issues" by Ajantha Dahanayake of Delft University of Technology (The Netherlands) concentrates on using a representation formalism to construct a problem specific CAME environment. Such an automated support environment must be provided for the information systems design state in particular for the required UpperCASE tools according to the methods chosen for the problem specific environment.

Chapter 3 entitled, "Future Directions in CASE Repositories" by Ajantha Dahanayake of Delft University of Technology (The Netherlands) reports on how CAME environments provide a fully flexible environment for method specification and integration and can be used for information systems design activities. The chapter then discusses how this theory can lead to the design of the architecture of such an environment.

Chapter 4 entitled, "Audit of a CASE Environment" by Mario Piattini of the Universidad de Castilla-La Mancha and Jesús García Tomás of Universidad Politecnica de Madrid (Spain) addresses the questions that must be answered when auditing a CASE environment. The chapter reflects upon themes that have been dealt with in the literature from the perspective of an information systems audit. The authors introduce the basic concepts of an information systems audit and analyze the risks that need to be addressed when installing a CASE tool.

Chapter 5 entitled, "Process Model for Round-trip Engineering with Relational Database" by Leszek A. Maciaszek of Macquarie University (Australia) identifies difficult round-trip scenarios and defines the processes needed to handle those scenarios. The processes conform to the current state-of-the practice in forward and revere engineering. The chapter then discusses the limitations of a tool-driven round-trip engineering.

Chapter 6 entitled, "Achieving Effective Software Reuse for Business Systems" by Daniel Brandon, Jr. of Christian Brothers University (USA) reports on software reuse including discussions of both literature research and design/coding research. The chapter further presents an approach for software reuse in the development of business systems. The approach discussed in the chapter is based on object-oriented technology and provides for both the specification and enforcement of software reuse and corporate standards.

Chapter 7 entitled, "The Future of Software Development" by Karen Church and Geoff te Braake of Port Elizabeth Technikon (South Africa) discusses the results of two surveys as they illustrate the trends in software development. The authors look at the history of software development and its evolution. The authors discuss the evolution of programming languages, coding styles and software architecture. It further looks at the growing importance of user interfaces and describes future trends.

Chapter 8 entitled, "Understanding the Role of Use Case in UML: A Review and Research Agenda" by Brian Dobing of the University of Lethbridge and Jeffrey Parsons of Memorial University of New Foundland (Canada) focuses on two components of UML: use cases and class models. The authors consider the appropriateness of use cases as a component of an object-oriented modeling language by examining their role as a tool for communicating with users. The authors further consider the relationship between use cases and the class models that are developed from them. Finally, the authors offer a framework for empirical research to evaluate the value of use cases and their relationship to class models in UML.

Chapter 9 entitled, "Enhancing a Rigorous Reuse Process with Natural Language Requirement Specifications" by L. Felice, C. Leonardi, L. Favre and V.

Mauco of the Universidad Nacional del Centro de la Pcia. de Buenos Aires (Argentina) proposes a systematic reuse approach that integrates natural language requirement specifications with formal specifications in RAISE Specification Language. It addresses the problems associated with reusability techniques, discusses the reusability process and provides a concrete example of the principles discussed.

Chapter 10 entitled, "Extended Spatiotemporal UML: Motivations, Requirements, and Constructs" by Rosanne Price of Monash University (Australia), Nectaria Tryfona and Christian Jensen of Aalborg University (Denmark) presents a conceptual modeling language for spatiotemporal applications that offers built-in support for capturing spatially referenced, time-varying information. Specifically, the well-known object-oriented unified modeling language is extended to capture the semantics of spatiotemporal data. The chapter gives examples to illustrate the simplicity and flexibility of this approach.

Chapter 11 entitled, "A Design Method for Real-Time Object-Oriented Systems Using Communicating Real Time State Machines by Eduardo B. Fernandez, Jie Wu and Debera R. Hancock of Florida Atlantic University (USA) proposes an object-oriented analysis and design methodology that augments the traditional Unified Modeling Language dynamic model with real-time extensions based on high-level parallel machines and communication notations from Communicating Real-Time State Machines. The chapter also provides an example of the proposed methodology as it applies to an automated passenger train system.

Chapter 12 entitled, "Java Integrated Development Environments' Support for Reuse-Oriented Software Development" by Jenni Ristonmaa, Jarmo Ahonen and Marko Forsell of the University of Jyväskylä (Finland) reports on the authors' study of three Java IDEs and how they support reuse-oriented software development. The authors derived the evaluation criteria from a known reuse model. They conclude that current Java IDEs need to improve their support for the reuse process.

Chapter 13 entitled, "Information Modeling and Method Engineering: A Psychological Perspective" by Keng Siau of the University of Nebraska-Lincoln (USA) proposes the use of cognitive psychology as a reference discipline for information modeling and method engineering. The chapter reviews theories in cognitive psychology and applies them to information modeling and method engineering.

Chapter 14 entitled, "Load-Testing of Web Site Applications: Analysis and Recommendations" by Vijay Raghavan of Northern Kentucky University (USA) discusses the need and benefits of load testing. The author provides criteria for developing a metrics program for load testing Web site applications. Finally, the chapter concludes that it is critical for organizations deploying Web sites to develop a load-testing plan that includes all aspects of site development.

Chapter 15 entitled, "Component-Based ERP Design in a Distributed Object Environment" by Bonn-Oh Kim of Seattle University and Ted Lee of Memphis State University (USA) outlines strategic steps needed to wield a dominant power in the future Enterprise Resource Planning (ERP) market. The steps discussed are: knowledge modeling, componentization of domain knowledge, implementation of componentized domain knowledge, and marketing strategies for domain knowledge components.

Chapter 16 entitled, "Knowledge and Object-Oriented Approach for Interoperability of Heterogeneous Information Management Systems" by Chin-Wan Chung and Chang-Ryong Kim of the Korea Advanced Institute of Science and Technology (Korea) and Son Dao of Hughes Research Laboratory (USA) incorporates concepts and constructs associated with the knowledge and object-oriented paradigms with abstract views, procedures, encapsulation, inheritance and class composition hierarchies to resolve problems

Chapter 17 entitled, "A Recursive Approach to Software Development" by Shirley Becker of the Florida Institute of Technology and Alan Jorgensen of Advanced Engineering Technology (USA) proposes that a recursive software development process be used as a means of managing the complexity of today's software systems. The authors advocate that the recursive approach has the flexibility needed to perform development activities in any order to ensure that systems requirements are met.

Chapter 18 entitled, "Adding Alternative Access Paths to Abstract Data Types" by Xavier Franch and Jordi Marco of the Universitat Politecnica de Catalunya (Spain) presents a proposal for developing efficient programs in the abstract data type programming framework, keeping the modular structure of programs and without violating the information hiding principle. The proposal focuses in the concept of shortcut as an efficient way of accessing data, an alternative to using primitive operations of ADT.

Chapter 19 entitled, "Relational Data Modeling for Geographic Information Systems" by Lawrence West, Jr. of the University of Central Florida and Brian Mennecke of East Carolina University (USA) addresses data modeling problems inherent in the use of geographic information systems that are not adequately covered by traditional modeling techniques. This chapter proposes relational modeling techniques that document organizational data integrity rules when systems that include spatial data are developed for more widespread use.

Chapter 20 entitled, "Software Process Models are Software Too: A Domain Class Model for Software Process Models" by Daniel Turk of Colorado State University and Vijay Vaishnavi of Georgia State University (USA) focuses on the domain class model as an example of one type of model that could be produced if an approach such as the Unified Process were used in the process modeling domain. While identifying the conceptual needs of process modeling systems, these models leave open the choice of how to formalize and implement actual solutions. The authors develop a domain class model for process models as an example.

Chapter 21 entitled, "A Process Model for Certification of Product and Process" by Hareton Leung and Vincent Li of Hong Kong Polytechnic University (Hong Kong) identifies two process models, one for process certification and another for product certification. The authors then propose a certification process for Commercial Off the Shelf (COTS) product and its development process. Finally, the authors develop a model of certification process for both product certification and development process certification.

As businesses seek to improve their use of software, the chapters in this book will provide insightful theoretical discussion as well as practical examples and case studies illustrating the concepts discussed. Researchers, academician, students, or software engineers will find the information contained herein invaluable as a starting point or a supplement to their research and practice. From how to improve reuse techniques to how to more efficiently develop and use models, this book contains practical and theoretical information which is essential to those seeking to fully understand the emerging field of software engineering.

IRM Press
January 2002

Chapter 1

Computer Aided Method Engineering

Ajantha Dahanayake
Delft University of Technology, The Netherlands

The relationship between information systems development methods, organizational information systems engineering requirements, and the advantage of flexible automated support environments is presented. CASE technology is presented as a possible solution to provide flexible automated support. In this chapter the major topic is a conceptual model to specify the functionality of a support environment. First a review of a number of basic concepts and approaches for deriving models for CASE environments are given. An informal description of service component concepts used to derive a generic framework is presented. Further, a configuration of service components, to support Computer Aided Method Engineering (CAME), is outlined.

MODELS OF SUPPORT ENVIRONMENTS

There are a number of approaches attempting to develop a better understanding of CASE technology to support information modeling. Some of these will be discussed below to formulate the rationale behind the approach adopted in this book.

Models Based on Integration Issues

Integration issues are discussed in Wasserman (1990), Brown et al., (1992), and Wallnau et al. (1991), from the viewpoint that integration can be thought of as a set of characteristics of a CASE environment. These charac-

Previously published in *Computer-Aided Method Engineering: Designing CASE Repositories for the 21st Century*, edited by Ajantha Dahanayake. Copyright © 2001, Idea Group Publishing.

teristics are seen as independent dimensions, namely data integration, control integration, and presentation integration, along with which integration issues can be examined.

Subsequently, the data, control, and presentation dimensions have been expanded by adding platform and process integration dimensions (Zarrella, 1990). Platform integration refers to the technical capability of tools that execute on different hardware and system software platforms to interoperate effectively. Process integration refers to the ability of a CASE tool to represent and support the development process. This dimensional view of tool integration is further enhanced by distinguishing between integration of tools with a platform and integration of tools with a process. Tool-process integration is subdivided into life-cycle processes and development processes. Platform and process integration is seen as orthogonal to data, control, and presentation integration (Thomas et al., 1992). This multidimensional view of integration is somewhat problematic. It is not clear what is meant by: "the dimensions are orthogonal" and whether they can, or should be considered separately.

An approach discussed in Thomas et. al. (1992) treats integration not as a property of a component, but rather as a property of a relationship between components. Goals are defined for the properties of each relationship such as the relationship between a tool and a framework a tool and a development process, and among tools. A framework is the platform where the tools operate according to this interpretation; this framework is similar to the NIST/ECMA reference framework (Brown et al., 1992).

Although this view is useful to highlight integration issues as being distinct environment characteristics in their own right, it has its own limitations. The integration relationships are expressed as goals, which an environment may achieve. Unfortunately, there is no discussion about how to achieve these goals, what dependencies there are between them, and what trade-offs have to be made. This approach is helpful to consider the potential relationships between every pair of tools in the environment; but there is little direction to addressing the environment as a whole.

Repository Based Models

A view focused on a central repository as a key mechanism for data integration in CASE environment is preferred by many. This has formed the basis of several efforts to develop environments. There are a number of CASE environments offering repository-based models, for example, PCTE (Portable Common Tool Environment) and its object management service (European Computer Manufactures Association, 1990). Some other examples are proprietary tools, such as IEW and IEF (Staring, 1989), object management

Figure 1. Four conceptual levels of a CASE repository that are important for providing a flexible andextendable mechanism for integration

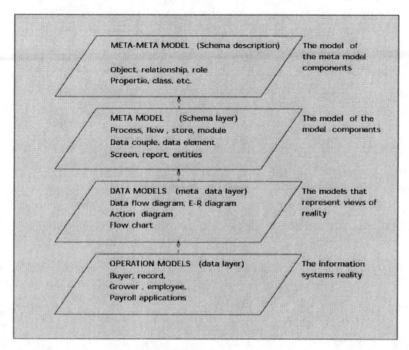

workbench, software through pictures (Wasserman, 1990), research based Daida (Jarke et al., 1992), and Ithaca (Mey et al., 1993). There is a belief that a repository of some sort at the heart of a CASE environment should be the primary means of tool integration (Welke, 1988).

A data storage mechanism, an interface to persistent data, a set of schemata, an information model, and a concept of operations to manipulate the data characterize a repository. The description of the stored data, called a schema, is the main concept that makes it different from a database. A schema typically records information about the different types of data in the repository and how these data are interrelated. The schema itself will be stored somewhere, often together with the instance data and will require an interface to access it, often the same interface as the instance data. The schema information may be specific to a particular application domain or may be more general to a wide set of domains. As a description of all the data stored in the repository, the schema has an important role to play. In effect, a representation of the schema acts as the definition of the data stored in the repository, explaining the design of the data structures. The schema can be used as the basis for determining access. The ability of the schema as a representation of a real-world application domain is critical to the success of the repository. Figure 1 gives the definitions following this explanation of Welke (1989).

Current MetaCASE tools based on repository models enable modification of diagram elements and associated storage and manipulation functionality. Modification of advanced aspects such as consistency verification, diagram technique definition according to the requirements of an arbitrary technique, and generation or model execution is still non-existent. Practice has been based on providing method component libraries, method reuse, and runtime adaptability. The existence of a schema, or a meta model within an environment, is itself not adequate, even though meta model integration leads to increased flexibility (Verhoef, 1993; Dahanayake, 1997). There are many issues that need to be resolved. These issues fall into two main categories: syntax issues, e.g. naming, notation, convention; and semantic issues, e.g. what is stored, where is it stored, and what does it mean?

There have been a number of attempts at schema level to define generic models that can be used as the basis for semantic agreements between tools across an application domain. A great deal of research is taking place in this area, with "enterprise modeling and integration" being the phrase that unites much of this work. To date, none of these generic schemata have achieved wide success, although the IBM AD/Cycle Information Model (IBM, 1989) and ISO Information Resource Dictionary Systems (IRDS) (ISD/IEC, 1990) represent extensive efforts in this area.

Frameworks

A generic framework for CASE environments with all types of integration are presented in Brown et al. (1994), combined with the NIST/ECMA Frameworks Reference Model (Brown et al., 1992) in a coherent manner. It is the result of joint standardization efforts of ECMA (European Computer Manufactures Association) and NIST (National Institute for Standardization and Technologies). Similar architectures are discussed in Wasserman (1990), Zarrella (1990), Thomas et al. (1992), and Olle et al. (1988).

According to Brown et al.'s (1994) description, the reference model is a catalog of service descriptions spanning the functionality of a populated environment. The service descriptions are grouped in various ways, either by degrees of abstraction, granularity, or functionality. The highest level division classifies services either as end-user or as framework services. The former services include services which support the execution of a project directly. These are the services that tend to be used by those who directly participate in the execution of a project, such as engineers and managers. These services are technical management, technical engineering, project management, and support services. The latter services pertain to users who facilitate, maintain, or improve the operation of the computer system, such as a human user performing a tool installation task.

Framework services form a central core with a potential relationship to all other services in the environment. These services comprise the infrastructure of the environment. They include those services that jointly provide support for applications, for CASE tools, and are referred to as 'the environment framework.' It contains detailed descriptions of 50 framework services. These services are classified as: object management, process management, communication, operating system, user interface, policy enforcement, framework administration, and configuration services.

The environment framework does not take into consideration that different CASE environments have different facilities and categories of requirements. In addition, different CASE environments have their own way of defining interactions between requirement categories. Although this framework describes a basic architecture for standardization, its focus is more or less on an inventory list of approaches (Dahanayake et al., 1992). It is not easy to acquire exact requirements to describe a flexible architecture. It says little about the requirements for integration at the semantic level (Brown et al., 1992). In Brown et al. (1994), these deficiencies are discussed in terms of a service-based conceptual model, and this suggests that it is necessary to distinguish conceptual issues, the services, from implementation issues, and stress the need for a design context, the process that the environment must support. Then the integration can be regarded as the specification of which services are provided by the environment, and how these services are related.

Even though actual environments show mixing of services and functionality, it is becoming more and more clear that the services tend to be a relatively fixed set of infrastructure services needed for modeling environments, regardless of domain or tool content (Brown et al., 1992). From a conceptual point of view, the capabilities of environments are referred to as services, which are abstract descriptions of the work that can be done. The separation of the 'conceptual' world of the model from the 'actual' world of existing tools and environments is of fundamental importance.

The conceptual viewpoint provides an abstract description of the functionality that may be found in the environment. An actual viewpoint would describe a particular realization of the conceptual viewpoint in terms of environment architecture with specific tools and standards. Figure 3 illustrates the distinction between conceptual service description and a set of actual tools, many of which may overlap in their functional capabilities.

Summarizing this section, one can say that the information modeling process needs to address issues involved in an integrated modeling environment, regardless of the available technology. The basic question, 'What does this environment do?' can be answered when the services correspond to an

Figure 2. Relationship Between Conceptual and Actual Worlds

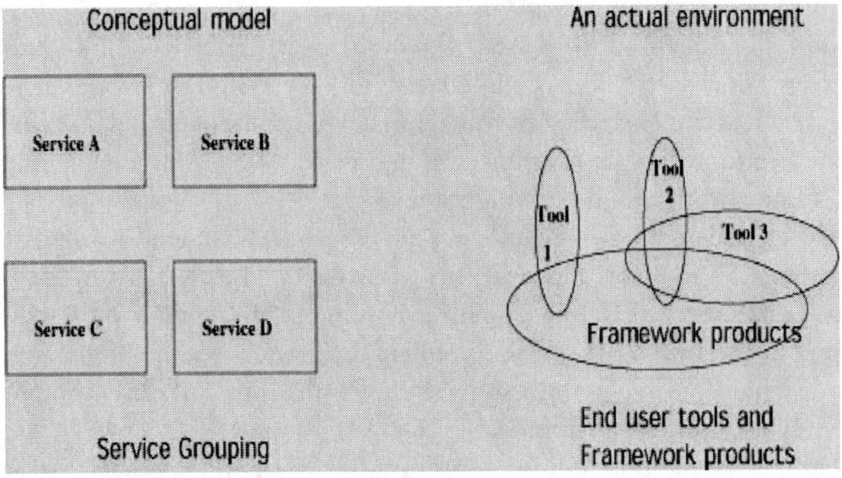

abstract description of the functionality of the environment that is offered to its user. The conceptual model as opposed to actual models, the service descriptions, tends neatly to partition the functions of an environment. When an actual environment is examined, however, these neat conceptual groupings are seldom found. Therefore, this functional overlap is the reason why a conceptual model is necessary: one of the principle values is that it provides a common conceptual basis with which to define problem-specific information modeling environments.

TOWARDS A SERVICE OBJECT-BASED MODEL

In the field of information systems development, there is a strong belief that an understanding of the information systems analysis and design process is important before bringing up solutions. Information modeling is the process concerned with in this study. Central to this process are the services available to the users of an environment. The mechanisms are a way of implementing services, and are concerned with the technology available and the techniques that can be applied to connect different service components.

Opposed to this, the process encodes the set of goals of a project, providing the context in which the services must be related. Figure 3 gives an illustration of this interpretation.

When one wants to model an information modeling environment that has flexibility to supporting arbitrary modeling techniques for analysis and design activities, there is a need for a set of concepts, which guarantees this objective. The service-based models offered so far have not succeeded in describing the

Figure 3. Relationships Between Processes, Services, and Mechanisms

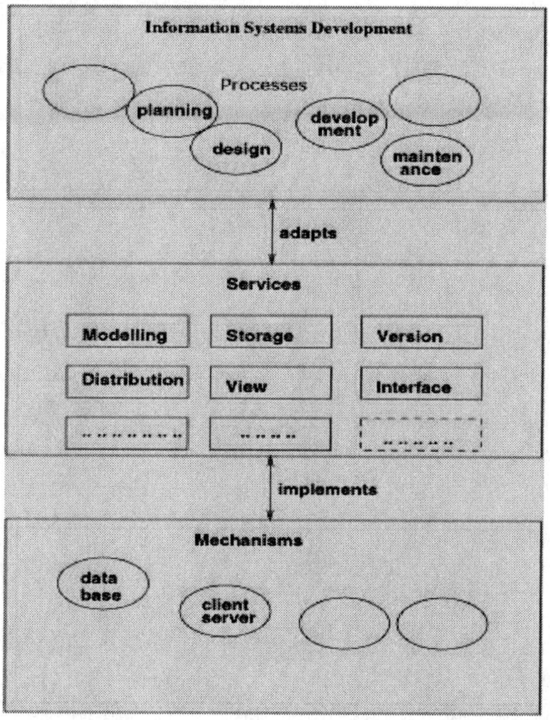

required flexibility needed for analysis and design activities. It is evident that to derive a list of services, one needs to have some form of a CASE environment architecture to define the relationships between the main areas of requirements. One possibility was to take a number of architectures of existing CASE environments and then to see how far these could be combined into one; this approach was partly adapted in NIST/ECMA. Another possibility is to use an object-oriented approach.

An Object-Oriented Service Model

A framework based on an object-oriented approach is presented in Dahanayake et al. (1992). This service model is used to formulate the conceptual model of an information-modeling environment that provides method flexibility. It originated from the need to evaluate object-oriented database support for systems engineering environments at SERC (Software Engineering Research Centre) (Dahanayake et al., 1995). The approach is advantageous, as the object concept allows modularity. When a model increases in modularity, it enables a flexible architecture, which can be modified more easily in view of maintenance and reuse of modeling techniques.

The general idea is that a particular repository is a 'configuration' of functionalities, where such functionality can be expressed as a service with its associated concepts and behavior, called a 'service object.' Each service object interacts with the world outside the environment as well as with the other service objects around it. It is not necessary for each CASE environment to offer all the services defined by this object model. Any actual CASE environment has the freedom to decide on its service objects and its services. The repository object is a configuration of service objects and gives the capability to model the interfaces such that they satisfy the service users' demands without having to redefine the service.

The Dahanayake et al. (1992) framework offers a good basis for discussing what functionalities a CASE environment must provide. It serves as a starting point for obtaining agreement on what an 'ideal' CASE environment would do in terms of the services it should provide versus other, less useful approaches, such as defining its architecture or saying what tools it should work with, or how it should be constructed.

Its application as a means of uniformly highlighting specific distinctive characteristics of existing CASE environments is particularly useful in the evaluation of such environments, and has been demonstrated in Dahanayake et al. (1992; 1995). Figure 4 illustrates the major services of a CASE environment engaged in information systems development activities. A detailed description of the framework is available in Dahanayake et al. (1992).

The approach adopted here is to identify main CASE functionalities and to evaluate their requirements and interactions and to see whether there is a possibility to relate these, according to the situation in a particular CASE environment. The major functionalities of a CASE environment can be summarized as follows.

The services required for a systems analysis and designing environment are rather complex. A CASE environment that supports systems development activities has to support multiple development methods suitable for problem situations. It needs *a modeling service* that is able to support a wide range of methods. When such models are developed, they need to be stored successfully, and should be easily accessed and manipulated. The requirements of this functionality are described by *the storage and manipulation service*. The models and their represented data have to be consistent. For example, if a designer removes an object type or adds a relationship type during the design stage, consistent states have to be restored. It is necessary to have a reliable *integrity and consistency service*. When the development team needs to use different tools, they handle different views of the systems. It is necessary to have a suitable *view service* to generate tools with their required modeling

Figure 4. Service Model of a CASE Environment

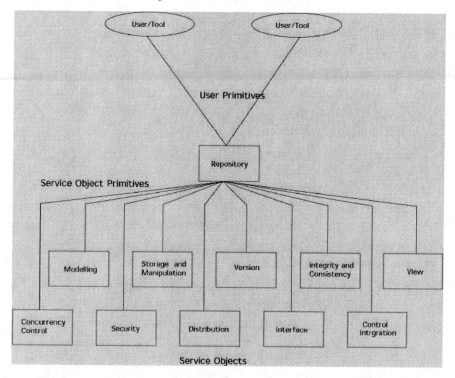

environment. This provides access to commonly used objects. An interface gives all users of a CASE environment access to user interfaces. System development is not possible without a user *interface service*. It is also natural to have a distributed development environment. Such requirements can be defined by *a distribution service*. When teams are working on different parts of the system, it is necessary to have *concurrency control and security services*. It is also necessary to have parallel developments of models. Then there is a need for a capable *version service*. When teams are working with different tools, they can share the same data; therefore, it is necessary to notify any changes, what is called *a control integration service*. This gives a summary of expected services from a CASE environment for information systems analysis and design activities.

The object concept is used to define a major functionality as a service. Therefore, the definition of an object is formulated as follows:

- An **object** consists of a unique identity, a number of properties, and a number of actions. An action has an internal specification in terms of assignment and interaction steps, which change the state of the object, i.e., the value of its properties, and cause additional actions to be executed.

Basic concepts for a CASE environment are defined using this object model. This formulates an informal description of the framework's concept and it constitutes the basis for further reasoning.

Repository Object: RO is a tuple **(SO, UP, T)**

- **SO: Service Object** is defined as an object describing an essential functionality that abstracts the essence of a CASE environment in terms of primitives used to describe a functionality and the associated actions, to provide that functionality.
  - **SOP: Service Object Primitives** is a collection of primitives a service object supports in order to provide functionality. Each such primitive defines what concepts are associated with it, independent of other service objects.
- **UP: User Primitive** allows a user or a tool to invoke from the service object the desired actions according to its need to enact activities.
- **T: Thread** is the manner in which certain services of service objects will be involved to obtain the necessary action. The order in which such service objects are activated is the Thread that provides the way a particular repository implements a user-primitive.

The major information systems development functionalities of a CASE environment are defined in Dahanayake et. al. (1995; 1992) using the service object concept. The CASE environment is described as a configuration of service objects, and each service object gives a detailed list of service object primitives. The modularity of the service object is helpful in the identification of the required functionality, and it provides opportunities to specify service object primitives of varying degrees of priority to satisfy required CASE environment services. Therefore, this approach presents a concept structure for a generic framework to describe a CASE environment, to fulfill the flexibility requirements.

In the following section this framework description is used to identify the constituent of a CAME (Computer Aided Method Engineering) environment.

COMPUTER AIDED METHOD ENGINEERING SERVICES

Information Systems Development (ISD) is a change process taken with respect to an object system in an environment by a systems development group using tools and an organized collection of methods to produce a target system. The object systems are usually modeled using notations and techniques, which are governed by the methods and supported by tools, which implement these methods and provide assistance in their use. To be able to successfully model and define methods, one needs tools and techniques at the method development level. These tools have to be capable of describing the method concept structures and of specifying new tools that support methods. These method development tools and methods together form a Computer Aided Method Engineering (CAME) environment.

The scientific area of customized modeling support for information systems development is popularly known as Computer Aided Method Engineering (CAME). This area aims at the development of a flexible support environment for information engineers engaged in information systems analysis and design activities. By this, one means the stage where an automated support environment has to produce the necessary information modeling tools. The decisions influencing the type of method to be used for a particular analysis and design activity are dependent on the problem area. Once the modeling tools are available, the actual analysis and design takes place. Therefore, there exists a distinction between putting together relevant modeling tools to attain flexibility within the environment, and further proceeding with actual systems analysis and design activities with these tools (see Figure 5).

The overall functionality of the CAME environment is to provide the services necessary to define the required modeling tools. The environment should not only support different methods; it should also be able to support the integration of models developed by these different modeling techniques. Therefore, it is necessary for the environment to be able to support independent modeling techniques in a consistent manner. The team should be able to specify the analysis and design technique they want to use in an environment. Therefore we use the framework given in Dahanayake et al. (1992) to identify the basic services of a CAME environment.

Basic CAME Services

The concepts used to model the problem area plays a central role in each description of a modeling tool.

Therefore, we need a suitable **modeling service** that can describe the range of concepts used in analysis and design tools. When we develop modeling tools, the data models developed by such tools need to be stored, and such stored data needs to be accessed and manipulated. This explains the need for a **storage and manipulation service**. When data is created, be it tools' meta models or operational models, the consistency and integrity of such data needs to be maintained. This service is called the **transaction service**. To create different modeling tools, one needs an **interface service** to allow users

Figure 5. The analysis and design stage comprises method engineering and systems analysis and design in a CAME environment

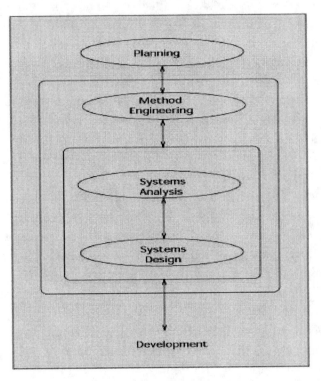

access to user interfaces. Such user interfaces share different views of the databases. Without a **view service** one cannot handle multiple modeling tool facilities. This allows us to limit our attention to the services, modeling, storage and manipulation, integrity and consistency, views, and interfaces, which are considered to be the basic services that are important for our research (see Figure 6).

The services distribution, control integration, security, concurrency control, and version are as important to an environment as the services mentioned earlier. Their contribution is more predominant when information engineers are actually developing data models during the systems design phase. As the area of interest is designing a CAME environment to provide an automated facility to design problem-specific analysis and design tools, the design and generation of such tools is the primary concern of this book.

SUMMARY

A theoretical view on information modeling environments and their required flexibility is presented in the preceding sections. An informal

Figure 6. Basic Services Relevant to Computer Aided Method Engineering

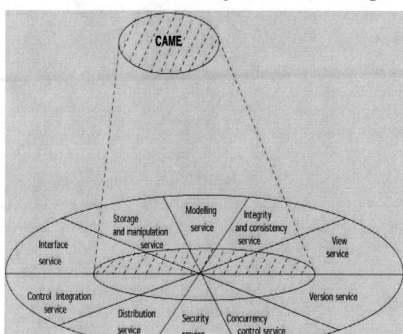

definition of the key concept 'service object' is given. Finally, a CAME service model using this concept to specify a flexible information-modeling environment for analysis and design activities is outlined.

Various problems around systems development methods and CASE tools are discussed. Today, information systems development activities need the adaptation of automated support to problem situations. By this, one means that information engineers should be in a position to define the techniques they want to use within an automated support environment. By considering CASE technology as a possible direction and directed attention towards the information systems analysis and design stage of information systems development.

This chapter explored the question, How can one describe a flexible information modeling environment so that the concepts of the framework are adequate to address the functionality of information systems analysis and design according to a particular problem situation? Recent developments in meta model-based repository architectures and the service-based framework approaches induced to consider an object-oriented service framework to specify the functionality of a CAME environment.

The concept service object to define the major functionalities of a CAME environment in a consistent way is used. This is a crucial assumption, therefore, recall the essential steps in reasoning. In the reasoning is identified that the process of analysis and design could be used to set the goals of a project and to provide the context in which services are to be supported. These services have to represent major functionalities in a modular manner, to provide the flexibility for the selection and definition of the necessary primitives used in a particular modeling technique. These techniques are referred to in a broader sense as methods in this book. Therefore, the concept of object is used to define a service, which allows one to define the required flexibility, using service object primitives.

CASE environments directed at the modeling and generation of specific tools will be referred to as CAME (Computer Aided Method Engineering) environments. An elaboration of the theory aimed at improving the automated support for information modeling using tailorable environments for analysis and design activities is given in this book.

REFERENCES

Brown, A.W., Carney, D.J., Morris, E.J., Smith, D.B., Zarrella, P.F. (1994). *Principles of CASE Tool Integration*. Oxford University Press, New York.

Brown, A.W., Earl, A.N., McDermid, J.A. (1992). *Software Engineering Environments. Automated Support for Software Engineering*. McGraw-Hill.

Brown, A.W., Feiler, P.H. (1992). *An Analysis Technique for Examining Integration in a Project Support Environment*. Technical Report CMU/SEI-92-TR-3, ADA253351, Software Engineering Institute, Carnegie Mellon University, Pittsburg, PA.

Dahanayake, A.N.W. (1997). *CAME: An environment to support flexible information modeling*. PhD thesis, Delft University of Technology, The Netherlands.

Dahanayake, A.N.W., Bosman, J.B., Florijn, G. (1992). *Requirements for Software Engineering Environments Repositories*. Technical Report, SERC, Software Engineering Research Centrum, Utrecht, The Netherlands.

Dahanayake, A., Bosman, J., Florijn, G., Welke, R.J. (1992). *A Framework for Modelling Repositories*. In Proceedings of the 3rd Workshop on NEXT Generation of CASE Tools, Manchester, UK.

Dahanayake, A., Florijn, G. (1995). *Evaluation of Object-Oriented Database support for Software Engineering Environments*. In Proceedings of the Software Engineering Environments Conference, Noordwijkerhout, The Netherlands.

IBM (1989). *Systems Application Architecture–AD/Cycle Concepts*. First edition.

ISO/IEC (1990). *Information Resource Dictionary System Framework.*

Jarke, M., Mylopoulos, J., Schmidt, J.W., Vassiliou, Y. (1992). *DAIDA: An Environment for Evolving Information Systems.* ACM Transaction on Information Systems, 10(1),1-50.

de Mey, V., Nierstrasz, O. (1993). *The ITHACA Application Development Environment.* In D. Tsichritzis, Ed., Visual Objects, pages 265-278. University of Geneva.

Olle, T.W., Hagelstein, J., Macdonald, I.G., Rolland, C., Sol, H.G., van Assche, F.J.M., Verrijn-Stuart, A.A. (1988). *Information Systems Methodologies: A Framework for Understanding.* Addison-Wesley.

Staring, W.R. (1989). *Comparison of Information Engineering Facility (IEF) and Information Engineering Workbench (IEW) (in Dutch).* Informatie, 31(5),321-408.

Thomas, I., Nejmeh, B. (1992). *Definitions of Tool Integration for Environments.* IEEE Software, 9(3),29-35.

Verhoef, T.F. (1993). *Effective Information Modelling Support.* PhD thesis, Delft University of Technology, Delft, The Netherlands.

Wasserman, A. (1990). *Tool Integration in Software Environments.* In F. Long, Ed., Software Engineering Environments. Lecture Notes in Computer Science, 467, 138-150, Berlin, Germany.

Welke, R.J. (1988). *The CASE Repository: More than another database application.* In Proceedings of 1988 INTEC Symposium on Systems Analysis and Design: A Research Strategy, Atlanta, Georgia.

Welke, R.J. (1989). *Meta systems on meta models.* Case Outlook, 89(4).

Wallnau, K.C., Feiler, P.H. (1991). *Tool Integration and Environment Architectures.* Technical Report CMU/SEI-91-TR-11, ADA 237810, Software Engineering Institute, Carnegie Mellon University, Pittsburgh, PA.

Zarella, P.F. (1990). *CASE Tool Integration and Standardization.* Technical Report CMU/SEI-90-TR-14, Software Engineering Institute, Carnegie-Mellon University.

Chapter 2

Architecture and Implementation Issues

Ajantha Dahanayake
Delft University of Technology, The Netherlands

Historically the focus is on the theory of how problem-specific systems design tools can be supported by a Computer Aided Method Engineering (CAME) environment based on service object representation. To arrive at an implementation model, the conceptual model of the service object representation must be formalized. This theory is feasible when there is adequate computer support. Many researchers have emphasized strongly that requirement specification languages should have a rigorous formal basis; however, this need for formality has not been generally acknowledged in the field of information systems development. Most organizations and research groups tend to define their own methods using techniques advocated within such methods that often have no formal foundation. Discussions of modeling techniques are based on numerous examples, mostly using diagrams and notational conventions, to provide a popular style for the definition of new concepts and their behavior. In a CAME environment however, which gives the freedom to specify a modeling technique from scratch, it is difficult to avoid deficiencies such as inconsistency, lack of structure, over specification, incompleteness, ambiguity, and redundancy without using a formal approach. In automated support a formal model is used to provide stable specifications for implementation. In fact, an implementation can be seen as another, enormously detailed formal description, usually in an imperative programming language. To implement this sophisticated automated support, formal specifications of the CAME service description with adequate formal reasoning were derived earlier.

In this chapter the concentration is on using representation formalism to construct a problem-specific CAME environment. Such an automated support environment must be provided for the information systems design stage in particular for the required UpperCASE tools according to the methods chosen for the problem situations. The vision is that CAME environments must function as a service-based, object-oriented MetaCASE environment that offers the services required for modeling tools, and using a mechanism to interpret the required modeling knowledge and changing the visual representation to the required form using a graphic object binding mechanism. Further, this environment must offer a mechanism for the populations of models specified according to such UpperCASE tools.

According to the service description, a CAME environment consists of five major services. Figure 1 provides a general architecture of a service object based CAME environment that is able to support the activities of users. Two types of users can be identified: one, the 'method engineers' that apply a *meta model editor* to specify meta models of design tools according to problem specific design activities.

Figure 1: The general architecture of a service object based CAME environment

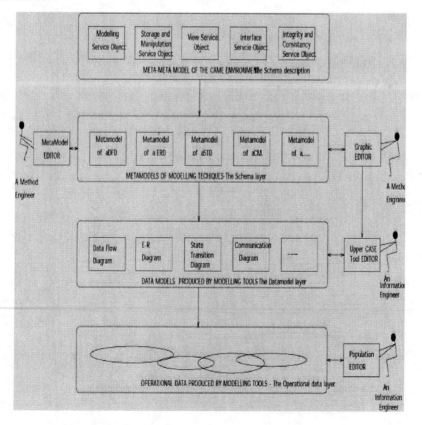

When the meta model of a particular modeling technique is ready, the method engineer associates the required graphic representations to the concepts and constraints using the *graphic editor*. The second type of user is the 'information engineer' who uses *UpperCASE tool editors* to develop models of the problem domain. The data models produced by UpperCASE tools are populated using the population editor when an object base is required. Such populations are the operational models of the required information system (see Figure 2).

The structure of the CAME environment is determined mainly by the structure of the *meta model editor*. The basic service objects of the CAME environment form the schema description layer of the object base. The meta models that describe the process and product knowledge of modeling techniques constructed by the *meta model editor* form the schema layer of the object base. The data models constructed using UpperCASE tools according to the graphic representations specified by the *graphic editor* form the data model layer. The data models' associated populations constructed using the *population editor* form the operation data layer. An evolutionary development strategy was chosen during the development of the CAME environment; the required functionality is added gradually at the appropriate stages. The first stage is to design and develop a *meta model editor* which forms the core of the environment and then to expand the environment gradually with a *graphic editor* and a *population editor* (see Figure 2).

The CAME environment prototype implemented in NeXTSTEP/Objective C is used in this book to highlight the architectural and implementation issues. This is the NeXTSTEP environment normally found on the NeXT workstations of Intel-based PCs, and it is a complete object-oriented environment built on Unix. NeXTSTEP supports object-oriented programming principles and is centered on the concept of objects using Objective C language. NeXTSTEP can be seen as a sophisticated object-oriented development environment. It embodies three pre-

Figure 2: The main support functions of the service object based CAME environment and the prototype development strategy

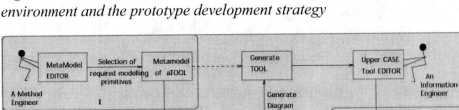

ferred major components for such an environment, namely: a library of software kits, a set of development tools, and an object-oriented language. NeXTSTEP is provided with an extensive library. It includes several software kits which can be used to create or adapt your own objects. These kits include, among others, an application kit for building graphical user interfaces, and an indexing kit for interaction with standard index structure database server.

The selection of an object-oriented development approach is not surprising when one is trying to implement an object-based description of a CAME environment. The approach adopted is used to distinguish conceptual modeling consisting of object modeling and interaction modeling, user interface modeling, implementation modeling, and programming activities. These activities are performed in an iterative top-down fashion. The existing set of object classes is taken as the starting point in each iteration cycle. During implementation modeling the results of conceptual modeling and interface modeling are translated into class definitions of an Object Oriented (OO) environment. This results in a class tree together with pseudo code definitions of each object class. These class definitions are implemented subsequently in the OO programming environment as part of the programming activities. This design and development approach is similar to the OO systems analysis and design methods, which increase incrementally the functionality and structure of the system in implementation. Further, this design has the capability to generate method-specific UpperCASE tools according to problem situations.

The remainder of this chapter is organized as follows: first is an elaboration on the functionality of a CAME environment followed by the architecture of the CAME environments *meta model editor*, in which meta models of UpperCASE tools can be specified according to this theory is given. Then follows the architecture of the *population editor,* which populates data models according to tools, which are generated for the problem situations and based on a meta model or the modeling knowledge of the technique associated with the design tool. The architecture of the *graphic editor* is followed by a summary, and conclusions end this chapter.

FUNCTIONALITY OF THE CAME ENVIRONMENT

According to this theory the CAME environment supports the construction of UpperCASE tools. First, it is necessary to define the meta model associated with the modeling knowledge of a technique required according to the problem situation. Secondly, the required tools for the information systems design process have to be generated according to the defined meta model. Once the tools are available, the real information systems design process and the population of the data models will take place. The main modules—the meta model editor, the graphic editor and the population editor—primarily describe the functionality of the CAME environment which supports the generation of specific UpperCASE tools as required for problem situations. These modules need to communicate and interact to function in the required manner. The user interface of the environment has a considerable influence on the object types' interrelationships and interactions; therefore, first the user interface of the CAME environment is taken into account using the simple prototype to explain its functionality.

The user interface of the CAME environment is based on layers of interfaces. The highest layer, called the MAIN, allows the user to communicate through menus. When the MAIN is started, a menu will appear on the screen with some items to choose: Repository, Population, Representation, Hide, Quite, etc.; an example of a MAIN menu is given in Figure 3. If the user chooses a command from a menu where the command name ends with an arrowhead, the MAIN will prompt the user to obtain more information. The items **population** and **representation** give access to the *population editor* and *graphic editor,* respectively. The Repository item gives access to the *meta model editor.* The informal module structure of this CAME environments' MAIN shell is given in Figure 4, where METAED, GRAPHICED, and POPED represent the underlying modules of the *meta model editor*, graphic editor, and *population editor,* respectively, and the gray lines are used to represent the communication paths.

The discussion here will focus on the functionality of the *meta model editor, population editor,* and the

Figure 3: The MAIN Menu of the CAME Environment

META-CAME	
Info	▷
Repository	▷
Population	▷
Representation	▷
Edit	▷
Windows	▷
Print...	p
Hide	h
Quit	q

Figure 4: The Module Structure of MAIN and its Underlying User Interfaces

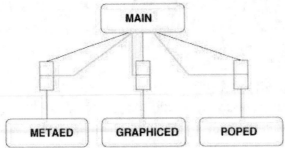

graphic editor.

The Meta Model Editor

The meta model editor forms the kernel of the CAME environment. The service object model forms the functional specifications of the meta model editor of the CAME environment. Figure 5 shows the important functional separations that are embedded according to this service description.

In the remainder of this subsection, we focus on the functionality of the meta model editor that must support the construction of meta models. To do this, the meta model editor requires the following services:

- The Modeling Service Object specified as:
  - a **meta model base**

    Describing mainly the services of the *modeling service object*. The meta model base consists of an *OS_basis* providing the *object structure* and graphical *constraints* for designing a meta model, and an *OS_editor* to verify the *population derivation rules* for a specific meta model according to syntax rules of *object structure* populations. Figure 6 represents the interactions and the informal module structure of the main modules of the *modeling service object*.
- The Storage and Manipulation Service Object specified as:
  - a central **repository** that stores all data of the Meta model editor. This central repository should supply a simple *store-query-add-delete-read* mechanism providing facilitates for the developed models and modeling components to be stored and manipulated. The non-graphical constraints

Figure 5: The Main Functional Separations of the Meta Model Editors' Architecture

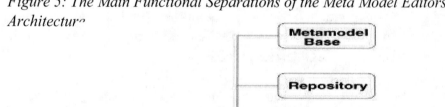

Figure 6: The Module Structure of the Meta Model Bas

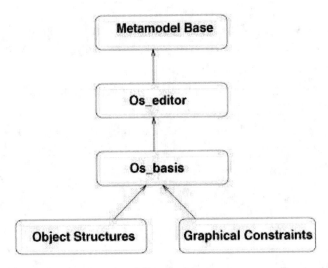

are not used at this stage of development, and have restricted the main concern to the populations of object structures; therefore, one only need the *storage and manipulation structure* interpretation that is relevant to the object structures and their complex data structure populations.

- The transaction Service Object specified as:
  - An **application control base** will supply access to the repository in a methodically correct way. Specifically, it will check the pre and post priori rules of a technique by communicating with *OS_editor*, and initiate *transactions* providing the Integrity and Consistency to incorporate the information passing process required for the developed meta models to be stored and manipulated. The *Transaction Structure* required for the process of information passing is explored in the underlying transaction model of the platform where the CAME environment will be implemented.
- The Interface Service Object specified as:
  - a **graphic base**
    Describes mainly the service of the *interface service object*. The graphic base consists of a *graphic_basis* providing *graphic structures* and *graphic constraints* and a *graphic_editor* in a similar fashion as found in **meta model base**. A graphic user interface to edit and modify all types of meta models is called a *Diagram Editor* (DED). A DED will provide this graphic interface to an OS_editor. Since the OS_editor already takes care of methodical constraints, DEDs need to be concerned only with the *graphic structures* and *graphic constraints*, and the mapping of user

Figure 7: The Main Objects that Define the Character of the User Interface

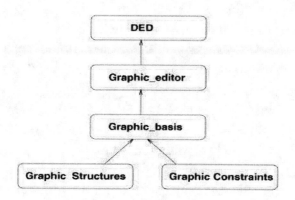

actions to the associated OS_editor to provide *user interface service*. A *graphic_basis* and a *graphic_editor* are introduced in a similar fashion as for a *modeling service object* for this purpose. This also explains the separation of modeling concepts from their graphic representations during meta modeling to allow a modeling concept to appear in the required graphic form. The interactions and the informal module structure of the main modules of the user interface are given in Figure 7.

Figure 8: View Representator and its Position with Respect to the Other Modules

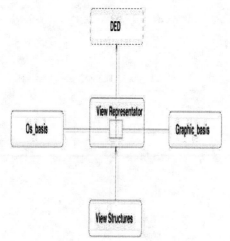

- The View Service Object specified as:
  - a **view representator**
    Allows the components of meta models as well as fragments of meta models to appear in different modeling techniques. It represents *view structures* of *view service object* to create multiple representations of *object structure* populations in relation to UpperCASE tools, and to relate them to the underlying metamodel of the modeling technique in the required manner. The view representation is illustrated in Figure 8.

The Population Editor

The population editor supports the population of meta models as well as data models. The population editor extends the kernel service of the meta model editor to support the generation of populations within a CAME environment. The services that are part of the population editor have to interact with the kernel services to function in the required manner. There are a number of extensions required for all these interactions to help the user to generate UpperCASE tools in an easy way. The important functional extensions required to extend the meta model editors' kernel description are discussed in this section.

For the population of such schemas, the population editor requires:

- extension to the **Repository** to provide:
  - An object browser
    An object browser gives access to all objects in the active repository defined under a meta model by following certain paths. This is similar to *path expressions*. This enables a user to select the required object types to be populated.

Figure 9: Populatable Object Types and Population Managers

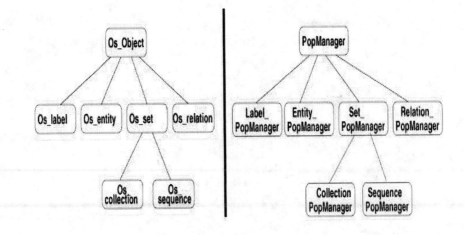

- A population manager

  An object PopManager is introduced to store an object's population and to provide access to it. This can be seen as the *Store* mechanism. Each type of object that may be populated has its own type of PopManager (see Figure 9), because each type of object needs different services from its PopManager.
- extension to the **graphic base** to provide a number of graphic objects:
  - Pop editor

    An editor that allows the user to add instances to database populations.
  - Add instance dialog

    To provide basic update interactions.
- extension to the **application control base** to provide:
  - Population Manager Control Meeting Point

    An object *PopManContrMPoint* to take over the *transactions* required during the information passing process.
  - Instance Validation checker

    To maintain pre and post conditions for the consistency management according to *population derivation rules*.

The Graphic Editor

The graphic editor supports the binding of visual representations of the meta model components to the necessary representational requirements to arrive at the required modeling technique, specified according to the requirements of the problem situation. This stage involves the generation of UpperCASE tools. For this purpose the graphic editor requires:

- extension to the **graphic base** to provide a number of graphic objects:
  - Library of graphic objects

    To select the required graphic representations according to the specifications of the modeling technique.
  - Edit representation

    An editor that can be used to select the required meta model of the UpperCASE tool.
  - Select representation

    An editor to select and bind graphic objects to the modeling concepts described under the meta model of the modeling technique.
  - Draw representation

    To select the required UpperCASE tool and to assign a name.
  - Diagram Editor

An editor that acts as the required UpperCASE tool editor.

THE META MODEL EDITOR

The theory that describes the functionality of the meta model editor is feasible only when it is implemented in a programming environment. In this section the focus is on the architecture of the meta model editor. The object model of each module discussed under the functional description of the meta model editor provides the important architectural building blocks that are required for this purpose. Figure 5 shows the important functional separations that are embedded in the architecture.

Architectural Issues

The object model of the meta model base consists primarily of object structure components and graphical constraint components. The object model consists of object types bearing the same name as the component (system) being modeled. This is such that a component can be considered to be an instance of an active object class that exchanges messages with other components, as well as something that has static relationships with other objects.

The object model of the repository consisting of a schema description layer (or service object descriptions) and a schema layer, will be referred to as the repository object. The repository will register any instance of object types derived from the meta model base. Figure 10 shows part of the object model of a repository. The relationship registration is filled by sending a register message to the repository. Each instance of object type is required to know the name of the class of which it is an instance. This allows the repository to handle queries that include class information.

Figure 10: Part of a Repository

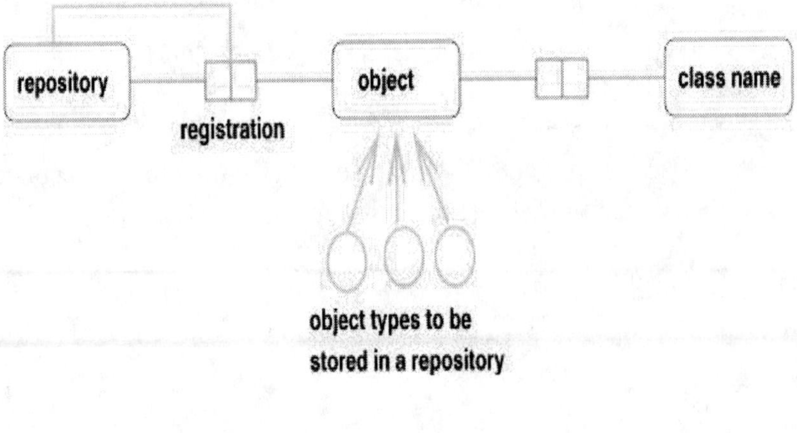

Figure 11: Additional Administration for an Active Repository

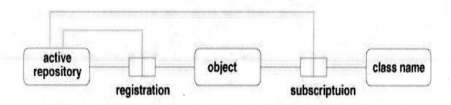

An active repository extends a repository by adding messages, which may be sent by a Diagram Editor (DED). These messages are "subscribe" and "un-subscribe". A DED subscribes to an object when it has at least one representation of that object. Similarly, it will un-subscribe from an object when it no longer holds any representation of that object. Active repositories require extra administration. Each subscribe message results in the creation of a subscription relationship instance. An active repository keeps track of all the subscriptions it has created (see Figure 11).

The object model of the meta model editor's graphic base or the user interface is a three-layer module structure. In this module structure there is one main object for each layer of interfaces, i.e., the Meta Model Editor (METAED), the Group Editor (GED) and the Diagram Editor (DED). The METAED layer is the highest layer of the meta model editors' user interface. The DED is the actual diagram editor. At this point an additional editor is introduced between the METAED and DED: the Group Editor (GED). A GED provides access to a number of DEDs of the same type, e.g., a number of meta model editors. This allows a user to keep

Figure 12: Overall Class Tree of the User Interface

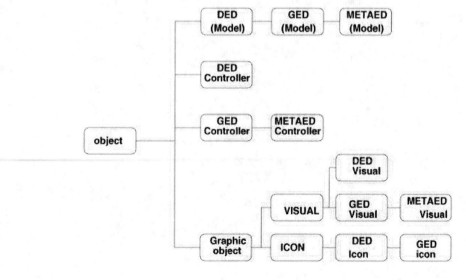

short-cuts to frequently used diagrams or to have several different diagrams organized in a group. A GED is a DED restricted to show icons that represent DEDs instead of general graphic objects.

The kernel model of the system is extended by a visual and a controller component according to the model view control principle as introduced in Smalltalk (Goldberg, 1982). Visual object is used to refer to a view in the model view control principle, as it is misleading to use view here alongside the concept of view given in this book. These components can be described in terms of editors as follows:

- Model: This object represents the internal data of the DED. It is responsible for altering internal data held by the model, which may in turn activate an update message.
- View: The visual object handles output to the screen, which is a visual representation of the models' data. The different control objects are contained in the visual object to allow users to modify the access data.
- Controller: The controller object processes user input. Every user action corresponds to a modification of a visual object. These actions are translated by the controller object into specific action messages, which are sent to the model.

Figure 12 represents the overall class tree of the user interface. Figure 13 shows the interactions with the active repository along the editor hierarchy.

The interaction of the main modules of the meta model editor plays an

Figure 13: Editor Hierarchy and Interactions with Active Repository

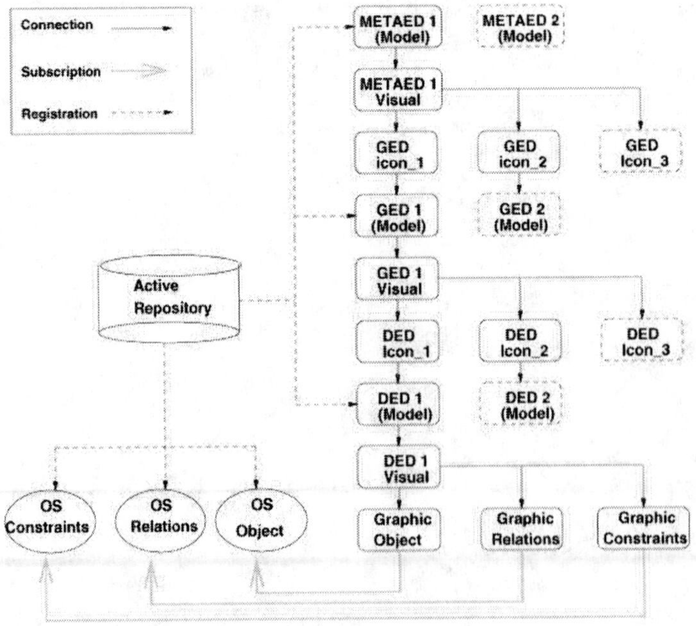

important role during the design of the CAME prototype. The overall interaction model of the meta model editor is given in the Figure 14. The solid arrows represent message flows and grey arrows correspond to control flows. In this figure a number of new objects are visualized together with the main modules and objects discussed under the functional model of the meta model editor. The position and role of all these components will be explained when appropriate.

DEDs need their own administration to keep track of the representations of the objects in the repository. Since a DED is an abstract concept, the representation type it will handle also needs to be abstract. Therefore a generalized graphical object type (graphic object) is introduced, which plays a basic role for the representation of view types of all concrete graphical editors. Figure 15 shows the representation relationship. Not all graphic objects are generalized objects, because the repository will store any instance of a type that is eventually generalized to object (or, in OO terms, the type is derived from object), and this allows the DEDs to store representation data in the repository. The representation relationship type object acts on behalf of the view representator.

At this point it is necessary to discuss the application control bases' function on different editors or objects. A controller object called Application Controller is introduced. This object is unique for each session, i.e., there is always only one Application Controller object active no matter how many repositories are open. Its main task is to provide the user with a means to create, open, and perform other functions on repositories. It also initializes some other objects, which are necessary

Figure 14: Overall Interaction Model of the Meta Model Editor

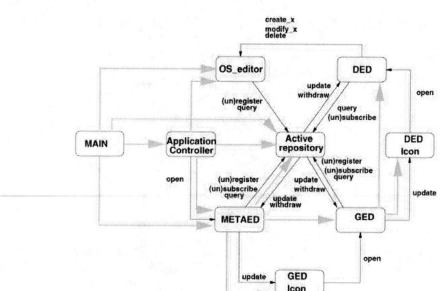

for the DEDs. The Application Controller object maintains a list of active repositories and is connected to the MAIN of the user interface via each corresponding repository.

First of all, DEDs, METAEDs and GEDs must store their interface information somewhere to keep it available across working sessions. The obvious storage place is the repository. This way, a repository keeps a record of a complete working environment. A repository may receive three kinds of messages. The first two, register and unregister, add an object into the repository and delete an object from the repository, respectively. The third message, query, asks the repository to return a list of objects satisfying a specified condition.

The object OS_editor is used to validate requests and to determine consequences of manipulations. The outcome of these calculations is used to keep the repository consistent. All the information the OS_editor needs to perform this task is stored in the repository. Therefore it only needs to know the repository. The METAED on the other hand needs to keep track of the OS_editor, all active DEDs, GEDs, and the repository. This leads to the object relation model given in Figure 16.

Only an OS_editor should (un)register objects, as they are responsible for the consistency of the repository. Both the OS_editor and DEDs can query a repository. To enable a DED to be notified about changes, it recognizes the message update and withdraws. An active repository will send an update message when it has determined a change in an object subscribed to by the DED. When such an object is removed from the repository, the repository will send a withdraw

Figure 15: Administration of Objects Visualized by a Diagram Editor (DED)

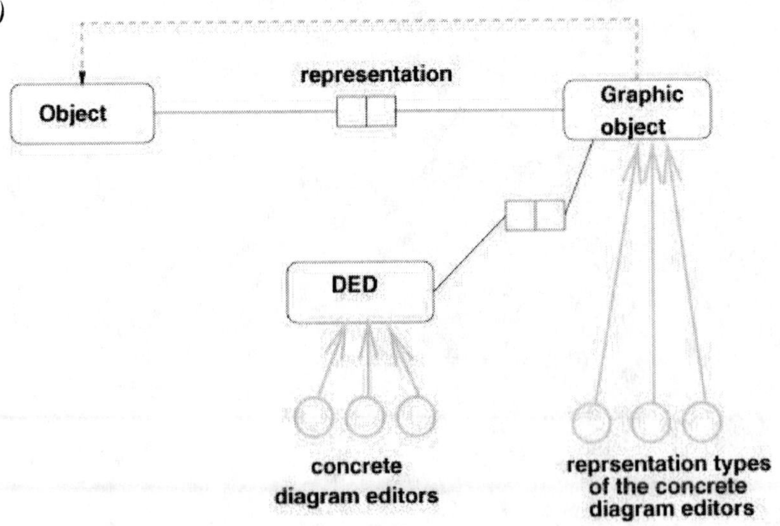

message.

The creation of objects is done through OS_editor. Since object creation can require any number of parameters, it cannot be solved generically by an OS_editor. Each Object type that an OS_editor manages therefore requires its own creation message. An advantage of this explicit handling of instance creation of each object type is that it provides a good point to do prior checks on the operation. Deletion can be handled generically by an OS_editor and is done through the delete message. Every layer in the user interface (METAED, GED, or DED) is updated to the repository separately. This became necessary because it is not necessary to update the whole user interface hierarchy to the repository. For example, a simple update of the title on the name panel of DED undergoes the message chain between DED and repository, but in the case of changing the name of GED-icon, it carries a whole set of messages way down to the last layer.

The object model of the meta model editor's overall design is given in Figure 17. Note the new concepts, which are introduced solely to explain the gradual extension of data and functionality. A window just shows some graphic objects. An editor actively manages the representation relationship of these graphic objects by subscribing to the represented object. An icon is just a picture representing something; a named icon adds a name to this picture. A DED_icon limits the things the named icon can represent to DEDs. Likewise, a GED_icon limits representation to GEDs.

Meta Model Editors' User Interface

An overview of meta model editors' user interface is provided in Figure 18. The Repository item is for the opening of the meta model editor, which activates the Repository submenu. A window will appear for initialization of a repository file for the meta model. Once a repository is created it gives access to the underlying interface structure of the meta model editor.

Figure 16: Relations METAED Have to Maintain

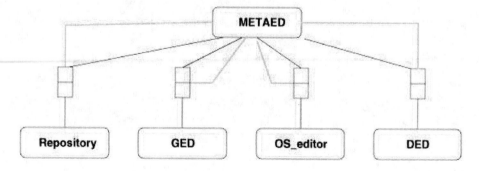

Figure 17: Overall Object Model of the CAME Environment

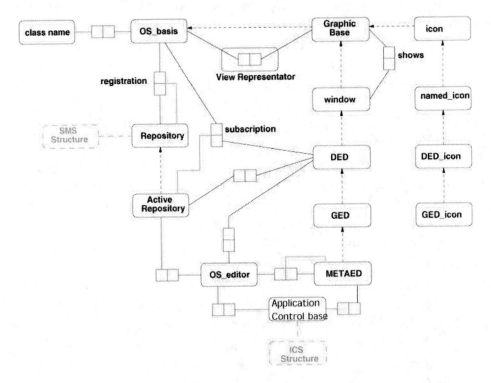

Apart from creating and opening a repository, the sub menu items provide two other facilities: Snapshot to make a back-up of an opened repository, and Delete to select a repository file from the disk to remove it completely. After creating a new (New) or opening (Open) an existing repository, the METAED window shown in Figure 18 appears; this is the top-most interface layer of the meta model editor. The repository item allows more than one repository to be opened at any given time.

On the top of the editor pane appears the window title = 'pathname' + editor title. The top part of the METAED window shows the type of the next level editors and an image to indicate the METAED. There are two types of editors that can be activated, Object Structure Editors (OSE) and Task Structure Editors (TSE). The TSE will be not discussed here, because only the OSE is required at this stage to develop meta models and to describe the functionality of this CAME environment. A Group Editor (GED) can be created by dragging and dropping the OSE_icon on to the bottom part of the repository window. Otherwise an available OSE_icon can be highlighted, to open a GED. Figure 19 presents a part of the object model of the METAED user interface. The METAED contains a number of icons, and each icon represents a GED instance.

Figure 18: The Meta Model Editor's User Interface

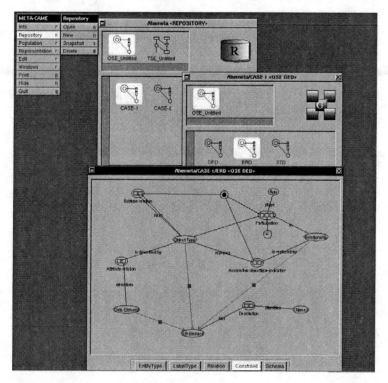

The group editor

Group editors manage a number of diagrams. A diagram is for example a schema defined in object structures. Each diagram is edited through a Diagram Editor (DED). When an OSE_icon opens a GED, a window appears as in Figure 18. The title bar contains a name that identifies the kind of GED and a name that is the same as that of the icons in the METAED window. Under the title bar is a GED_icon and an image for identifying GEDs. This GED_icon gives the user

Figure 19: Object Model of METAEDs' User Interface Parts

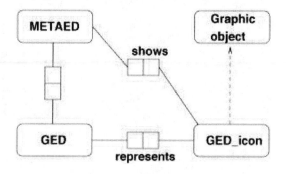

control over the GED. The drag drop facility creates a new DED in the scrollable area where the active diagrams are represented by an icon. A name uniquely identifies each icon. The user communicates with a GED through icons. The drag-drop of a GED_icon generates a unique message to the GED to generate new diagrams, a DED_icon. A double click on a DED_icon opens a diagram editor. When the user clicks on the name of the diagram icon, the GED gets the update message followed by the new name as input from the user.

From the discussion above it is clear that DEDs, GEDs, and METAEDs have much in common. In fact, a METAED is a specialized form of a GED. GEDs are specialized DEDs. Therefore, the object model of GEDs generalizes a METAED's object model. Figure 20 shows this model in which some extra constraints are needed: a GED icon represents a GED, a GED may only show DED icons, and METAED may only show GED icons.

The diagram editor

The user interface of a DED, shown in Figure 18, is much the same as the GED user interface, except that it's scrollable area may contain any graphic object. The only difference between a DED and a GED is that DEDs must know the OS_editor they must use to manipulate the repository. The DED communicates with the user

Figure 20: Object Model of the GED and METAED User Interface

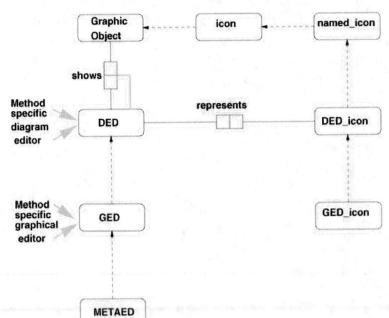

by means of buttons, Pop Up Menus, and dialog boxes. The Pop Up Menus appear usually when the right button is held down. What particular Pop Up Menu appears depends on the position of the mouse cursor. If the cursor is positioned over an object, a Pop Up Menu specific to that kind of object appears.

A button item can be selected by holding the mouse button down, putting the arrow over the desired item, and then releasing the mouse button. After an item is chosen, for example Entity, it can be positioned on the diagram editor; a window for selection or for entering the name normally follows. Some items have their own sub menus, and they appear automatically when the mouse cursor is placed over such an item. Selecting an item from one of these sub menus is done in the same way as selecting an ordinary item. If the editor needs information from the user to perform the selected action, one or more dialog boxes appear. When the mouse cursor is positioned over the dialog box, the requested information can be entered by typing text and/or clicking on a button.

To add graphical constraint a special button is available in the DED. When clicked on it this button will be highlighted. To select the required constraint, a Pop Up Menu below the constraint button has to be dragged on to the desired constraint. After a constraint is selected, it can be added into the schema by clicking on the position where it should be added. Constraints are connected to the role it relates to by dragging a line using the left mouse button. If it drags to an incorrect role, it will not be connected. A double click on the constraint checks if the current population satisfies the constraint. A panel appears allowing a user to perform some operations on the constraints.

Implementation issues

An important realization of the meta model editor is in the implementation of the DED which handles the separation of modeling concepts and visual aspects of objects which are described as graphic structures. Each object has one modeling concept associated with it, and can have any number of visual representations. The visual representations, which are called graphic objects, know which modeling concept object they are associated with, and this enables them to handle changes to the object. To keep the visual aspects and modeling concepts consistent with each other, a list of mappings is kept in a central place. If one visual representation changes the state of the modeling concept object, this change is forwarded to all other visual representations.

When a user opens or creates a DED, a window with the graphic_editor appears on the screen, which is the top-most module. This is used to implement a major part of the user interface, and to control most of the interaction with the user.

The creation of a new object type for example, is handled by the graphic_editor. The graphic_editor sends a message to the OS_editor, which performs the actual creation of the new object type. The graphic_editor stores global data about the visual aspects of the object structure it maintains. This data consists of a reference to the OS_editor that handles the modeling concept side of the object structure, the visual to modeling concept mapping mentioned above, and an administration of all visual objects. The need to store the OS_editor is self-explanatory. The mapping is used to pass relevant information along from the user to the conceptual counterpart, which interacts with the visual objects. It is also used backwards: if a modeling concept object is destroyed, all associated visual objects will also be destroyed. The administration of all visual objects is used to save and load complete object structures; a visual representation of this is presented in Figure 21.

OS_editor

The OS_editor is the place where all data about the modeling concept objects is stored. It is responsible for the consistency of all data, and can provide derived information. To do this, the OS_editor has procedures to create new objects, to retrieve or to destroy existing ones, and to derive information.

The OS_editor can provide the following derived information:

- The pater familias of a given object
- Whether or not a given object may be generalized or specialized

The OS_editor knows which objects are part of the object structure at hand, and is able to derive some information about them. Therefore, to describe the object Structure completely, additional information is needed. For example, it is not enough to know that role A is part of the object structure; it is also necessary to

Figure 21: DED and its Underlying Interaction Modules

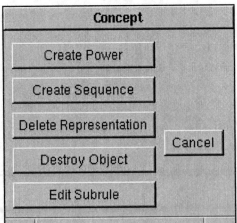

know which (if any) object is its base, and in which relationship type it is contained. This kind of information, the structure of the model, is kept in the conceptual objects, which are subclasses of OS_basis.

Controller objects

The user communicates with the program through DEDs. When the user wants something which effects a conceptual object, the DED sends a message to the OS_editor. Creation and destruction or deletion of a conceptual object is done though an OS_editor. Creation and deletion of visual objects or graphic counterparts of conceptual objects is done through a DED, consisting of an object Ose Controller and an object graphic_editor. In the tool, only one OS_editor is required. Several DEDs can be opened or created. A Repository Controller creates an OS_editor when the user opens or creates a repository. Repository Controller passes the OS_editor to the Application Controller. The Application Controller, when opening or creating a DED, passes this OS_editor to the Ose Controller.

OS_basis and graphic_basis

The OS_basis and graphic_basis trees capture the structure of the meta model that is being edited. All object structure concepts have a counterpart in OS_basis and graphic_basis trees. The structure that is kept in the OS_basis object is manipulated by the OS_editor, while the structure contained in the graphic_basis objects is manipulated by the graphic_editor. The OS_basis hierarchy of object structures, where a similar graphic_basis hierarchy exists for its counterparts in graphic structures, is given in Figure 22.

Specification of graphical constraints

The graphical constraints are introduced in a similar fashion to object structures, to enter and administer graphical constraints. The graphical constraints differ in three points: syntax, semantics, and graphic representation. This consists of extensions to the OS_basis and graphic_basis, and some additions to the OS_editor and the graphic_editor. OS_item is the super type of all object structure object types, and this OS_item is taken as the root of the extension tree of constraints. OS_item handles all required administrative functions, such as access to the OS_editor. OS_constraint is an abstract type upon which all constraints are based. To determine the subtypes of OS_constraints, all constraints are compared and their requirements are matched. Based on this matching, groups of constraints are distinguished (see Figure 22).

Figure 22: OS_basis Hierarchy of Object Structures

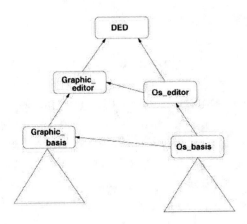

An important criterion is the type of object the constraints are allowed to associate with. This is created by generalizing constraints into six groups and adding a group type resulting in a hierarchy tree as shown in Figure 23. This distribution of constraint types over abstract super types allows a maximum shearing of procedures and data. For example, all standard constraints use the same procedure that associates the constraint with a set of roles, whereas the collection type constraints share the procedure that associates the constraint with a concept type or collection type.

The structure of the extension of the graphic_basis tree is the same as the structure of the extension of the OS_basis tree. These extensions implement the user interface and handle the visual representation of constraints. The extensions consist of procedures to create, store, and retrieve objects of type graphic_constraint and OS_constraint. These procedures are analogous to the existing procedures that handle all other object types of object structures.

The final implementation model is obtained after applying the transformations for generalization and specialization to the object models so far discussed, retaining the functional separations according to the theory formulated in previous chapters. The detailed class trees are not included here, as most of them have been already explained in detail.

THE POPULATION EDITOR

The functionality of the population editor is given above. In this section the focus is on the architecture of the population editor. The important architectural building blocks that are required for this purpose are put forward in the following section.

Figure 23: Resulting Graphical Constraint Hierarchy

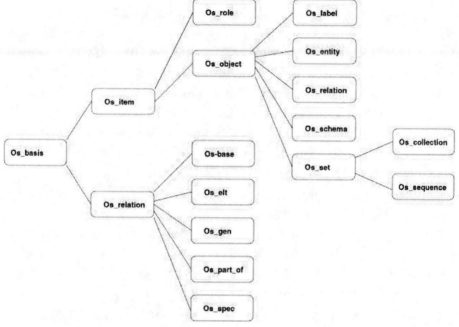

Constraint kind	Connects to
Standard	1 set of role
set	2 sets of roles
collection	concept or collection type
subtype	entity type
enumeration	concept
schema	set of concepts

Constraint types and their allowed connections

Architectural Issues

This section describes the extensions needed for the administration of populations. In the first case the object model of the repository is extended with an extra object PopManager which is central to maintaining the relevant populations, and in the second case the object model of the graphic base is extended with a pop editor.

Thirdly the extensions required for the application control base will be discussed under the object PopManContrMPoint.

The interaction between objects are concerned with the adding of an instance to the population of an object which causes interaction between the PopManager and pop editor. The scenario is triggered by a graphic_object, which sends a message to its associated OS_object to edit its population. The OS_object creates a pop editor, which handles the actual adding of a new instance by telling the PopManager to add an instance to the population of OS_object which is kept in the PopManager. The PopManager creates a dialog box, the user enters the value of the new instance, which is then retrieved by the PopManager and propagated to the pop editor to keep the display up to date: Figure 24 provides a general interpretation of this description. There are four objects of concern when interfering with populations; this is visualized in Figure 25.

The PopManager is an object that stores a population and provides access to it. Each type of object that can be populated has its own subtype PopManager, because each type of object needs its different services from the PopManager. For example, the PopManager of an entity type must propagate the value of new instances to objects higher in the generalization hierarchy. The general interaction model relating to population generation is shown in Figure 26.

The PopManager is the actual abstract data type and is continually saved to and restored from disk. Instead of direct communication with the PopManager, all communications are handled by a central Population Manager Controller Meeting Point (PopManContrMPoint). This PopManContrMPoint provides an easy interface to the PopManager by handling all disk access transparently. Further this object is guaranteed to have only one instance per population on disk. The PopManContrMPoint is also responsible for keeping the population consistent by communicating with the OS_editor. The population derivation rules are used to make sure the population is consistent if the schema is consistent. PopManager Controller is the actual object that most of the graphic base objects will use to interface to populations. The PopManager Controller inherits the relevant methods and data from PopManager and from OS_object. Due to the technical impossibility of implementing multiple inheritance directly we have introduced PopManContrMPoint to take over this responsibility with the help of a forwarding mechanism. Figure 27 shows an interpretation of the PopManContrMPoints role in relation to communication and interactions with other object modules.

The main purpose of PopManager Controller is to provide groups of related user interfaces as an easy way of keeping the overall graphic base consistent. In addition to this, PopManager Controller provides a means to have an active

Figure 24: Interaction Model of the Adding of a New Instance

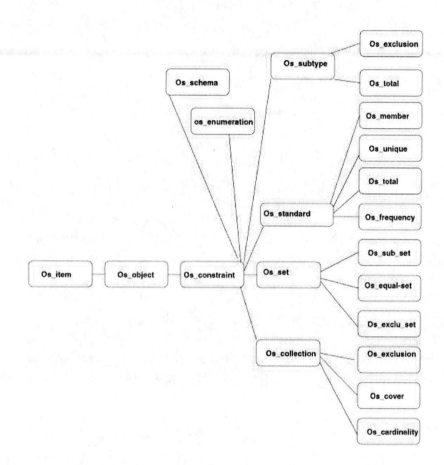

Figure 25: Population Related Objects

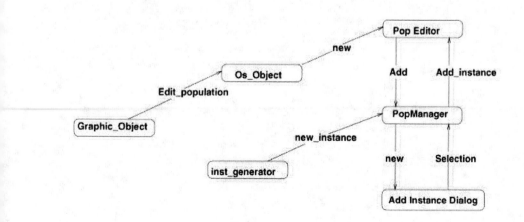

Figure 26: General Interaction Model of Population Generation

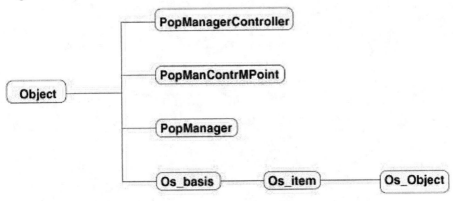

instance, and in the case of Collection types, of making distinctions for editing sets or separate instances, in a way that is easy for separated objects. By doing this PopManager Controller imposes a standard of how the user interface should work. Further to this the PopManager Controller does not add much extra functionality.

Population Editors' User Interface

When the CAME environment is activated, the Population item gives access to the instance generation part of the CAME environment. As shown in Figure 28 a sub menu appears. The editor is started by selecting the Edit Population item in the Population sub menu.

Figure 27: The PopManContrMPoint's Role in Relation to Other Objects

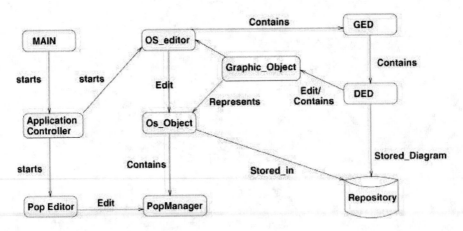

Selecting an object

The population editor first gives the object browser to select an object that will eventually be populated. The object browser is supported by a Choose Object window (see Figure 28) which shows a list of all objects in the active repository from which the population can be edited. All object types are populated in the same way. An object can be selected by clicking on an object name or, if required, the whole action can be cancelled with the use of the Cancel button, which returns the user to the Population sub menu and enables the Edit Population button. The pop editor is opened by clicking on the edit population, and this forms the main part of the population editor's user interface. The pop editor and add instance dialog windows are updated automatically when a new object is selected.

Figure 28: Population Editor's Access Menu and Object Browse

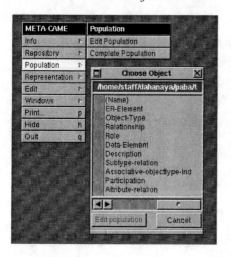

Pop editor

The pop editor consists of a scroll view showing the instances and two buttons to edit the population. At the top of the scroll view is a bar with the titles of the column of instances. The title of the first column is the name of the current object because it never contains instances defined in another object. If a collection type is being edited, the second column shows the name of the element object. In the case of a relationship the names, of the roles are shown.

An instance can be selected by clicking on it. In the case of a relationships or an entity, the entire instance is selected. A set can be edited by selecting one instance by clicking on the element, the second column of the instance, or an entire set by clicking on the set, the first column. An instance can be de-selected by clicking on it again.

The Delete button in the pop editor window can be used to delete instances from a population of an object. It is disabled if nothing is selected in the scroll view. If the user is not allowed to edit a population, this button is disabled. Deletion of instances may have an effect on the populations of other objects that are connected to the object that the instance was removed from, for example, generalization, specialization, relationships, and collections. Instances related to these instances will be deleted, and the population will be updated automatically.

The 'add instance dialog...' button can be used to add instances to a population. When a user is not allowed to add instances to population, this button is disabled. If a valid instance is entered, a new instance will be made above the currently selected instance, or at the bottom of the list if none is selected.

When the object concerned is a collection type, there are special rules included for positioning the add instances activity. When the whole set is selected, the instances will be added at the end of the currently selected set. If an element of a collection type is selected, an instance will be added in front of the selected instance. A new collection can be created by not selecting anything. The action of the 'add instance dialog' will add a new set at the end of the list.

Add instance dialog

The add instance dialog window lets the user add new instances to the population of a selected object. Often the names of these instances are created automatically. The user has to enter the chosen instances from other objects that form the elements or roles of the object which are being currently editing. A newly created instance is added to the population using an 'add to population' button, or by pressing enter after entering the last column. The add instance dialog is updated automatically when a new selection is made in the pop editor.

Implementation Issues

The population editor supports the development of operational models by generating instances to the objects defined in the meta model editor. Once the meta model is ready, the UpperCASE tool can be built around it, by knowing the overall structure of the CASE tool and using the interface to the population database. There are several important elements; the first is dealing with repositories. These are the actual files that contain the data of one project. This data includes the abstract meta models, including their populations among other data. The required CASE tool must be able to add its data, such as graphic representations, to the repository. It should also be able to make a distinction between a populated repository (project file) and an empty one, which can be loaded when a new project is started. Secondly, the UpperCASE tools must be able to deal with the populations of relevant object types, i.e., entity, label, collections, sequences, relationships, and schemas, in the meta model, which actually represent the design that is made by a future user of the UpperCASE tool. In fact the following groups of interactions must be performed by the UpperCASE tools built around the meta model editor:

- Provision of a mechanism leading to Loading and Saving repositories, carrying

the capabilities of the Store mechanism
- Using the knowledge of the meta model to link the repository to the relevant parts of the UpperCASE tool model
- Interfacing with population, leading to Update, Assign, and Query

We will first introduce these interactions as they form an important part of the storage and manipulation activities. Then we will give a brief summary of the important issues concerning interfacing to populations and managing of populations.

Loading and saving

The Application Controller and Repository Controller objects are of importance to load and save repositories. The Application Controller provides a higher level interface which handles the opening of the required object files and puts requesters on screen to ask the user which repository they intend to use. Repository Controller provides the internal interface which handles the access to the repository, by keeping a list of open DEDs, and taking over the opening and creating of the repository.

Retrieving the meta model structure layout for interfacing

Since we decided to make use of the available facilities of the platform for data manipulation, the following is considered:
- To get a list of all objects as the same kind of the meta model, one can obtain the list in the form of an IXpostingList from the repository. The way to do this is:

      positionList = [repository queryClass: obj_GetClass("TheClass")]
- or alternatively to get a list of different objects:

      positionList = [repository queryClass: [TheClass class]]
- simply to append additional lists to the former is done in the following way:
  positionList=[appendList:[repository queryClass:[OtherClass class]]]

Once the lists are obtained from the repository, one can use them to access the objects on the disk. Alternatively, the name of an object at a certain position can be obtained. For further understanding of how the indexing kit works, see NeXT Publications.

Editing populations

There are three basic categories of operations, namely delete, add, and read for editing populations. In PopManager, PopManContrMPoint, and in PopManager Controller, there are methods to add or delete instances. Most of the read methods are particular to PopManager and PopManContrMPoint, but are accessible via the

PopManager Controller due to a forwarding mechanism. Usually the user interfaces should only use PopManager Controller to edit populations.

The functionality is distributed across the hierarchy in the following way. At the bottom level there is the PopManager which is the actual abstract data object to be edited. It does some syntactical and semantic checking and basically adds or deletes instances to or from the population.

On top of that lays the PopManContrMPoint, the main purpose of which is to access the PopManager, which mainly resides on disk, by adding the necessary functionality needed to handle the database. In addition to that, PopManContrMPoints form the heart of the notification system. If any operation on the population succeeds, and thereby causes a change, it will send its subscribers, usually PopManager Controller, a notification message. Finally PopManContrMPoints do additional checking on the parameters they pass on to the PopManager and also provide a means of generating the unique instance names, in case they are needed.

Retrieving data from populations

The main method for this activity is the method, readInstancesOfPopulation:with: provided by the PopManContrMPoint, which can be called directly via the PopManager Controller. The use of this method is rather simple. Furthermore, it is possible to retrieve all kinds of data such as the number of names in an instance (numberOfColumns), the number of instances in the population (numberOfInstances), check for existence of an instance Id (instanceExists), and the names that can be associated with different columns of instances (getRowOfInstance:name).

In addition to this there are methods for getting information about characteristics of the abstract object most notably typeOfObject, getClassName, addPossible, deletePossible, noUniqueName, popEditTitle, isLable, isGeneralisation, and isSpecialisation.

Finally the Id of each of the objects that are concerned with handling the abstract object can be retrieved by the methods meetingPoint, PopManager and osObject, for getting the Id of PopManContrMPoint, PopManager and OS_object, respectively.

The methods for getting unique instance names need a little explanation. Whenever the result of noUniqueName is No, the user interface should take care that the instance Id name that is added to the population is unique. Note that none of the objects actually check the uniqueness of the name Id added for performance reasons. To do this the user interface can perform the generateNexInstName method to obtain a guaranteed unique name.

Adding to populations

The most commonly used method for adding instances is the addInstance: method. The position of the instance, which is actually only of real importance in the case of a sequence, is determined by the active position and set selection mode, which can be set using the setActiveInstanceAt: and the setFirstColSelection: methods.

It is also possible directly to pass the position and set mode to the method addInstance:row:mode: of PopManContrMPoint, which is actually the meth-od that is called by the PopManager Controller when passing it an addInstance: message. In both cases all user interfaces are notified of any changers.

Deleting from populations

The method that is normally used for deleting a population is deleteInstance where the instance at the active position is deleted or none if the active position is -1. When in set mode and if firstColSelection is YES, then the entire set is deleted, in all other cases only one instance is deleted.

The notification mechanism

The notification system is activated for each operation that causes a change in the population among some other events, The order of action methods is described in Figure 29. Note that each action method also has a return value, so there is also an information flow in the opposite direction of the action methods. This, in fact, has nothing to do with the actual notification. There are also some variations on the pattern, where an action within PopManager Controller causes a notification to be sent.

Subscribing and unsubscribing

A few steps need to be done to get notifications of changes in the population from the PopManager Controller. First of all a user interface object needs to implement the notification methods for the kind of events it wants notification for. These are defined in PopManNotification protocol. Second the user interface object needs to tell the PopManager Controller that it is ready to receive notification by sending it a subscribeForNotif: message. To cancel a subscription, the unsubscribeForNotif: method should be used, where the Id must be the same as

Figure 29: The Notification Path During Normal Operations

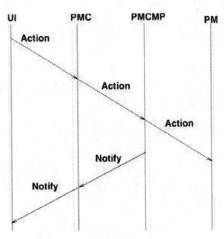

was used when subscribing.

Accessing PopManager directly

Sometimes it is simply unwanted, while editing the population, that the user interfaces are updated continuously. This is the case when editing a large amount of the population at once, for example with the complete population option. Currently there is no other way than accessing PopManager directly if one wants to work around the notification mechanism. Of course one could also turn of the updating of the user interface as an alternative, but one needs the PopManager Id, to be fetched, since the methods that are not supported in PopManager Controller or PopManContrMPoint are forwarded automatically to PopManager and OS_object, respectively. When editing a PopManager directly, one must take certain extra actions into account, namely:

- Enclosing the entire operation within a nestTransaction/ unnestTransaction pair
- Saving the object back to disk when finished
- Notifying all user interfaces that use the object of the change, usually with an sendrenewAll or sendRenewAllToAllInstances to PopManContrMPoint

Interfacing to populations

Usually the only object a user or an UpperCASE tool has to use for editing the population is PopManager Controller. This object hides the inner structure of the population editing structure by releasing the user from the task of calling the other relevant objects. By doing this PopManager Controller hides all disk access, including transaction schemes, and ensures consistency within the population. Furthermore, PopManager Controller provides a notification scheme to its users that keeps them up to date of any changes in the population. In fact, all users of the same PopManager Controller instance form a logically grouped set of interfaces. The entire notification system is designed in such a way that different user interface objects need to communicate as little as possible with the other interface objects. This makes the designing of graphic user interfaces for UpperCASE tools a lot easier and consistent. Other relevant objects that are used for editing populations are PopManContrMPoint, PopManager, and OS_object. All of these are, directly or indirectly, used by PopManager Controller. They can be accessed directly in the rare case it is really necessary, but most of the time using PopManager Controller is sufficient.

Managing populations

The PopManager Controller object enables separated user interface parts to handle the PopManager. For example, the pop editor and add instance dialog user interfaces are different objects that handle the same PopManager Controller. The Choose Object window sends the pop editor the message whenever the user chooses a new object to edit. The pop editor then sends a message to the PopManager Controller. The PopManager Controller notifies its subscribers, in this case the add instance dialog user interface, to renew all methods. This means that the pop editor does not need to notify the add instance dialog of any changes. This is of course a welcome feature, especially when a lot of different user interface parts are present, since the communication between the user interface objects is kept at minimum. As it is possible to have multiple groups of interfaces, which can use several different PopManager Controllers, it is also possible to have several PopManager Controllers that manage the same PopManager, as shown in Figure 30. To avoid inconsistencies, and to give the automatic notification a bigger scope, the additional object PopManContrMPoint is introduced.

Just as user interfaces can have subscriptions for notification on PopManager Controllers, PopManager Controllers have subscriptions for notification on PopManContrMPoints. There is at most one PopManContrMPoint per PopManager, which assures that all PopManager Controllers that handle the same object are connected to the same PopManContrMPoint. Since all operations on the PopManager that are performed by the PopManager Controller are carried out via the PopManContrMPoint, the latter can notify all its subscribers (all PopManager Controllers that handle that object) of any changes. All together, all groups of user interfaces are always kept up to date; it does not matter who makes the change. An

Figure 30: An Example Arrangement

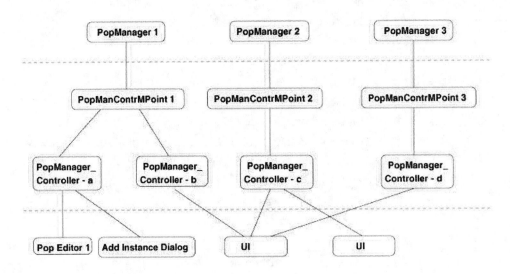

exception of course is when some object accesses PopManager directly from disk. The reason for making a distinction between PopManagers and PopManContrMPoints is simply because PopManagers are contained on disk, while PopManContrMPoints have codes to access this disk, which obviously could not be put in the PopManager. The overall class hierarchy of the population editor is given in Figure 31.

THE GRAPHIC EDITOR

The graphic editor (GRAPHICED) is responsible mainly for the extensions of the user interface. The important architectural issues that extend the object model of the CAME environment are the next topic of discussion.

Architectural issues

First the graphic_basis of the graphic base module of the CAME environment is extended with a number of graphic object types, to form the library of graphic objects. These graphic object types can be assigned to the objects types of a meta model. The graphic object types are the new graphic representations that will be

Figure 31: Organization of the Population Editor Related Class Tree

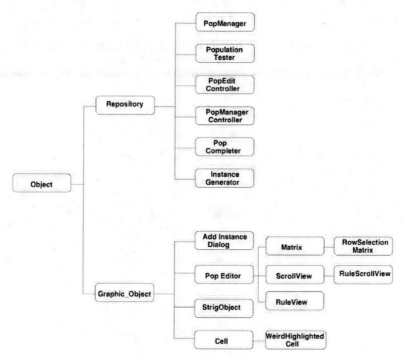

used in the diagram editor to support specific modeling techniques according to the requirements of the problem situation. Figure 32 gives an example of such a class hierarchy.

According to our interpretation of view structures, each meta model which is of a schema type is a view of the UpperCASE tools' required modeling primitives. The object types gathered together as a schema type are the objects that will change their representations to arrive at the required diagrammatic representation. For this purpose, first a user interface is designed that allows the user to select a specific schemafootnote{ Which is a meta model of a modeling technique from the repository. Once a schema is selected, a second user interface is designed to select the components of the meta model and the required graphic object types, and to combine them. The edit representation and its underlying select representation user interface carry this responsibility. The edit representation and its interaction model with other components of the CAME environment is shown in Figure 33.

An UpperCASE tool editor is designed so that it has access to a specific schema capable of creating or opening a specific diagram technique. The name of the diagram technique is already stored in the repository, and the UpperCASE tool editor obtains an assigned name. This UpperCASE tool editor has to offer all functions that are necessary to create data models. The draw representation module

Figure 32: Part of the Class Hierarchy of the Graphic Object Library

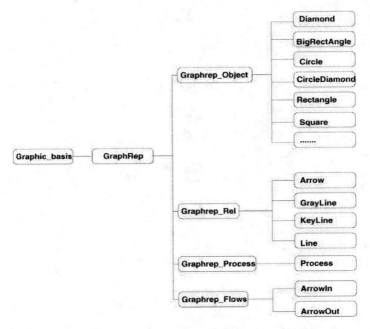

Figure 33: Interaction Model of Edit Representation

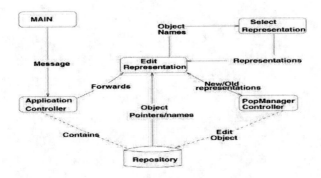

Figure 34: Interaction Model of Draw Representation

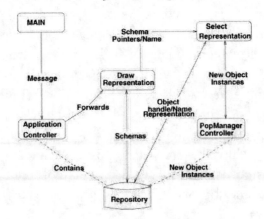

associated with the graphic base module of the CAME environment guarantees the access to UpperCASE tool editors. Figure 34 shows the interaction model of the draw representation and UpperCASE tool editor with the rest of the module structure of the CAME environment.

Graphic Editors' User Interface

In this section we introduce a brief description of the user interface of the graphic editor. The item representation of the MAIN menu gives access to the components of the graphic editor. The MAIN menu, together with representation sub menu, contain the edit representation and draw representation elements.

A single click on the edit representation item opens a new panel to browse through the schema types that can be selected (see Figure 35). When the choice is made, a new panel select representation appears immediately which allows the user to assign graphic_object instances to OS_objects.

Figure 36 shows this select representation user interface. The required graphic representation can be typed or selected with the use of the Help button. The Help button gives access to a browser (see Figure 37) which visualizes the available graphic object types. The Save button can be used to add this required information to the repository, or the button Cancel can be used.

When the user's attention is required until some condition is met certain attention panels pop up. For example, if a user tries to alter the graphic representation of an OS_object in a schema which is been used to design data models, an alert panel will point out this incident. It prevents the user from changing the previously stored graphic_objects, because it is possible that populations already exist with that graphic representation. In such a situation it is quite natural to delete the data model if required.

The item draw representation gives access to a new panel to select a schema;

Figure 35: Edit Representation Panel

Figure 36: Select Representation Panel

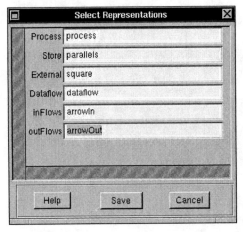

Figure 37: Browser of the Help Button

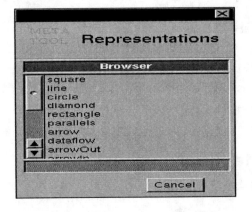

Figure 38 gives an example of this panel, which is a two-column browser. The first column contains the schema types, and the second column contains the created data model instances of a specific schema type. To create a new data model, first its name has to be assigned followed by a return key action, which will automatically open an UpperCASE tool editor or simply a diagram editor with the assigned name. It is also possible to select a name of a model instance to open an existing diagram instance. Similarly, Delete and Cancel buttons can be used if their services are required.

The UpperCASE tool is provided by diagram editor windows containing a title bar:

<DIAGRAM EDITOR>
/ < Schema_type_name > /
<Diagram_instance_name>.

This diagram editor offers possibilities to select required modeling concepts in the appropriate graphic form to design models according to UpperCASE tool's specifications. This selection is supported with a Pop Up List.

The selected concept is assigned a name before placing it on the diagram editor with the help of the panel (see Figure 39) containing an instance browser, which allows a new named instance to be assigned or an available instance to be selected. This diagram editor supports, among other required functions, deleting as well as moving an object within the editor.

Implementation Issues

An overview of the class hierarchy that captures the structure of all added components concerning the graphic editor is given in Figure 40. Besides the objects

Figure 38: Draw Representation Panel

Figure 39: Panel to Enter the Object Names

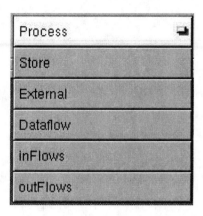

that this figure shows, there are other transient user interface objects which are created and used within a specific object. These are mainly panels or browsers, such as the browser generated with the Help button in edit representation. The object GraphRep represents the graphic object library.

The diagram editor is a window where the modeling tool is displayed. The object ShowReps is the controller of the diagram editor. A Draw_area is a place in this window called ShapeView, and each new graphic representation is considered to be a sub Draw_area. All Draw_areas within a window are arranged in a hierarchy, each sub area having a single super area and zero or more sub areas. A particular Draw_area has its own coordinate system, expressed as a coordinate transformation of its super area's coordinate system. A subclass of a Draw_area is created which implements the mouse-event method to process mouse events. Then the instance of the custom Draw_area is added to the window hierarchy. These custom Draw_areas are the super classes of the graphic object library.

At the same time as a new graphic representation is created, a new element of the population of the active OS_object is generated and tested, to determine if the element is a valid member of its population before being added. The active OS_object is given via the Pop Up List of the diagram editor window.

The following functions are embedded into the ShowRep object:
- the selection and activation of OS_objects
- the creation of the new instances of the OS_objects
- the assignment of names to graphic_objects
- the creation of instances of the graphic_object associated to OS_object

Figure 40: Overall Class Hierarchy of the Extra Objects Required for the Graphic Editor

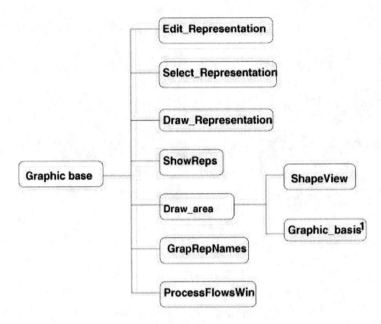

- the adding of the sub draw_areas to the draw_area hierarchy
- the moving of graphic_objects
- the deletion of graphic_objects
- the deletion of related instances of the OS_objects
- the saving of the diagram editor window in the repository

SUMMARY AND CONCLUSIONS

The lack of a tailorable automated support at the level of information systems analysis and design stage according to information modeling needs of a problem situation continues to pose a considerable challenge to both academics and practitioners. This chapter demonstrated how a CAME environment prototype is designed to deal with this situation. A platform was developed to try out a tool construction principle, based on a high-level specification of modeling techniques, with an easy-to-use method specification language. The environment is represented as a configuration of service objects of major functionalities of information systems analysis and design activities. The specifications of these service objects are used as the architectural building blocks of the CAME prototype.

This prototype, based on the service object base theory, demonstrates that it is possible to develop an automated modeling support environment for the method engineering activities required in information systems design work by mapping the service object description onto an available object-oriented technology.

REFERENCES

Goldberg, A. (1984). *Smalltalk-80: The Interactive Programming Environment.* Reading, Massachusetts: Addison-Wesley.

Chapter 3

Future Directions
in CASE Repositories

Ajantha Dahanayake
Delft University of Technology, The Netherlands

Today, components and Component Based Development (CBD) is seen as one of the important events in the evolution of information technology. Components and CBD offer the promise of a software marketplace where components may be built, bought, or sold in a manner similar to components in other industries. In the light of the ongoing developments, in the manner and art of developing software systems, it is important to consider how the Computer Aided Systems Engineering (CASE) environment that supports building these systems can be produced on a CBD approach.

In spite of the fact that CASE environments have been around since the '70s, there are still many problems with these environments. Among the problems of CASE environments are the lack of conceptual models to help understand the technology, the poor state of user requirements specification, inflexible method, support and complicated integration facilities, which contribute to the dissatisfaction in CASE users.

During the '90s there has been a growing need to provide a more formal basis to the art of software development and maintenance through standardized process and product models. The importance of CAME (Computer Aided Method Engineering) in CASE led to the development of CASE shells, MetaCASE tools, or customizable CASE environments that were intended to overcome the inflexibility of method support. The declining cost of computing technology and its increasing functionality, specifically in graphic user interfaces, has contributed to the present re-invention of CASE environments.

Previously published in *Computer-Aided Method Engineering: Designing CASE Repositories for the 21st Century*, edited by Ajantha Dahanayake. Copyright © 2001, Idea Group Publishing.

CASE research in the last decade has addressed issues such as method integration, multiple user support, multiple representation paradigms, method modifiability and evolution, and information retrieval and computation facilities. Considerable progress has been made by isolating particular issues and providing a comprehensive solution with certain trade-off on limited flexibility. The requirement of a fully Component Based architecture for CASE environments has been not examined properly. The combination of requirements of flexibility in terms of support for arbitrary modeling techniques, and evolution of the development environment to ever-changing functionality and applications never the less needs a flexible environment architectures.

Therefore, the theory formulation and development of a prototype for designing a next generation of CASE environments is addressed in this book. A CAME environment is considered as a component of a CASE environment. A comprehensive solution is sought to the environment problem by paying attention to a conceptual model of such an environment that has been designed to avoid the confusion around integration issues, and to meet the specification of user requirements concerning a component-based architecture.

A CAME environment provides a fully flexible environment for method specification and integration, and can be used for information systems design activities. A large part of this book reports how this theory leads to the designing of the architecture of such an environment. This final chapter contains a review of the theory and an assessment of the extent to which its applicability is upheld.

A REVIEW OF CAME THEORY AND ARCHITECTURE

The concept of CAME as the solution to the issue of supporting information systems analysis and design work by providing tailorable automated support according to the information systems modeling needs in a problem situation is addressed in this book. The automated support tools have become the primary means of support at the systems analysis and design stage, and also the automated support tools currently used by information systems engineers such as CASE, UpperCASE, MetaCASE, or IPSE do not meet the expectations of the information systems designers. This observation, stimulated to approach the issue of a modeling support environment, can be tailored according to arbitrary modeling techniques used for information systems analysis and design activities.

The overall objective was to find a way to integrate the conceptual model of the flexible information modeling environment, that represents the way of modeling and working of information systems modeling techniques, and the computer aided systems engineering environment technology. The theory is based on the supposition that the service object based conceptual model that represents the way of modeling and working of information systems design techniques can provide the architectural building blocks of a tailorable automated support environment to provide CAME support for design and generation of modeling techniques according to the problem situations. Based on this premise a theory was defined for formulating and structuring the functionality of an information systems analysis and design environment that combines the services required according to a problem situation and their automated support in a consistent way. The theory leads to a conceptual model of a flexible and tailorable CAME environment through implementation of the conceptual framework.

Recall that the process of information systems analysis and design is viewed as the stages of method engineering of required modeling techniques, and the analysis and design of the information system using such generated tools. The method engineering of the required modeling techniques involves the identification of the required modeling primitives that are required according to the problem situation, as well as the design of a meta model of the desired modeling approach. The resulting meta model constitutes a conceptual model that describes the information architecture of the required modeling tool according to the problem situation. During the generation of the modeling tools, the information architectures or the identified building blocks of the required modeling tools are provided with the required graphic representations according to the notational conventions of the modeling tools. This results in an UpperCASE tool or in an automated way of support for information systems analysis and design activities according to the problem situation requirements. The actual analysis and design of the information systems architecture of the problem area takes place using the generated tools. The crux of this tailorable way of support is as follows.

Chapters 2, 3, and 4 outline the theory that a flexible modeling environment can be represented adequately by considering it to be a configuration of service objects of main functionalities of information systems analysis and design activities.

It has been explained that the functionality of an information system modeling environment refers to a configuration of main services. This set provides the required combinations to represent flexible modeling environments. The services give an indication as to how to specify the boundaries within which certain functionality can be looked for. Their purpose is to help in identifying the required functionality of an information system modeling environment that can be tailored to the requirements of problem specific modeling techniques. Therefore, a configuration of service objects represents the main functionality of the information systems analysis and design activities that is required according to the problem situation within flexible modeling environments.

In Chapter 2 it is shown that it is possible to define a service object concept that allows the main functionalities of a CAME environment to be represented. The case example reported in Chapter 3 indicated that the service object based CAME environments functional description can indeed provide a good basis to identify the required service objects to fulfill a particular functionality. Chapter 4 shows that it is possible to define a set of concepts, constraints, and interactions that allow a sharp distinction between service objects to specify the services within such a service object. The service object model proves to be a useful instrument for delineating the boundaries and the services of the solution environment that are required eventually.

Chapter 5 provides a confirmation of the feasibility of a service object based environment to support design of information architectures of modeling techniques and generate modeling tools for analysis and design activities. That is, it is possible to develop an automated method engineering environment for information systems analysis and design work by mapping the service object description onto an available object oriented technology.

The specifications of the architectural building blocks of a flexible way of support for information systems analysis and design activities revealed the need for an automated means of support. The feasibility of a service object based Computer Aided Method Engineering environment for engineering information systems modeling techniques has been demonstrated. The prototype META-CAME implemented in the NeXTSTEP/Objective C platform confirmed that the service object based conceptual model is executable, such that flexible modeling support can be realized.

Perhaps the most important contribution of this work is from an information systems engineer's perspective, a service object based CAME architecture offers problem-specific design tools for information systems analysis and design activities. There were number of test cases conducted to assess the extent to which this upheld. The test cases that were conducted with respect to this hypothesis can be found in Chapters 6, 7, and 8. In view of the results obtained in the case studies reported in Chapters 6, 7, and 8, this hypothesis can not be rejected. The case studies evaluated the extent to which the environment is flexible according to a problem situation. The design and generation of information systems analysis and design tools for the financial and administration systems design activities resulted in a modeling support that could be tailored according to the problem situation needs of a structured analysis and design approach. The design and generation of information systems design tools for the automobile map system resulted in a modeling support that could be tailored according to the problem situation needs of an object oriented modeling approach. The design and generation of information systems design tools described yielded a support tailorable to an uncommon modeling approach and to the identification of shortcomings with respect to executability of the representational aspects of a modeling approach. Finally, the design of a database and generation of database presentation tools yielded support for a modeling approach according to the problem requirements, and resulted in support for representational independence by providing graphical, matrix, and tree structures. Those case studies have shown that it is possible to define a set of tightly integrated tools that is useful for defining an integrated modeling approach, and that the theory and the supporting technology have the capability to evolve into full life-cycle support for information systems development.

CASE OUTLOOK FOR THE 21ST CENTURY

Today, business issues are global in nature; information technology, and the function it can deliver, is just another tool in the arsenal to improve and accomplish more quickly the desired organizational goals. From an organizational context there is the perceived need for new functionality. The time needed to develop and implement a solution is increasingly out of step with the speed at which organizations must respond to, or initiate, change. They need Information Systems (IS) professionals to design, develop, produce, distribute, service, and improve product components according to their demands.

The emergence of novel application areas such as Geographic Information Systems, Data Warehouses, Enterprise Resource Planning, e-commerce, and the diffusion of advance information technologies such as multimedia, WAP, and n-tier architectures have necessitated a continuous search for identifying how they can be assimilated for the benefit of the organization. The paradigm shifts to new development approaches--such as Object Orientation, Component Based Development, and incremental approach--have necessitated a continuous search for new ways to identify how they can improve the affectivity and efficiency of systems development methodology in line with the ever-changing business demands.

The information systems development methodology has always been unsatisfactory, and over and over it is been evaluated. These evaluations resulted that there is no way to standardize the information systems development methodology, but to allow it to be composed of a modular structure satisfying the requirements of flexibility, scalability, and reuse (Kumar and Welke, 1992; Dahanayake, 1997; Tolvanen, 1998). In light of this modular structure of the methodology and the demand on systems to anticipate business evolution, a theory and a construction principle of CASE tools is put forward for the methodology construction that supports present systems development activities. The construction of CASE tools based on this Computer Aided Methodology Engineering theory will support cross-cultural information systems development methodologies and will bring about discipline as well as guidance to solve today's systems development challenges.

Method engineering covers all those processes by which an ISD method is developed, and later customized and instantiated in an organization, in order to make the method fit the tradition, culture, and infrastructure of the organization and to meet the specific needs of a particular project. One of the major considerations within the Method Engineering is to ensure that a method forms a coherent and integrated composition, and the structure and the content of the methods are properly changed during the engineering process.

This customized method construction gave rise to combine and integrate different methods to satisfy the requirements of flexibility, scalability, and reuse (Kronlof, 1993; Kumar & Welke, 1992; Goldkhul et al., 1998). A method with a modular structure is composed of models and techniques that are integrated by a common phase structure and a compatible set of approaches and paradigmatic assumptions. Examples of such methods are Multiview (Wood-Harper et al., 1985), Fusion (Coleman et al., 1994), and UML (Jacobson et al., 1999) where models and techniques have frequently been drawn from other methods. Composing a method from components offers the capability of offering appropriate support for specific tasks.

Relation Between Modeling Methods, Tools and Techniques During Method Engineering

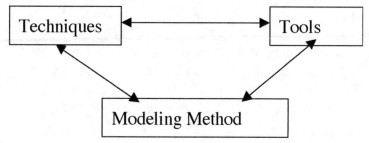

*The Cross-Cultural Modeling Methodology that can Anticipate Business
Evolution*

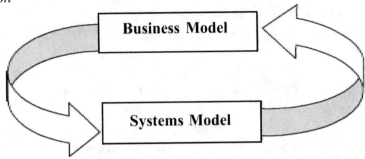

The methodology for systems development today encompasses the
construction of the future conceptual model of the business, which must be
related to the (implicit) present conceptual model of the application or
(information) systems model.   Information requirement specification is
constructed in the framework of business model and system model. Information required for reaching the solution is described in the business model (e.g.,
workflow, dynamic models, flow-charts, communication models, process
models, etc.). Information available is defined in the system model (e.g.,
entity relationship models, data-flow models, state transition diagrams,
object models, functional models, dynamic models, etc.) so that the business
model is derivable from the system model. These two models are inter-related
and are the two sides of the same coin. The affectivity of the Information
Systems Development approach depends on the corporation and interoperability between these two dimensions. Then the ISD approach needs to
customize as well as improve the corporation and inter-operability of the
modeling methods according to these modeling dimensions to stay in tuned
to these cross-cultural modeling needs.

The main challenge for information systems design and development in
general is the continuous changing business needs and the slow and inefficient
anticipation of information system. It is the thesis of this paper that the lack
of consistency between the business modeling approaches and systems
modeling approaches has to be properly treated and solved in order to
anticipate business needs through systems evolution. The anticipation to
business evolution through systems evolution needs to be treated through a
(modeling) method integration requirement within the design methodology.
Failures in this aim cause incoherence and disintegration that in the practice
of information systems development appear as obscurity, mistakes, and
general inefficiency, or even leads to the avoidance of the methodology.

The methods fail to support the modeling needs because within the framework of business modeling and systems modeling, the modeling approach lacks integration during method construction. The prerequisites that have to be fulfilled for such an integration of modeling dimensions to be successful have to be identified and their inherent complexity has to be considered at early stages of a method construction exercise.

A modular structure gives the opportunity to investigate the credibility of a methodology in anticipating the evolution of information system according to changing business processes. Also a modular structure creates special demands for integration and consistency among the components of a methodology that promotes evolution of information system according to business needs. First of all a methodology that anticipates the evolution of the systems has to take into consideration that there are no gaps in support of modeling relevant features in the domain concern, i.e., the business requirements modeling and systems requirements modeling have to assure structural integrity. Second, it should provide smooth guidance to proceed from one process to another guaranteeing functional integrity. Third, the terminology related to process, domains, and deliverables has to be compatible.

A customized method construction at the maximum flexibility level is typically supported by a CAME environment, allowing the design, storage, retrieval, and assembly of these method components. This substantial degree of flexibility in the construction of new methods requires, among other items, integration of methods according to the situation of the project. It is quite reasonable to think that the modeling approaches are properly integrated within an effective methodology, but this is not true even for the Unified Modeling Language (UML) (Jacobson et al., 1999). The integration of models of different conceptual bases is required to improve the modeling support required for today's fast-changing systems modeling requirements, and the way forward for such development needs can be successfully attained when the CASE environment is constructed according to the theory presented in this book.

CONCLUDING REMARKS

First of all, this work has demonstrated the feasibility of a basic CAME environment. The support environment requirements, which have been determined for arbitrary modeling technique support according to a problem situation in Chapter 4, concentrated on modeling, views, storage and manipulation, and user interfaces services. The full implementation of storage and manipulation, and the transaction services were avoided to reduce the programming time. When using a CAME environment in reality, in information systems design and development activities, the services such as version, distribution, concurrency, and security control services must be supported on top of the services already specified to provide services in a distributed and multi-user CAME environment. Such an environment can be realized by concentrating on the theory presented here and extending it with adequate programming activities. The realization of a fully functional CAME environment in a CASE that supports the method engineering and full life-cycle phases of information systems design and development is not beyond current capabilities and technologies.

Secondly, many flaws found in current CASE environments are addressed in this book, which has introduced a basis for common terminology to allow useful scientific and commercial initiatives to take place. The service object based architecture, which separates the conceptual specifications and the representational differences of tools, conveys a high level object oriented application program interface for tool repository interaction. The meta-meta model of this environment provides flexibility and evolution of the modeling technique specification and use, which is unmatched by any existing MetaCASE tool. The novel modeling technique specification and generation mechanism presented in this book meets the needs of the highly diverse representational paradigms and the information processing capacity that are demanded from systems engineering environments. The integrity and consistency of repository data during concurrent access by different tools is guaranteed in the architectural specifications of the environment. In this respect a major paradigmatic revision of how CASE environments are conceived and implemented are provided offering considerable benefits for information systems engineers with easily adaptable generic services that adequately address flexible support for information systems design activities.

The third remark is that the method engineering approach of modeling technique generation has been directed at experienced practitioners with this PSM-based meta modeling technique. The affectivity of the tool generation depends on the practitioners' knowledge and experience in meta modeling. This approach can produce equally effective results when less experienced practitioners have mastered the art of meta modeling presented in this study. Learning this technique may take a few weeks for a qualified information systems engineer. Once the meta modeling technique is understood, the generation of a required tool is a matter of a few minutes. The environment can also be used for the process of learning the method engineering approach and its meta modeling technique.

The fourth remark concerns the trade-off between the development of a CAME prototype and a commercial tool. This work focused on arriving at an adequate prototype to present the theory in a reasonable period of time. The theory described in this book was developed over a period of four years, and the CAME prototype was implemented within a time period of two years. The fine-tuning of the user interface and performance was not considered as prime target. Therefore, a decision was made to avoid fine-tuning of the tool for high performance or for a highly commercial user interface. In the future, one can use this theory for the development of a full life-cycle support environment for information systems development activities.

A concluding remark is that there remains a substantial gap between the design and the development of information systems. Frequently there is a lack of guidance in finding the suitable information systems analysis and design approach that can be used to integrate the results into the information systems development phase. This is not due to shortcomings in the modeling technique generation and use of the theory described in this book. The CAME environment and the underlying theory provide the basis for tailoring a support environment according to problem requirements. Consequently the design of information architectures of modeling techniques and the generation of modeling techniques to support information systems design according to a problem situation leads to the realization of a tailorable way of modeling and information systems designing. This tailorability will always be obtained regardless of whether the subsequent design approach is successful. This tailorable way of automated modeling support will provide an efficient way of specifying an integrated set of tools in an information systems analysis, design, and development approach that will increase performance in information systems design and development work.

The primitives of a service object represent the actual environment's functionalities, and provide adequate architectural building blocks of information systems analysis and design processes to work into a cumulative tradition of component based CASE tool development. Obviously, testing this hypothesis will be an excellent subject for future research.

REFERENCE

Coleman, D., Arnold, P., Bodoff, S., Dollin, C., Gilchrist, H., Hayes, F., Jeremaes, H. (1994). *The Fusion method, Object-Oriented Development.* Prentice-Hall.

Dahanayake, A.N.W. (1997). *CAME: An Environment to Support Flexible Information Modeling.* PhD Dissertation, Delft University of Technology, The Netherlands.

Goldkhul, G., Lind, M., Seigerroth, U. (1998). *Method Integration: The Need for a Learning Perspective. IEE Proceedings -Software,* 145(4), 113-117.

Jacobson, I., Booch, G., Rumbaugh, J.   (1999). *The Unified Software Development Process.* Addison-Wesley.

Kronlof, K. (1993). *Method Integration, Concepts and Case Studies.* John Wiley,Chichester.

Kumar, K., Welke, R.J. (1992). *Methodology engineering: A proposal for situational specific methodology construction.* Challenges and Strategies for Research in Systems Development. (W.W. Cotterman and J.A. Senn, eds.) John Wiley.

Tolvanen, J-P. (1998) *Incremental Method Engineering with Modeling Tools.* PhD Dissertation, University of Jyvasklyla, Finland.

Wood-Haper, T., Antill, L., Avison, D. (1985). *Information Systems Definition: the Multiview Approach,* Blackwell Scientific Publication, London.

Chapter 4

Audit of a CASE Environment

Mario Piattini
Universidad de Castilla-La Mancha, Spain

Jesús García-Tomás
Universidad Politécnica de Madrid, Spain

INTRODUCTION

The diffusion of CASE tools, along with the ever more pressing problems surrounding the management of the systems development department, has meant that themes related to internal control and audit of a CASE environment are of increasing interest.

In fact, the high cost of introducing CASE technology added to the potential improvement in productivity and quality have made it one of the most important areas for the Information Systems auditor.

In this paper we will deal with some of the questions that have to be taken into account when auditing a CASE environment. Our aim is not to offer exhaustive checklists of factors of influence in this kind of environment, but rather to reflect upon some themes that have been dealt with throughout in the literature but from a different perspective to that of the information systems audit. In order to do this we will begin by briefly introducing the basic concepts of the information systems audit, giving a brief explanation of the different methodologies that are used in this area. We will also analize the risks that must be taken into account when installing a CASE tool.

Previously published in *Managing Information Technology in a Global Economy*, edited by Mehdi Khosrow-Pour. Copyright © 2001, Idea Group Publishing.

INFORMATION SYSTEMS AUDIT

By the term "internal control" we understand the policies, procedures and norms as a whole, which are established by the management group of a company in order to carry out its activities in an orderly and efficient way, safeguarding the assets and guaranteeing the completeness and reliability of its records. In the field of information technology, the aim of the internal control system is to guarantee the adaptation of the management of the computer assets and the reliability of the activities of the information systems (ISACF, 1998)

The concept "audit" can be defined as "the examination of an activity and the expressing of an opinion about the quality of the performance of an activity, undertaken by persons independent of the team responsible for the performance and supervision of the activity" (Clark et al., 1991).

Until a few years ago this function was related almost exclusively to the financial aspects and management of the companies; however due to their ever-increasing automation, the need has arisen for highly qualified technical personnel able to understand the risks that exist in the automated environment of information systems: these are the information system auditors (Piattini, 2000). Although at the beginning this person was considered as an "assistant" to the finance auditor, for whom he/she prepared programs which would make certain tests easier to carry out, nowadays they are increasingly more autonomous due to the growing complexity of information systems.

The computer audit can be defined, as according to Weber (1999), as "the process of collecting and evaluating evidence to determine whether a computer system safeguards assets. Maintains data integrity, allows organizational goals to be achieved effectively, and uses resources efficiently."

Usually the information system audit is applied in two different ways; on the one hand the principal areas of the computer department are audited: the exploitation, the management, the development methodology, the operating system, telecommunications, databases, etc. and on the other hand the applications that work in the company are audited – internally developed, sub-contracted or acquired.

The audit of the CASE environment would form a part of the audit of the development process. The importance of the audit of the development environment arises from the fact that it is the starting point for the execution of the audit of the applications.

INFORMATION SYSTEM AUDIT METHODOLOGIES

Although different methodologies exist that can be applied in information system audit given that almost all firms of auditors and individual companies develop their own – these can be divided into two groups:

- Traditional Method: that in which the auditor examines the environment with the aid of a checklist, which is made up of a series of questions to be answered. For example:

Is there a development methodology? **Y   N   NA**

The auditor must record the result of his investigation: Y, if the answer is affirmative, N, if it is the contrary, or NA (not applicable)

- Risk Oriented Approach Methodology: as that proposed by the "Information System Audit and Control Association" (ISACA), the most prestigious international association in the field of information system audit. In this methodology, first the control objectives are established which minimize the potential risks to which the environment is subjected.

Referring to these risks, the following could be defined as an example:

Control Objective:
The CASE tool must increase the productivity of the development personnel.

Once the control objectives have been established, the specific techniques corresponding to those objectives are specified:

Control Technique:
The methodology and procedures for the use of the CASE tool must be established.

A control objective may have several associated techniques (controls) which give it complete cover. These may be of the following types: preventitive, detective, or corrective.
When controls exist, tests are designed – known as "compliance tests" – which allow the consistence of these controls to be verified.

Compliance Tests:
Examine the manuals related to the methodology and the procedures.

If these tests detect irregularities in the controls, or if there are no controls, a further kind of test is designed – known as "substantiating risk tests – which allow the impact of these deficiencies to be estimated.

Substantiating test:
Check if the applications have been developed following the methodology prescribed, by examining the documentation produced by the CASE tool.

Once the results of the tests have been evaluated, conclusions are drawn, and these are discussed with the persons directly responsible for the areas affected with the aim of corroborating the results. Lastly, the auditor must communicate a series of comments in which he describes the situation, the risk that exists, the defect to be corrected and the recommendations.

As a result of the audit, a final report will be submitted in which the most important conclusions which have been arrived at are presented, as well as the scope of the audit.

Therefore, the auditor must have knowledge of:
- The risks associated with CASE technology, as in order to set the objectives of the audit, it is necessary to be able to identify the risks associated with this technology, evaluating the controls established in order to minimize them.
- The areas of the audit involved, which are principally focused on system development.
- The different categories of CASE tools and their principal characteristics (see, for example, McClure, 1989). This is an aspect on which Moeller (1989) insists: "System developers, users and auditors must have a good knowledge of the CASE tools that they are using, including their documentation characteristics and the link with the code generators."

If the auditor is not familiar with the CASE tool he/she will not be able to carry out certain verifications and therefore an independent expert in the tool would be required, although that person were not the auditor.

RISKS OF CASE TECHNOLOGY

As pointed out by Perry (1992), two types of risks associated to CASE technology exist – the first includes the risks inherent in the installation and use of CASE, and the second is the risk involved in not using CASE.

In fact it is unlikely that an organization that is not using CASE technology, would be rigorously following a methodology and therefore the auditor should control the development of the software. Moreover, the auditor should reflect this fact in his final comments, as the absence of CASE will impede improvement in productivity and quality of the development, will increase maintenance cost, and the risk may exist of losing the most competent members of staff (as they may leave the company in order to keep up to date)

In reference to the risks involved in the installation of CASE technology, these can be analized as they arise during its installation or its daily use.

Risks During the Installation

The auditor must control the following aspects during the installation:

- The selection process should be carried out in accordance with the procedures already existing in the company (see, for example, ISO). In this process, it is important (or even essential) to take into account the level of maturity of development of the company in order to select the most appropriate CASE tool for it. Another important aspect in the selection is that the auditor should be consulted about what audit facilities the CASE tool should have, and these should be borne in mind in the selection.
- The prestige and solvency of the manufacturer and distributer. They should be able to provide sufficient support.
- The terms of the contract (see Perry, 1983)
- A training program should be established and carried out as planned.
- An installation plan is proposed and this is approved by the management member responsible for this area.
- The new posts and responsibilities created by the CASE technology must be defined.
- If a pilot project is carried out, its development must be followed.
- In the conversion of a system to the new tools, the auditor must ensure that the necessary controls have been carried out in order to guarantee the integrity of the information related to the system.

Risks Arising During Use

Once the tools have been installed, the auditor must be careful to ensure that:

- The tools are under constant evaluation, in order to check that they have adapted as well as possible to the company and that they are being used to their full potential. It is also necessary to ensure that the procedures established are being carried out correctly and their cost-effectiveness
- The CASE tools are integrated with the rest of the software in the company
- The integrity of the data transferred between CASE products or process manuals and the CASE tool is controlled and maintained.

- The procedures of confidentiality are respected. When part of the information that before was kept on paper is substituted by information stored in the repository of the tool, this aspect may be neglected. It will be necessary to ensure that the designs are only modified by authorized persons, leaving only clues that allow independent inspection by the internal control or the auditor.
- Strict control is kept of versions in the dictionary or repository
- The results of the installation of CASE technology must be measured quantitatively.
- The CASE tool is being used in those applications where its use is clearly beneficial
- The changes undergone by the applications are reflected in the CASE tool

CONCLUSIONS

The great influence that CASE technology has on the development environment, has a considerable effect on the work of the auditor. This power of automation changes the nature of the development process, eliminating or combining some steps and altering the means of verification of the specifications and applications. The auditor needs to recognize the changes in the development process caused by the CASE. A clear example of these changes could be the automatic generation of the code from diagrams.

We have briefly summed up the principal aspects related to the information system audit, all of which can be applied in a general way to both internal and external audits, bearing in mind the essence and periodicity of each.

Lastly, we should emphasize that CASE tools can be of help to the auditor in his work as they store a large quantity of information about how the applications have been designed and therefore the information system auditor should understand the new focus for the development of systems, such as CASE, and the way in which documentation is constructed.

REFERENCES

Clark, R et al. (Ed.). (1991). *The Security, Audit and Control of Databases.* Aldershot, UK: Avebury Technical.

ISACF. (1998). *Control Objectives for Information and Related Technology.* The Information System Audit and Control Foundation, Illinois, EEUU.

ISO. (1995). *Guideline for the evaluation and selection of CASE tools.* ISO/IEC IS 14102. Geneve. International Standarization for Organization.

McClure, C. (1989). *CASE is software automation.* Englewood Cliffs, NJ: Prentice Hall.

Moeller, R.R. (1989). *Computer, Audit, Control and Security.* New York, EEUU, John Wiley & Sons.

Perry, W.E. (1991). *Ensuring the Integrity of the Data Base*. Auerbach Publishers, Warren, Gorham & Lamont.

Piattini, M. (Ed.). (2000). *Auditing Information Systems*. Hershey, PA: Idea Group Publishing.

Weber, R. (1999). *Information Systems Control and Audit*. Upper Saddle River, NJ: Prentice Hall.

Chapter 5

Process Model for Round-trip Engineering with Relational Database

Leszek A. Maciaszek
Macquarie University, Australia

Iterative and incremental development of client/server database systems requires a round-trip engineering support, in particular in a design-implementation cycle. This paper identifies some more difficult round-trip engineering scenarios and defines processes needed to handle those scenarios. The processes conform to the current state-of-the-practice in forward and reverse engineering with relational databases.

The paper identifies limitations of a tool-driven round-trip engineering. The limitations can be linked to three reasons: (1) the inability of a CASE/4GL tool to always generate correct incremental code after schema has been changed, (2) the need for a CASE/4GL to understand the reverse-engineered procedural parts written (or modified) in the implementation phase, (3) the requirement that a database content (extension) be re-instated at the end of each design-implementation cycle.

Technical limitations introduce a risk that design models and a database implementation become misaligned and the design-implementation cycle cannot be continued for iterative and incremental software production. Project managers need a process model to impose necessary rigour on design and programming teams to alleviate technical restrictions. The paper defines a project management strategy that enforces appropriate automated and manual processes on database development teams.

Previously published in *Challenges of Information Technology Management in the 21ˢᵗ Century*, edited by Mehdi Khosrow-Pour. Copyright © 2000, Idea Group Publishing.

INTRODUCTION

Modern software development processes are invariably incremental and iterative. System models are refined and transformed through analysis, design and implementation phases – details are added in successive iterations, changes and improvements are introduced as needed, and incremental releases of software modules maintain user satisfaction and provide important feedback to modules still under development. As Rational Unified Process states: "An iterative process is one that involves managing a stream of executable releases. An incremental process is one that involves the continuous integration of the system's architecture to produce these releases, with each new release embodying incremental improvements over the other" (Booch et al., 1999, p.33).

Iterative and incremental processes need a strong round-trip engineering support between adjacent development phases. This is particularly true for lower engineering processes – design and programming phases. Changes in design models have to be forward-engineered to existing implementation and changes in implementation have to be reverse-engineered to design models.

In this paper, we determine the limitations of commercial automation to support round-trip engineering between a database design model and an incrementally implemented relational database. We identify various incremental changes to design and implementation, and we show how they can be round-trip-engineered. The changes include declarative and procedural aspects of database intention (schema). We require that round-trip engineering is constrained by the database extension, i.e., the latest database content must be re-instated in a new database. We define processes that have to be imposed on the design and programming teams so that round-trip-engineering can be properly managed. The process management aspect can be enhanced if a change monitoring system is implemented in the database and if it is itself a subject of round-trip engineering (so that a record of design and implementation changes, still subject to round-trip engineering, is kept current at all times).

BACKGROUND AND RELATED WORK

The objective of round-trip engineering is to support evolutionary development of software systems. The term was coined, I think, by Grady Booch who defines it as combining of forward code generation and reverse engineering that gives "...the ability to work in either a graphical or textual view, while tools keep the two views consistent." (Booch et al., 1999, p.16).

Round-trip engineering is concerned with an evolutionary development of new systems and it therefore differs from re-engineering which examines and alters a legacy system to recover its design and re-implement it in a new form. Nevertheless, round-trip engineering shares the technologies of re-engineering (Olsen, 1998; Waters and Chikofsky, 1994), such as:

- forward engineering
- reverse engineering
- redocumentation from source code
- restructuring of program logic
- retargetting the system to a modern platform
- source code translation to another language
- data re-engineering (as opposed to process re-engineering)

There is a large body of literature on re-engineering. The working "blueprint" for how to use re-engineering for cost- and time-effective systems integration is given in Mischke (1998). Other major source of information on re-engineering is Arnold (1993). A process methodology for planning and implementing incremental re-engineering from legacy systems is described in Olsem (1998). Systems re-engineering patterns are discussed in Stevens and Pooley (1998).

Forward engineering with visual modeling tools is discussed in any major textbook on software engineering and on systems analysis and design. Research issues with regard to both forward and reverse engineering are extensively presented in the Proceedings of IEEE Computer Society's International Conferences on Software Engineering (ICSE conferences, with more than twenty years history). There are also specialized conferences on reverse engineering by IEEE Computer Society - Working Conferences on Reverse Engineering (WCRE conferences, with five years history).

Failures of Computer-Aided Software Engineering (CASE) tools to deliver promised benefits, and the reasons for these failures, are documented in Jarzabek and Huang (1998). Desired capabilities of reverse-engineering tools are described in Jarzabek and Wang (1998). These two papers emphasize the need for process-centric (rather than method-centric) CASE frameworks. Other contributions to process-oriented software engineering include Ambriola et al. (1997) and Greenwood et al. (1996).

Re-engineering and reverse engineering can benefit from artificial intelligence techniques and from construction of knowledge bases to assist in program and database understanding. Early work in this area is reported in Kozaczynski and Ning (1989). Tool requirements for database reverse engineering are identified in Hainaut et al. (1996). Database design recovery as an integral part of an iterative and incremental software production is discussed in Kozaczynski and Maciaszek (1990). An approach to reasoning with fuzzy nets for reverse engineering from databases is presented in Jahnke et al. (1997).

This chapter builds on this extensive body of research results and on the capabilities of current technology. The motivations for the chapter, and its potential contributions, are based on the following requirements:

1. iterative and incremental development pre-supposes that the design documentation reflects the current state of the database implementation at all times (or at least at some pre-specified "synchronization" times),
2. reverse engineering tools identify and model the recovered design with all details (as currently implemented),
3. forward engineering tools re-instate fully the database extension after changes to design models,
4. round-trip engineering applies to both data and procedural parts of a database.

ROUND-TRIP-ENGINEERING SCENARIOS

Round-trip-engineering with the database involves a Physical Data Model (PDM) at the design end, and a Database (DB) at the implementation end. A PDM model is a variant of a physical Entity-Relationship (ER) model. In our experiments, we used the representation supported by a commercial CASE tool - PowerDesigner Data Architect (version 6.1) from Powersoft. PowerDesigner was also used in all forward and reverse engineering activities with the DB (managed by Sybase System 11).

Figure 1 provides a high-level state model for round-trip engineering with database. The model uses State Transition Diagrams (STD) of the Unified Modeling Language (UML) (the diagram has been prepared with Rational Rose CASE

Figure 1. State transition diagram for round-trip engineering with

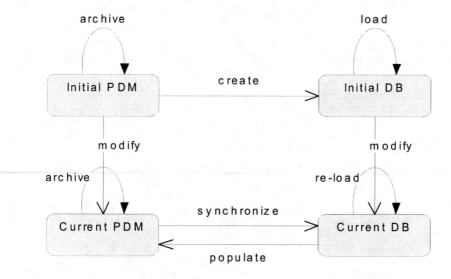

tool). After the PDM model is constructed (Initial PDM state), it can be archived (archive event) so that the future changes to the model (modify event) can be recognized by the CASE tool through comparisons with the archived PDM. Forward engineering of the PDM to the Initial DB is triggered by the create event. A DB extension is created as a result of load event. A modify event on Initial DB causes a database transition to Current DB state. At this stage, two possibilities exist: changes to Current PDM have to be synchronized with Current DB (synchronize event) or vice versa - changes to Current DB have to be populated back to Current PDM (populate event). Eventually, Current PDM may need to be archived and Current DB may need to be re-loaded.

The rest of this section is organized in six "change scenarios". Each scenario is discussed in the following points:

- categories of changes that fall in the scenario,
- the process of the automated forward and/or reverse engineering,
- example,
- limitations and conclusions.

In the scenario descriptions, the acronym FE stands for Forward Engineering and RE - for Reverse Engineering.

Scenario 1 - FE of relatively straightforward schema additions
Categories of changes:

- Addition of a null-allowing column to a table
- Addition of a table
- Addition of a user data type

Figure 2. Intention of T_Employee

T_Employee			
emp_id	<pk>	char(3)	not null
first_name		varchar(20)	not null
middle_initial		char(1)	null
family_name		varchar(40)	not null
phone		varchar(8)	null
commence_date		smalldatetime	null
terminate_date		smalldatetime	null

Figure 3. T_Employee with added null-allowing column

T_Employee			
emp_id	<pk>	char(3)	not null
first_name		varchar(20)	not null
middle_initial		char(1)	null
family_name		varchar(40)	not null
birth_date		smalldatetime	null
phone		varchar(8)	null
commence_date		smalldatetime	null
terminate_date		smalldatetime	null

- Addition of a view definition

  The process:
- Archive PDM
- Add a new object (e.g. a table) to PDM
- Generate SQL database modification script
- Execute the script on DB (ie. synchronize DB)
- Archive PDM

  Example 1 – addition of a null-allowing column to a table:
- Suppose that the following table (Fig.2) has been archived in PDM and the extension of the table exists in DB.
- New column (birth_date) added (Fig.3) in PDM.
- Modify Database script generated (alter table…) in PDM.

  alter table T_Employee
  add birth_date smalldatetime null
  go
- The script executed on DB - table intention modified and the extension of the table restored.

  Example 2 – addition of a table:
- Suppose that the previous addition of a column has been archived in PDM.
- New tables added in PDM.
- Modify Database script generated in PDM and executed on DB. The DB consists now of three tables with five relationships and a number of triggers to support referential integrity. The extension of T_Employee remains intact.

  Limitations and conclusions:
- Although the existing DB content remains intact, it may not be correct. This is

Figure 4: T_Task and T_Event tables added to the schema.

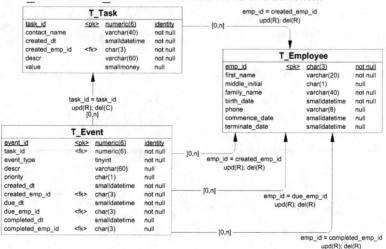

because the new integrity constraints, whether declarative or procedural, will not validate existing data.
- Populating new columns with data using SQL Update command may be more troublesome than re-loading the entire table with SQL Insert command (or with a DB Load utility).
- New columns include any foreign key columns created automatically in PDM to enforce referential integrity between existing and new tables. However, foreign key columns can only be added in Scenario 1 if they can accept null values. Otherwise, Scenario 2 applies.
- The recomended process is that PDM designers modify the database, archive PDM and inform DB programmers about the recommended ways to re-populate the database (as per risks and problems listed above).

Scenario 2 - FE of more problematic schema additions

Categories of changes:
- Addition of not-null column to a table (with or without the default value for the column).
- Addition of a referential integrity that requires a not-null foreign key in an existing table.

The process:

Adding a new column to a table in PDM and generating Modify Database script will not work (see Example below). For this reason, the FE process is more complex:
- Cut (remove) the table that requires new column(s) from PDM.
- In PDM, modify any invalidated indexes on foreign keys that pointed to the primary key of the table just removed.
- Archive PDM.
- Paste the table back to PDM and re-establish foreign keys and indexes.
- Add a not-null column.
- Generate SQL database modification script.
- Execute the script on the database.

Figure 5: Not-null birth_date column added to T_Employee.

T_Employee			
emp_id	<pk>	char(3)	not null
first_name		varchar(20)	not null
middle_initial		char(1)	null
family_name		varchar(40)	not null
birth_date		smalldatetime	not null
phone		varchar(8)	null
commence_date		smalldatetime	null
terminate_date		smalldatetime	null

- Re-insert the data into the re-created (ie. dropped and created) table.
- Archive PDM.

Example – addition of a not-null column to a table:
- In PDM, the NOT NULL birth_date column added to T_Employee table (Figure5).
- Modify Database script can be generated in PDM, but – as expected – does not execute on DB. Note that the setting of a default value on birth_date would not eliminate the server error (see below).

  alter table T_Employee
  add birth_date smalldatetime default '1-JAN-80' not null
  go

  Server Message: Number 4901, Severity 16
  ALTER TABLE only allows columns to be added which can contain nulls. Column 'birth_date' cannot be added to table 'T_Employee' because it does not allow nulls.

- The above means that the table has to be dropped (PDM and DB), re-created (FE) and data re-inserted with new insert scripts (DB). Note, however, that the indexes have to be repaired manually in PDM. Otherwise, the Modify Database script will not generate, as shown here:

  Error: The following indexes do not have any columns:
  -> Index "IND_FK_TASK_CRTEMPID"
  (IND_FK_TASK_CRTEMPID) of the table "T_Task" (T_TASK)
  -> Index "IND_FK_EVENT_CRTEMPID"
  (IND_FK_EVENT_CRTEMPID) of the table "T_Event" (T_EVENT)
  -> Index "IND_FK_EVENT_DUEEMPID"
  (IND_FK_EVENT_DUEEMPID) of the table "T_Event" (T_EVENT)
  -> Index "IND_FK_EVENT_CMPEMPID"
  (IND_FK_EVENT_CMPEMPID) of the table "T_Event" (T_EVENT)
  Result: 4 error(s).

Limitations and conclusions:
- Dropping a table with the primary key pointed to from other tables breaks the referential integrity of the database. The restoration of this integrity is not guaranteed when the table is re-created and data re-inserted. This is because the integrity is verified when foreign keys are inserted in "child" tables, not when the primary keys are inserted in "parent" table.
- The above risk can be alleviated by first deleting the records from the table and

then dropping it. The Delete action causes appropriate triggers to fire and requires remedial actions on child tables - thus allowing to drop the table later in a safe manner.

- Changes in Scenario 2 are troublesome and require a close cooperation between PDM designers and DB programmers. The FE process must conform to the sequence of events listed above.

Scenario 3 - FE of additional business rules on schema

Categories of changes:

- Addition of declarative business rules (such as data entry validation).
- Addition of procedural business rules implemented in triggers.

The process:

- Archive PDM.
- In PDM, set new business rules on columns, data types, or tables.
- Generate SQL database modification script.
- Execute the script on DB.
- Archive PDM.

Example – addition of non-modifiability on a column and making the column values conform to an entry pattern:

- The model is modified in PDM so that column birth_date must not be modifiable and phone must conform to the pattern: "9457[0-9][0-9][0-9][0-9]".
- Generate and execute SQL database modification script. The rule on phone generates a check constraint, but the rule on birth_date requires a trigger.

```
create table T_Employee
(
    emp_id          char(3)                     not null,
    first_name      varchar(20)     not null,
    middle_initial  char(1)                     null ,
    family_name     varchar(40)     not null,
    birth_date      smalldatetime   default '1-JAN-80' not null,
    phone           varchar(8)      null
       constraint CKC_PHONE_T_EMPLOY check
           (phone like "9457[0-9][0-9][0-9][0-9]"),
    commence_date   smalldatetime null   ,
    terminate_date  smalldatetime null   ,
    constraint PK_T_EMPLOYEE primary key (emp_id)
)


/* Update trigger "tu_t_employee" for table "T_Employee" */
create trigger tu_t_employee on T_Employee for update as
```

Figure 6: Schema after RE to a new PDM.

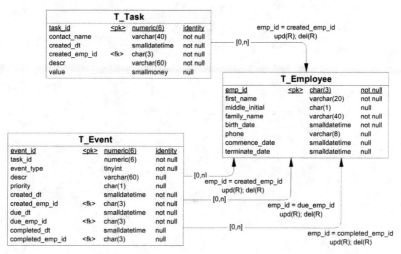

```
begin
  declare
    @maxcard int,
    @numrows int,
    @numnull int,
    @errno int,
    @errmsg varchar(255)
  select @numrows = @@rowcount
    if @numrows = 0
      return


    /* Non modifiable column "birth_date" cannot be modified */
    if update(birth_date)
      if exists (select 1
          from inserted I, deleted d
          where i.birth_date != d.birth_date)
        begin
          select @errno = 30001,
            @errmsg = 'Column "birth_date" cannot be modified.'
          Goto error
            end
          return
/* Errors handling */
error:
  raiserror @errno @errmsg
```

Figure 7: PDM after RE.

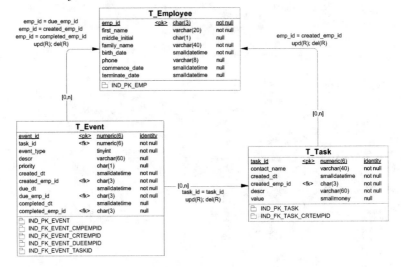

rollback transaction
end
go
commit
go

Limitations and conclusions:

* Newly generated database rules and triggers do not validate the prior database content.
* The recommended process is that PDM designers modify PDM and DB (with a prior warning given to DB programmers).

Scenario 4 - FE and then RE to a new PDM

Categories of changes:

* No changes, just FE to a new DB followed by RE to a new PDM.

The process:

* In PDM, forward-engineer to a new DB.
* In PDM, reverse-engineer from a DB.
* Archive PDM.

Example – RE to a new PDM:

* RE T_Employee, T_Event and T_task tables.
* Reversed-engineered graphical result in PDM is incomplete (Figure 6). The relationship between T_Event and T_Task "vanished" (cp. Figure 4) because the CASCADE DELETE constraint in the original PDM was implemented in DB procedurally through a trigger rather than declaratively (however, the trig-

ger itself is reverse-engineered, as expected – ref. Scenario 6).

Limitations and conclusions:

* RE creates a challenge for a CASE tool and the reverse-engineered PDM may contain some flaws. The flaws of a graphical nature can be rectified, but the flaws in the repository can be difficult to correct.
* This scenario has only theoretical significance. In practice, RE needs to be conducted after changes have been made to the DB intention.

Scenario 5 - RE to a new PDM after some changes made in DB intention

Categories of changes:

* Primary key (PK) and foreign key (FK) indexes specified on DB tables.
* System procedures to enforce PK and FK (sp_primarykey & sp_foreignkey) specified on DB (but all referential integrity constraints implemented procedurally through triggers).

The process:

* In DB, make necessary changes.
* In PDM, reverse-engineer the modified DB objects.
* Archive PDM.

Example – RE to a new PDM after changes made to DB:

* RE T_Employee, T_Event and T_task tables (ref. the original PDM in Figure 4).
* Changes made by the programmers on DB:
* PK and FK indexes created.
* Referential integrity constraints specified additionally through sp_primarykey and sp_foreignkey procedures (so that the relationships can be re-constructed in RE).
* RE graphical result (Figure 7):
* The indexes re-engineered properly but some relationships have not been re-constructed correctly - the CASCADE DELETE (del(c)) constraint between T_Event and T_Task changed to RESTRICT DELETE (del(r)), and the three relationships between T_Event and T_Employee re-engineered as only one relationship.
* Unless the above problems are corrected manually, a conflict exists in DB between declarative constraints (implemented through sp_primarykey and sp_foreignkey procedures) and procedural constraints (implemented in triggers).

Limitations and conclusions:

* As before, RE creates a challenge for a CASE/4GL tool and the reverse-engineered PDM may contain some flaws. The flaws of a graphical nature can

be rectified, but the flaws in the repository create serious problems.
- Indexes cannot be reverse-engineered on individual basis - the entire table would have to be reverse-engineered.
- The recommended process is that DB programmers modify the database and re-load the data. All changes are well-documented and passed to PDM designers who then conduct a selective RE at a specified synchronization time.

Scenario 6 - RE of triggers and stored procedures to a PDM
Categories of changes:
- Triggers modified in DB.
- Stored procedures created or modified in DB.

    The process:
- In DB, make necessary changes.
- In PDM, reverse-engineer the modified DB objects..
- Archive PDM.

    Example – RE of a modified trigger:
- In DB, td_t_task trigger modified so that rollback transaction has been changed to rollback trigger with raise error.
- The trigger is reverse-engineered from DB and it replaces the previous trigger in PDM. The trigger is then marked as User-Defined in PDM, so that it can be forward-engineer without changes.

    Limitations and conclusions:
- This RE too creates a challenge for a CASE/4GL tool and the reverse-engineered PDM may contain some flaws.
- A care should be taken so that the triggers once modified in DB are not auto-

Figure 8: Sequence diagram for the process model.

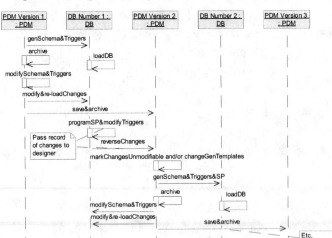

matically re-generated later in FE activities. These triggers can only be modified in DB, not in PDM (they need to be marked as User-Defined).

- Alternatively, if the scripting language of the CASE tool allows to "program" the modification in the templates used to generate the triggers, then the change can be automatically affected in each FE action.

   Limitations and conclusions:

- DB programmers modify the database and re-load the data. All changes are well-documented and passed to PDM designers who then conduct a selective RE at a specified "synchronization" time.
- The reverse-engineered triggers are marked as not modifiable in PDM or the generation templates are "re-programmed."
- Since in practice, in large-scale database systems, the referential integrity is implemented procedurally, the changes conforming to this scenario can heavily limit the reverse engineering activities.
- Note also that in some DBMS-s (e.g., Sybase), only DELETE RESTRICT and UPDATE RESTRICT can be implemented declaratively. In such systems, other options (CASCADE, SET NULL, and SET DEFAULT) have to be implemented procedurally.

PROCESS MODEL

The round-trip engineering process should take into consideration that:

- The PDM model can be archived and versioned by a CASE tool, but a typical relational DB does not have a built-in capability to maintain DB versions (other than by creating a new DB).
- After initial generation of DB, the need for changes to PDM is frequently "discovered" during programming; therefore, programmers should be able to modify DB as needed as long as the modifications are populated back to current PDM. The populate event (ref. Figure 1) should be done in bulk at specific synchronization times and PDM should be then archived.
- Any later changes to the archived PDM that need to be synchronized with DB, should be forward engineered to a new DB instance.

Figure 8 represents a UML sequence diagram for the round-trip engineering process model. The diagram shows three PDM object instances and two DB object instances.

First, in Design Phase 1, a PDM model is created (PDM Version 1) so that SQL scripts can be generated to create database schema and triggers in a DB (DB Number 1). PDM Version 1 is then archived, and DB Number 1 can be loaded with data.

As long as DB programmers (in Programming Phase 1) do not modify database intention, designers (still in Design Phase 1) can modify schema and triggers in PDM, and can generate new SQL scripts to modify database schema and triggers as well as to re-load the database following the modifications. At this point, a PDM model should be saved and archived in PDM Version 2.

Because PDM and DB are now in unison, DB programmers can be given a period of time (Programming Phase 2) for unconstrained development, including programming of stored procedures and making changes to triggers and to database intention. However, all such changes must be carefully documented and passed to designers at the end of Programming Phase 2 (and the beginning of Design Phase 2).

In Design Phase 2, the unconstrained programming is suspended and programming changes are reverse-engineered to PDM Version 2. Changes to triggers and stored procedures are marked in PDM as unmodifiable (ie. User Defined), so that future forward engineering actions do not overwrite those programs. Alternatively, and for triggers only, the code generation templates are "reprogrammed" so that newly-generated triggers are exactly as those modified in Programming Phase 2.

When still in Design Phase 2, designers can modify PDM Version 2 any way they like before generating new SQL scripts to create a DB Number 2. This brings to the end the cycle of changes organized in two design and two programming phases (and resulting in a brand new database instance). PDM Version 2 and DB Number 2 are now in sync, and the cycle can be repeated.

A cycle can begin with design phase or with programming phase - the process model requires only that the phases do not conflict, ie. the programmers do not modify DB in the design phase and the designers do not modify PDM in the programming phase. Any intended changes to DB or to PDM are recorded in a Change Monitoring System and affected in its own phase.

SUMMARY

In this paper, I identified a number of challenging issues that underpin round-trip engineering with databases and I defined a process model to manage the design-implementation cycle with a relational database. The paper addressed a range of issues in round-trip engineering of data and procedural parts of a database system. The scope of the paper did not include the design-implementation cycle with client programs (including any SQL code implemented in the client). A strong underlying assumption of the paper was that a database content (database extension) must always be restored after any round-trip engineering cycle.

In the true spirit of round-trip engineering, a process model was proposed that ensures that the PDM and the DB are synchronized at all times. The model has been successfully applied to guide development in a few medium-size software projects in a market research organization (ACNielsen Australia). The projects involved Visual C++ programs communicating with Sybase System 11 database via ODBC as well as through the native API (Sybase CL-Library). The development tools included PowerDesigner for round-trip engineering with Sybase and Rational Rose for round-trip engineering with Visual C++.

REFERENCES

Ambriola, V., Conradi, R. and Fuggetta, A. (1997). Assessing process-centered software engineering environments. *ACM Tran. Soft. Eng. and Methodology*, 3, 283-328.

Arnold, R. S. (1993). Software reengineering. *IEEE Computer Society*, 688.

Booch, G., Rumbaugh, J. and Jacobson, I. (1999). *The Unified Modeling Language User Guide*, 482. Reading, MA: Addison-Wesley.

Greenwood, R. M., Warboys, B.C. and SA, J. (1996). Cooperating evolving components: A rigorous approach to evolving large software systems. *Proc. 18th Int. Conf. on Soft. Eng., IEEE Computer Society*, 428-437.

Hainaut, J.-L., Englebert, V., Henrard, J., Hick, J.-M. and Roland, D. (1996). Database reverse engineering: from requirements to CARE tools. *Automated Soft. Eng.*, 1/2, 9-46.

Jahnke, J.H., Schafer, W. and Zundorf, A. (1997). Generic fuzzy reasoning nets as a basis for reverse engineering relational database applications. *ACM SIGSOFT Software Engineering Notes*, 6, 193-210.

Jarzabek, S. and Huang, R. (1998). The case for user-centered CASE tools. *Comm. ACM*, 8, 93-99.

Jarzabek, S. and Wang, G. (1998). Model-based design of reverse engineering tools. *Software Maintenance: Research and Practice*, 10, 353-380.

Kozaczynski, W. and Maciaszek, L.A. (1990). Design recovery as integral aspect of software engineering. *Proc. Fifth Australian Soft. Eng. Conf. ASWEC'90*, 87-92. Sydney, May 22-25.

Kozaczynski, W. and Ning, J.Q. (1989). SRE: A knowledge-based environment for large-scale software re-engineering activities. *Proc. 11th Int. Conf. on Soft. Eng.*, 113-122. Pittsburgh, PA, USA, ACM.

Mischke, M.A. (Ed.). (1998). Reengineering. *Systems Integration Success* (1999 Edition), 336. Auerbach Pub.

Olsem, M.R. (1998). An incremental approach to software systems re-engineering. *Software Maintenance: Research and Practice*, 10, 181-202.

Stevens, P. and Pooley, R. (1998). Systems reengineering patterns. *ACM SIGSOFT Software Engineering Notes*, 6, 17-23.

Waters, R. G. and Chikofsky, E. (1994). Reverse engineering: Progress along many dimensions. *Comm. ACM*, 5, 22-25.

Chapter 6

Achieving Effective Software Reuse for Business Systems

Daniel Brandon, Jr.
Christian Brothers University, USA

OVERVIEW

"Reuse (software) engineering is a process where a technology asset is designed and developed following architectural principles, and with the intent of being reused in the future" (Bean, 1999). "If programming has a Holy Grail, widespread code reuse is it with a bullet. While IT has made and continues to make laudable progress in our reuse, we never seem to make great strides in this area" (Grinzo, 1998). The quest for that Holy Grail has taken many developers over many years down unproductive paths" (Bowen, 1997).

This chapter reports on software reuse research (both literature research and design/coding research) and presents an approach for effective software reuse in the development of business systems. This approach is based on Object Oriented technology and provides for both the specification and enforcement of software reuse and corporate standards.

BUSINESS SYSTEMS

Business software systems are typically composed of three logical portions or layers as shown in Figure 1. The "presentation layer" involves the primary user interaction typically via a graphical user interface (GUI). The "business logic" layer provides database connectivity, validation, security, transaction control, and other sequencing or optimization control. This layer may be packaged by a vendor in an application or transaction server or written by a user. The "database layer" provides for the manipulation of persistent data, which for most business systems

Previously published in *Managing Information Technology in a Global Economy*, edited by Mehdi Khosrow-Pour. Copyright © 2001, Idea Group Publishing.

Figure 1

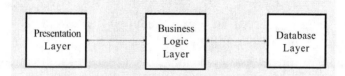

today is stored in a relational database. The interface to this process is a well defined standard application programming interface (API) like ODBC or JDBC using SQL.

NEED FOR REUSE

Today's software development is characterized by many disturbing but well documented facts, including:

Most software development projects "fail" (60% [Williamson, 1997])
The supply of qualified IT professionals is much less than the demand
The complexity of software is constantly increasing
IT needs "better," "cheaper," "faster" software development methods

"Object technology promises a way to deliver cost-effective, high quality and flexible systems on time to the customer" (McClure, 1996). "IS shops that institute component-based software development reduce failure, embrace efficiency and augment the bottom line" (Williamson, 1997). "The bottom line is this: while it takes time for reuse to settle into an organization – and for an organization to settle on reuse – you can add increasing value throughout the process" (Barrett, 1999). We say "object technology" not just adopting an object oriented language (such as C++ or Java), since one can still build poor, non object oriented, and non reusable software even using a fully object oriented language.

TYPES AND APPLICATIONS OF REUSE

Radding defines several different types of reusable components (Radding, 1998):

GUI widgets – effective, but only provide modest payback"
Server-Side components – provide significant payback but require extensive up-front design and an architectural foundation.
Infrastructure components – generic services for transactions, messaging, and database … require extensive design and complex programming
High-level patterns - identify components with high reuse potential
Packaged applications – only guaranteed reuse, … may not offer the exact functionality required

This article and the research behind it are concerned with the first three types of reuse.

Reusing code has several key implementation areas: application evolution, multiple implementations, standards, and new applications. The reuse of code from prior applications in new applications has received the most attention. However, just as important is the reuse of code (and the technology embedded therein) within the same application.

APPLICATION EVOLUTION

Charles Darwin stated that it was not the biggest, smartest, or fastest species that would survive, but the most adaptable. The same is true for application software. Applications must evolve even before they are completely developed, since the environment under which they operate (business, regulatory, social, political, etc.) changes during the time the software is designed and implemented. This is the traditional "requirements creep." Then after the application is successfully deployed, there is a constant need for change.

MULTIPLE IMPLEMENTATIONS

Another key need for reusability within the same application is for multiple implementations. The most common need for multiple implementations involves customizations, internationalization, and multiple platform support. Organizations whose software must be utilized globally may have a need to present an interface to customers in the native language and socially acceptable look and feel ("localization"). The multiple platform dimension of reuse today involves an architectural choice in languages and delivery platforms.

CORPORATE SOFTWARE DEVELOPMENT STANDARDS

Corporate software development standards concern both maintaining standards in all parts of an application and maintaining standards across all applications. "For a computer system to have lasting value it must exist compatibly with users and other systems in an ever-changing Information Technology (IT) world (Brandon, 1999). As stated by Weinschenk and Yeo, "Interface designers, project managers, developers, and business units need a common set of look-and-feel guidelines to design and develop by" (Weinschenk, 1995). In the area of user interface standards alone, Appendix A of Weinschenk's book presents a list these standards; there are over three hundred items (Weinschenk, 1997). Many companies today still rely on some type of printed "Standards Manuals."

ACHIEVING EFFECTIVE SOFTWARE REUSE

In most organizations, software reusability is a goal that is very elusive, as said by Bahrami "a most difficult promise to deliver on" (Bahrami, 1999). Radding stated: "Code reuse seems to make sense, but many companies find there is so much work involved, it's not worth the effort. ...In reality, large scale software reuse is still more the exception than the rule" (Radding, 1998). Bean in "Reuse 101" states; the current decreased "hype" surrounding code reuse is likely due to three basic problems (Bean, 1999):

Reuse is an easily misunderstood concept

Identifying what can be reused is a confusing process

Implementing reuse is seldom simple or easy to understand

Grinzo (1998) also list several reasons and observations on the problem of reuse, other than for some "difficult to implement but easy to plug-in cases" such as GUI widgets: a "nightmare of limitations and bizarre incompatibilities," performance problems, "thorny psychological issues" involving programmers' personalities, market components that are buggy and difficult to use, fear of entrapment, component size, absurd licensing restrictions, or lack of source code availability.

Some organizations try to promote software reusability by simply publishing specifications on class libraries that have been built for other in house applications or that are available via third parties, some dictate some type of reuse, and other organizations give away some type of "bonus" for reusing the class libraries of others (Bahrami, 1999).

But more often than not, these approaches typically do not result in much success.

"It's becoming clear to some who work in this field that large-scale reuse of code represents a major undertaking" (Radding, 1998). " An OO/reuse discipline entails more than creating and using class libraries. It requires *formalizing* the practice of reuse" (McClure, 1996).

Based upon both our literature research herein and experimental implementations, it was concluded that there were two key components to formalizing an effective software reuse practice both within an application development and for new applications. These components were:

1. Defining a specific Information Technology Architecture within which applications would be developed and reuse would apply

2. Defining a very specific object oriented "Reuse Foundation" that would be implemented within the chosen IT architecture

Figure 2

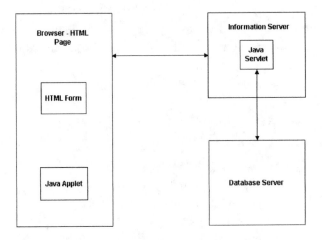

IT ARCHITECTURE

"If you want reuse to succeed, you need to invest in the architecture first" (Radding, 1998). "Without an architecture, organizations will not be able to build or even to buy consistently reusable components." In terms of IT architectures for business systems, there are historically several types as: Central Computer, File Services, Two or Three Tier Client Server, and Two or Three Tier Internet (Browser) based. Various transaction processing and database vendors have their own "slants" on these basic approaches, which may depend upon how business logic and the database are distributed.

It was decided to base our implementation research and development on the last of these categories as shown in Figure 2. Only vendor independent and "open" architectures would be used. The "multiple platform" dimension of reusability would be handled by using Java and Java generated HTML. Internet based applications are becoming the preferred way of delivering software based services within an organization (Intranets), to the worldwide customer base via browsers and "net appliances" (Internet), and between business (Extranets).

The presentation layer is represented by browser windows using HTML or Java Applets. The HTML is a static container for the Java Applet or is dynamically generated by a Java Servlet. The business logic layer is in the form of Java Servlets running on the information (Internet) server. The database, typically running on a separate server, is accessed via JDBC from the Servlets (or even from the Applets if a "type 4" pure JDBC driver was used).

Figure 3

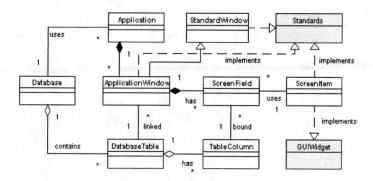

OBJECT ORIENTED REUSE FOUNDATION

As has been concluded by several authors, "A reuse effort demands a solid conceptual foundation" (Barrett, 1999). The foundation used here is shown in Figure 3, and is called the "Object Oriented Reuse Foundation" (OORF). It is based on the key object oriented principles of inheritance and composition. By establishing this foundation, an organization can effectively begin to obtain significant reusability since programmers must inherit their class from one of the established classes and they must only compose their class of the established pre-built components.

In the design of Figure 3, an application is composed of a number of Application Windows. Each of these is derived from the Standard Window (or from another window which was derived from the Standard Window) and is associated with a table or view in that database. The Application Window implements the Standards interface. The Application Window is composed of screen fields, which use a specific screen item and are bound to a column of the database table/view. Each screen item implements the Standards and also implements the GUIWidget interface. The GUIWidget interface defines the functions that all screen

Figure 4

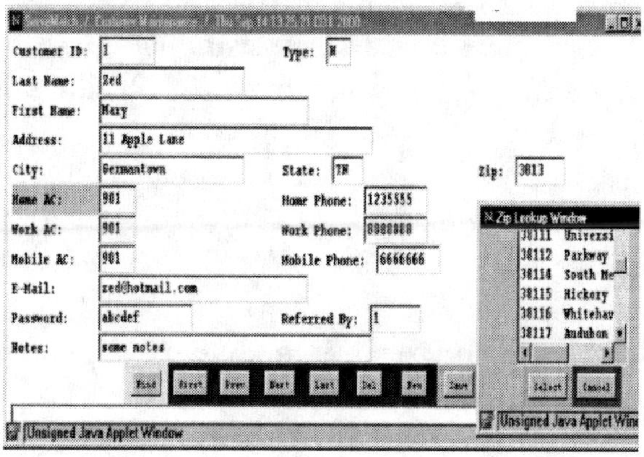

items provide (such as, requestFocus, setText, getText, isValid, etc.). The screen items can be from the Java AWT, Java Swing, or third party class libraries as long as these class library sources have been extended to use the data in the Standards. The Standards interface defines all the standards used throughout the system including: fonts, colors, styles, sizes, initial states, icons, etc.

While Figure 3 shows the conceptual OORF, there would typically be an inheritance hierarchy of Standard Windows including forms, tables, etc. Screen Items would be a hierarchy also for the different types of these widgets such as textboxes, radio buttons, choice buttons, etc. Each application could also create an inheritance hierarchy of application windows.

Figure 4 shows a generated application window which provides navigation and update support for a selected database table including automatic lookup of defined foreign keys to maintain referential integrity. The reusability for this example was 95%, that is 95% of the lines of code were already in the OORF. For the applications implemented thusfar, all obtained reusability of over 90%.

REFERENCES

Bahrami, A. (1999). *Object Oriented Systems Development*. New York: Irwin McGraw Hill

Barrett, K. and Schmuller, J. (1999). Building an infrastructure of real-world reuse. *Component Strategies*, October.

Bean, J. (1999). Reuse 101. *Enterprise Development*, October.

Bowen, B. (1997). Software reuse with java technology: Finding the holy grail. www.javasoft.com/features/1997/may/reuse.html.

Brandon, D. (2000). An object oriented approach to user interface standards. *Challenges of Information Technology in the 21st Century*. Hershey, PA: Idea Group Publishing.

Grinzo, L. (1998). The unbearable lightness of being reusable. *Dr. Dobbs Journal*, September.

Lim, W. C. (1998). *Managing Software Reuse*. Englewood Cliffs, NJ: Prentice Hall.

McClure, C. (1996). Experiences from the OO playing field. *Extended Intelligence*.

Paulk, M. (1995). *The Capability Maturity Model*. Reading, MA: Addison Wesley.

Radding, A. (1998). Hidden cost of code reuse. *Information Week*, November 9.

Reifer, D. (1997). *Practical Software Reuse*. New York: John Wiley & Sons.

Weinschenk, S., Jamar, P. and Yeo, S. (1997). *GUI Design Essentials*. New York: John Wiley & Sons.

Weinschenk, S. and Yeo, S. (1995). *Guidelines for Enterprise Wide GUI Design*. New York: John Wiley & Sons.

Williamson, M. (1999). Software reuse. *CIO Magazine*, May.

Chapter 7

The Future of Software Development

Karen Church and Geoff te Braake
Port Elizabeth Technikon, South Africa

Software development has changed dramatically in the last fifty years and will continue to change. Its future course is of particular interest to developers, in order to gain the correct skills, and to any person faced with a strategic information technology (IT) decision. It is commonly accepted that computers will play an ever-larger role in modern civilisation. There are many unknowns, but the IT decisions made today will affect the competitiveness and preparedness for tomorrow. Awareness of the central issues that will affect the future of software development is the best form of preparation. This chapter presents a view of the future of software development based on the history of software development and the results of two surveys.

INTRODUCTION

Software development tools and techniques have changed considerably in the last half century, are still changing, and will continue to change in the future as hardware capabilities improve and new technologies make new methods of processing and communication possible.

The aim of this chapter is to draw conclusions about the future of software development from trends that can be identified in its evolution to date. The results of two surveys will help to illustrate some of these trends. The first was a questionnaire survey aimed at software developers which compared their First and Last Project in terms of a number of criteria. The second was a survey of job advertisements in the *Computing SA* newspaper over a ten year period.

Previously published in *Managing Information Technology in a Global Economy*, edited by Mehdi Khosrow-Pour. Copyright © 2001, Idea Group Publishing.

This chapter addresses the advancing generations of programming languages which have gained and lost popularity over the survey period. The evolution of coding styles and software architecture will be briefly described. The growing importance of user interfaces will be explained, in addition to a brief description of the increasing complexity of applications from user and developer perspectives. The final section will describe the future trends that can be projected from these points.

LANGUAGE GENERATIONS AND USAGE

The first applications of computers were to gain some form of military advantage based on doing many mathematical calculations very quickly (Arnold, 1991, pp.32-35). Computers then began to be used in business to speed up administrative tasks (Leveson, 1997, p.130). Online transaction processing and later, the personal computer, introduced a whole new dimension to computing by allowing people without programming training to use computers.

The challenge for software developers is to create programs that enhance the lives and work of those who use them. This section begins by describing the software development evolution. The development of programming language generations and their usage is addressed.

LANGUAGE GENERATION

In the early generations of programming languages, machine and assembly languages, the code was written at the level of machine instructions. Many statements were needed to accomplish simple calculations. Programs were long and errors were easily introduced, but difficult to identify and remove.

High level languages (HLLs) were developed to hide the details of implementation from the programmer. This is known as abstraction and is a common theme in the history of programming languages (Watson, 1989, pp.4-10). Each HLL command is translated into any number of machine instructions. HLL coding is shorter, and programs are easier and quicker to write and debug. The commands are fairly easy to learn and meaningful names can be given to variables and subprograms.

Figure 1: Levels of abstraction in Visual Basic and C++

Visual Basic	C++
frmMain.MousePointer = vbHourglass	HCURSOR lhCursor; lhCursor = AfxGetApp()-> LoadStandardCursor (IDC_WAIT); m_bCursor = TRUE; SetCursor(lhCursor);

Table 1: Language Generation by Project

Style	First Project	Last Project
3GL	57.1%	15.4%
4GL	35.7%	76.9%
Other	7.1%	7.7%

HLLs differ in the amount of abstraction that they provide. Visual Basic (VB) offers a higher level of abstraction than C++, as can be seen in Figure 1, in the operation to change the mouse pointer.

The higher the level of abstraction, fewer lines of code are required to achieve the same goal. Less code in the program makes it easier and quicker to write and debug. However, there is usually a performance penalty when the level of the language is higher. Flexibility is also decreased as the level of the language increases because the programmer has less control over the exact way in which the processing is done (McConnell, 1996, pp. 345-368).

Non-procedural languages take abstraction even further, with the programmer coding the desired result, not the method for achieving it. Historically, procedural languages have been the most commonly used type of language, as other language types were slower and more resource intensive. However, recent improvements in computer performance and language optimisation has meant that currently, there is a greater use of the other types of languages. The most widely used non-procedural language is SQL (McDermid, 1991, p.44/3; Kimball, 1996, pp.xxi-xxii; Watson, 1989, pp.79-81).

Table 1 shows a definite trend towards higher level languages with over three quarters of the Last Project being done using fourth generation languages (4GLs). This can be attributed to increasing pressure to produce systems more efficiently together with the development of more powerful 4GLs (McConnell, 1996, pp.2,345).

Table 2: Most Sought-after Languages by Year

	1989	1990	1992	1993	1994	1995	1996	1997	1998	1999	2000
ASP	0.0	0.0	0.0	0.0	0.0	0.0	0.0	0.0	0.4	2.5	7.9
C	12.1	8.7	23.1	28.8	22.1	13.5	9.9	8.5	6.2	7.1	6.8
C++	0.0	0.0	4.6	8.0	19.4	18.5	16.2	11.7	12.9	16.2	14.7
COBOL	26.4	34.1	18.5	16.8	17.1	14.9	17.0	21.0	12.4	6.0	1.3
HTML	0.0	0.0	0.0	0.0	0.0	0.0	0.3	2.9	2.6	3.0	8.7
Java	0.0	0.0	0.0	0.0	0.0	0.0	0.6	3.2	4.7	7.0	12.3
JavaScript	0.0	0.0	0.0	0.0	0.0	0.0	0.0	0.0	0.4	1.1	3.1
Natural	12.1	19.2	15.7	12.8	14.4	8.6	8.8	9.8	9.4	3.3	0.5
RPG	18.3	19.2	21.3	15.2	6.8	9.6	5.4	5.6	6.0	4.6	0.8
SQL	2.9	0.9	7.4	7.2	5.0	10.2	6.5	4.0	9.4	10.2	11.0
Visual Basic	0.0	0.0	0.0	0.0	10.4	19.5	17.9	10.9	16.5	20.5	18.4

Figures = percentage of skills per newspaper issue.

LANGUAGE USAGE

Whilst hundreds of programming languages have been created, relatively few have been widely used. The advert survey (results below) aimed to discover which languages have been used the most in software development since 1989. A number of general trends can be seen from Table 2.

The most sought-after language in the early 1990s was COBOL, followed by RPG, Natural, and C. By the year 2000, the main languages were C++, VB, SQL, and the Web languages Java, HTML, and ASP.

Thus, there has been a move to higher level languages. There has been a shift away from some long established languages with the new computing environment dominated by the graphical user interface and the Web in particular. The next section will describe the evolution of coding styles.

CODING STYLE EVOLUTION

As seen in the previous section, languages have become more powerful and have raised their level of abstraction. The programming language chosen for development may either encourage or discourage certain programming practices depending on their features. This section highlights some of these coding styles.

Structured programming became the most popular programming style in the 1970s. It popularised the concept of modular programming (Yaeger, 1995, p.2). A source of many problems with structured programming was that variables could be inadvertently changed resulting in errors.

Since the late 1980s object-orientation has gained popularity amongst software developers. Object-orientation makes use of classes which encapsulate data and functions into a single unit. Object-orientation is an important paradigm for contemporary system developers and is supported in many widely used languages, such as C++ and Java (Salus, 1998, pp.5-11).

Graphical development languages (e.g., Visual Basic, Delphi) popularised the concept of component-based programming. Components should be built with standard interfaces so that they can be reused by other applications and any other language or tool that supports the interface method. This is widely used in Internet development. (Jacobson et al., 1997, pp.85,156).

Table 3: Coding Style by Project

Style	First Project	Last Project
Component	7.1%	23.1%
Object-oriented	28.6%	61.5%
Structured	50.0%	15.4%

It is common to build components using the object oriented style just as object orientation makes use of structured concepts. Thus the different styles can be seen as an evolution of better coding practices which aim to increase productivity, maintainability, reusability, and readability of code while decreasing the number of errors, and time required for coding and maintenance.

The coding style used by the respondents in the First and the Last Project shows considerable difference (Table 3). In the First Project the structured style was the most common, followed by the object-oriented style. Structured programming decreased considerably in the Last Project. Object orientation was the clear leader in the Last Project, followed by the component style.

The majority of object-oriented and component-based development is done using 4GLs . Projects developed using the structured style, however, mainly use 3GLs.

There has been an evolution in programming styles to promote modularisation, data hiding, and reuse. This allows systems to be developed more quickly, to have better quality and to be easier to maintain. Software architecture has also changed considerably resulting in different development opportunities and challenges which will be discussed in the next section.

SOFTWARE ARCHITECTURE

The previous sections showed that using modern coding styles can help developers to produce and maintain systems more efficiently. These styles have been supported by different languages in different eras. The evolution in software architecture is as a result of the changing capabilities of hardware, and increasingly distributed and integrated systems.

Most early data processing applications were isolated subsystems. Each application used its own flat data files. Online transaction processing increased the number of records in files and required random access to records. However, as the number of records in files increased, inconsistencies in data and accessing of records became major problems. Therefore a more integrated solution was sought and a number of database models were developed.

The network model was the first de facto database model in the late 1960s and early 1970s. The databases were, however, dependent on the application development language and many vendors produced incompatibile products (Fortier, 1997, pp.187-188). The relational model, proposed in 1970, was independent of the application development language using the database and many applications could access the same database (Deen, 1985, p.77). This meant that the organisation was not bound to a particular language for development (Hughes, 1988, p.4-5). The relational model has become popular due to the simplicity of

Figure 2: Three-tier Web architecture

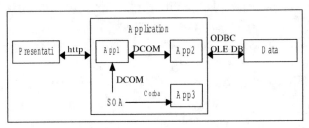

database structure, the flexibility of relationships, and the richness of data manipulation (Fortier, 1997, pp.207,244).

In the mid-1980s, Local Area Networks (LANs) were becoming popular and each department in a company installed its own LAN and developed its own departmental client/server applications. This resulted in redundant and inconsistent data within an organisation. In the early 1990s the development of enterprise client/server IT systems which replaced or augmented legacy mainframe systems and integrated departmental LANs, allowed companies to deliver the right information when and where it could best be used (Goldman, Rawles & Mariga, 1999, p.19).

These systems began using the three-tier application architecture (Figure 2), which is also the architecture of the Web. Applications are divided into three layers or tiers known as P-A-D, presentation, application and data. Each tier can be handled by different computers and developed in different languages. Not only can the layers of the application be split onto different computers, but each layer, especially the application and data layers, may also be split over multiple computers making it scalable. System maintenance and modification is facilitated by allowing changes to one tier or component without affecting the others (Edwards, 1999, pp.3-11). Providing the client with a Web interface greatly simplifies distribution and platform problems.

Thus software architecture has moved from a single unit on a mainframe computer to distributed data, application and presentation tiers. Data has moved from multiple, inconsistent data sources to single integrated databases. In dealing with large systems, such as the many enterprise scale systems presently being created, it is desirable to have an architecture that allows units to be worked on simulataneously and independently (Jacobson, 1997, p.171). An area of software development that has become very important in recent years, is the user interface, which is discussed in the next section.

Table 4: User Interface

Style	First Project	Last Project
GUI	35.7%	53.8%
Text-based	50.0%	0.0%
Web-based	14.3%	46.2%

USER INTERFACES

IT systems are commonly developed for access in a distributed environment, giving non-IT people access to information resources and data processing power. This makes the user interface particularly important in development. Changes in common user interfaces are described below.

The first few decades of computing focused on performance and functionality of applications. When millions of people began using productivity tools, it became apparent that a primary determinant of the success of an application was its ease of use for users of all levels of experience (Van Dam, 1997, p.64).

From the early 1960s through the mid-1980s text-based user interfaces were used almost exclusively. The WIMP GUI (graphical user interfaces based on windows, icons, menus and a pointing device), first began to gain popularity with the Macintosh in 1984 and later achieved its current dominance with Windows. When this event-driven paradigm was introduced it was difficult for developers to produce this type of application with the available tools. The Windows environment returned programmers to working in ways reminiscent of low-level programmers. A tool was needed to increase the level of abstraction to allow efficient Windows programming. Therefore languages such as Visual Basic and Delphi were developed to build GUI applications efficiently (Cornell, 1997, pp.xix).

Half of the First Projects reported in the questionnaire survey were text-based. Text-based systems development virtually disappeared in the Last Project whilst Web interfaces show the biggest gains, even though they are relatively new (Table 4).

Thus the user interface is one of the most important aspects of IT systems, especially as they are becoming more complex from a number of perspectives, which are discussed below.

GROWING APPLICATION COMPLEXITY

The user interface is one of the primary factors determining the success of a system. Applications are becoming more powerful but also more complex for developers to produce. This complexity arises from increasing integration with other systems and utilising the growing power of computers to produce better information. These trends are discussed in terms of groupware, multimedia, multiple language development, and team work.

Table 5: Number of Languages by Project

Style	Multi-language	Single Language
First Project	35.7%	64.3%
Last Project	92.3%	7.7%

Table 6: Number of Languages by Interface

Style	Multi-language	Single Language
GUI	66.7%	33.3%
Text	28.6%	71.4%
Web	87.5%	12.5%

GROUPWARE

Groupware is a relatively new set of technologies that allows for easier communication and collaborative work by means of a computer network. The Web is a very good medium for deploying groupware technologies, but needs to have enhanced security to make it viable (Goldman et al., 1999, pp.177-178, 217).

MULTIMEDIA

Multimedia provides a richer experience of the application for the user. This has become possible because of increased hardware capability. The Internet provides a container for presenting rich multimedia as well as providing the means of co-ordinating its distribution. Multimedia development tools have developed rapidly due to industry focus on the Web and its mass usage (Nicol et al., 1999, p.79).

An increasingly important feature of the software industry is gaming. Games tend to tax computer system resources to the maximum, making it imperative that developers access sound and graphics capabilities at low levels to increase the speed of performance. Graphics and sound are combined to create more real experiences. The simulation effects are becoming so realistic that games have large inventories of the objects and environments that are simulated. Some games require some level of artificial intelligence. Therefore, games development is driving new technologies, many of which will have applications in marketing, education and other areas (Tapscott, 1999; Walnum, 1995, pp.6-11,70-71).

MULTIPLE LANGUAGE DEVELOPMENT

It is evident from the advert survey referred to earlier that multiple technologies for a single project is not a new phenomenon. Many adverts for COBOL programmers included required skills in CICS and some database management system. In 2000 (Table 2) SQL was the fourth most sought-after skill. In Web development there are client side scripting and markup languages and application

Table 7: Team work by Project

Style	First Project	Last Project
Team member	78.6%	100.0%
Working solo	21.4%	0.0%

logic languages (Edwards, 1999, pp.3-11). Therefore, multiple language development is the rule, rather than the exception.

The questionnaire demonstrated that over 90% of the last projects (Table 5) were developed with multiple languages. This was particularly true of Web-based projects. It was less common in GUIs and the minority of text-based systems (Table 6). The component paradigm gives the possibility of being able to create a system built from components developed in the best language for the task. The components are connected using an interface protocol, the most common being COM/DCOM and CORBA (Finne, Leijen, Meijer & Jones, 1999).

TEAM WORK

A team can be defined as a group of people whose complementary skills, common purpose and approach enable them to complete a task for which they are mutually accountable. Team work has always been important, especially now with multiple languages and having to deal with the intricacies of networks and other technologies. This range of skills can only be provided by teams (Jacobson et al., 1997, p.54). Table 7 shows that the percentage of projects on which developers worked as a team, as opposed to doing the project on their own, rose from 78.6% to 100%. Thus while team work has been important in IT development in the past, it is has now become vital.

Thus applications are becoming more complex, both in terms of functionality offered and consequently in their development. Now that some of the important factors of the past and the present of IT systems development have been discussed, some thoughts on the future are presented.

THE FUTURE

With the rapid rate of change in the IT field it is very difficult for developers to see what the future trends might be. After analysing the past changes and current situation the following points are suggested as likely directions for the future of software development in the short term.

The trend of moving to higher level languages is sure to continue in the effort to produce quality systems efficiently. Hardware advances make the processing overheads incurred by these languages less significant.

There needs to be some consolidation in Web development and there are likely to be numerous tools and languages developed that attempt to do this. One technology that may prove important is Microsoft's ASP+ Web Forms, which will allow the development of Web applications in a similar way to Visual Basic. The ease with which these developers can produce complete Web applications and the increasing usage of ASP (see Table 2) makes this a technology to watch in the coming months. (Microsoft, 2000a; Microsoft, 2000b).

Java has progressed from experimental to implemented systems faster than any language except VB. Considering its rise in popularity and wide usage and successive releases to remedy the slowness in execution, Java can be expected to remain a mainstream programming language for some time to come (Berst, 2000a; Babcock, 2000).

Developers will experiment with other types of languages. Non-conventional languages may be used to produce specific components or applications in the areas for which the language is intended..

Object-orientation appears to remain dominant, but the component paradigm is likely to gain ground, especially with the importance of the Web.

The Web is likely to play a role in most systems development projects, especially as XML is developed to allow for more powerful applications. A specific example is the Simple Object Access Protocol (SOAP), a protocol that could provide the interface between virtually any two systems as long as they support both hypertext transfer protocol (HTTP) and XML. (Skonnard, 2000).

An emerging area of software development is that of mobile devices. The second generation of mobile phones, using digital networks, were introduced in the early 1990s and experienced exponential growth in numbers of users and services associated with them. The next generation of mobile telecommunications will include many more wireless data services (Väänänen-Vainio-Mattila & Ruuska, 1999, pp.24-25). It will be an important area of software development. It will create new requirements and limitations while still providing a rich multimedia experience for an even less computer literate audience than the Internet.

Thus the future of IT systems development will have increasingly stronger tools that allow developers to produce systems that address ever more complex functionality, thereby building applications that will enhance the user's productivity, not restrict it. As the tools become more powerful more of the technical correctness will be supplied by the tool, but more creativity will be required of the developer to adapt to and to use new technologies to produce better IT systems.

CONCLUSION

IT systems play a vital role in modern civilisation. There is virtually no industry that does not use some form of computerisation and many are totally dependent on computers to control their operations. Software development will change unrecognisably in the future, as it has in the past, and it is not possible to predict how with any certainty (Leveson, 1997, p.129). This paper attempts to present the future of software development, in terms of the factors from its past.

Programming languages have seen to be continually raising the level of abstraction, hiding the details of implementation from developers. This allows them to focus their efforts on achieving the best solution, rather than how to do it. The languages used have changed with the type of the majority of applications that are developed. Currently, as well as in the near future that means the most widely used languages will be visual development languages that produce Web applications. Coding styles have evolved methods for making programs easier and quicker to develop and to maintain by building them out of units which can be changed independently and reused in many systems. The independent units include the splitting of the application into data, logic and presentation tiers with interfacing protocols to make applications flexible and scalable. The user interface has become an increasingly important part of applications as they become more powerful and are used by people of all levels of experience to improve their efficiency.

Thus this paper has drawn some conclusions about the future of software development in order for current developers to make themselves better prepared to meet the challenges that lie ahead.

REFERENCES

Arnold, D. O. (1991). *Computers and Society Impact!* New York: McGraw-Hill.

Babcock, C. (2000). Java: Can Sun control the flood? *Inter@ctive Week*. [cited 3 July 2000]. URL http://www.zdnet.com/enterprise/stories/main/0,10228,2581701,00.html.

Berst, J. (2000a). *Scott McNealy's Java Jive*. [cited 3 July 2000]. URL http://www.zdnet.com/anchordesk/stories/story/0,10738,2582432,00.html.

Cornell, G. (1997). *Visual Basic 5 from the Group Up*. Berkeley, CA: Osborne/McGraw-Hill.

Deen, S. M. (1985). *Principles and Practice of Database Systems*. Hampshire: Macmillan.

Edwards, J. (1999). *3-Tier Client/Server at Work (Revised ed.)*. New York: John Wiley & Sons.

Finne S., Leijen, D., Meijer E. and Jones S.P. (1999). H/Direct: A binary foreign language interface for Haskell. *ACM SIGPLAN NOTICES*, 34(1), 153-162.

Fortier, P. J. (1997). *Database Systems Handbook*. New York: McGraw-Hill.

Goldman, J. E., Rawles, P. T. and Mariga, J. R. (1999). *Client/Server Information Systems*. New York: John Wiley & Sons.

Hughes, J. G. (1988). *Database Technology A Software Engineering Approach*. New York: Prentice Hall.

Jacobson, I., Griss, M. and Jonsson, P. (1997). *Software Reuse*. Reading, MA: Addison Wesley.

Kimball, R. (1996). *The Data Warehouse Toolkit*. New York: John Wiley & Sons.

Leveson, N. G. (1997). Software engineering: Stretching the limits of complexity. *Communications of the ACM*, February, 40, 129-131.

McConnell, S. (1996). *Rapid Development*. Redmond, WA: Microsoft Press.

McDermid, J. (1991). *Software Engineer's Reference Book*. Oxford: Butterworth-Heinemann.

Microsoft (2000a). *Microsoft Primes Millions of Developers for the Next-Generation Web*. [cited 3 July 2000]. URL http://www.microsoft.com/presspass/press/2000/feb00/nextgenerationpr.asp.

Microsoft (2000b). *Visual Studio Enables the Programmable Web*. [cited 3 July 2000] URL http://msdn.microsoft.com/vstudio/nextgen/technology/Webforms.asp.

Nicol, J.R., Getfreund, Y.S., Paschetto, J., Rush, K.S. and Martin, C. (1999). How the Internet helps build collaborative multimedia applications. *Communications of the ACM*, January, 42(1), 79-85.

Salus, P. H. (1998). *Handbook of Programming Languages*, 1. Macmillan Technical Publishing

Skonnard, A. (2000). *SOAP: The Simple Object Access Protocol*. [cited 1 August 2000]. Microsoft Internet Developer, January 2000.

Tapscott, D. (1999). The power of electronic play. *Computer World*, May 24, 32.

Väänänen-Vainio-Mattila, K. and Ruuska, S. (1999). Designing mobile phones and communicators for consumers' needs at Nokia. *Interactions*, September, 23-26.

Walnum, C. (1995). *Windows 95 Games SDK Strategy Guide*. Indianapolis, IN: Que.

Watson, D. (1989). *High-Level Languages and Their Compilers*. Wokingham, England: Addison Wesley.

Yaeger, J. (1995). *Programming in RPG/400 2nd ed*. Loveland, Co: Duke Press.

Chapter 8

Understanding the Role of Use Cases in UML: A Review and Research Agenda[1]

Brian Dobing
University of Lethbridge, Canada

Jeffrey Parsons
Memorial University of Newfoundland, Canada

A use case is a description of a sequence of actions constituting a complete task or transaction in an application. Use cases were first proposed by Jacobson (1987) and have since been incorporated as one of the key modeling constructs in UML (Booch, Jacobson, & Rumbaugh, 1999) and the Unified Software Development Process (Jacobson, Booch, & Rumbaugh, 1999). This paper traces the development of use cases, and identifies a number of problems with both their application and theoretical underpinnings. From an application perspective, the use case concept is marked by a high degree of variety in the level of abstraction versus implementation detail advocated by various authors. In addition, use cases are promoted as a primary mechanism for identifying objects in an application, even though they focus on processes rather than objects. Moreover, there is an apparent inconsistency between the so-called naturalness of object models and the commonly held view that use cases should be the primary means of communicating and verifying requirements with users. From a theoretical standpoint, the introduction of implementation issues in use cases can be seen as prematurely anchoring the analysis to particular implementation decisions. In addition, the fragmentation of objects across use cases creates conceptual difficulties in developing a

Previously published in the *Journal of Database Management*, vol.11, no.4, Copyright © 2000, Idea Group Publishing.

comprehensive class model from a set of use cases. Moreover, the role of categorization in human thinking suggests that class models may serve directly as a good mechanism for communicating and verifying application requirements with users. We conclude by outlining a framework for further empirical research to resolve issues raised in our analysis.

The Unified Modeling Language, or UML (Booch, Jacobson, & Rumbaugh, 1999), has rapidly emerged as a standard language and notation for object-oriented modeling in systems development, while the accompanying Unified Software Development Process (Jacobson, Booch, & Rumbaugh, 1999) has recently been developed to provide methodological support for the application of UML in software development. The adoption of UML brings focus to object-oriented developers faced with the task of choosing among dozens of proposed approaches to object-oriented analysis and design. In light of this activity, driven primarily by practitioners, it is important from an academic perspective to independently evaluate the capabilities and limitations of UML and the Unified Process. Such evaluations can contribute to the development of theoretical underpinnings of UML, to an improvement in its modeling power and usability, and to its appropriate application in systems development projects.

This chapter focuses on two components of UML: use cases and class models. In particular, we consider the appropriateness of use cases as a component of an object-oriented modeling language by looking at their role as a tool for communicating with users, and the relationship between use cases and the class models that are developed from them. We examine the variability in the amount of detail use cases should contain, according to various proponents, and introduce a theoretical rationale for including fewer task details than many proponents advocate. We discuss the lack of 'object'-orientation in use cases, and present a theoretical argument that use cases may, in fact, not be necessary or valuable in UML. Finally, we develop a framework for empirical research to evaluate the value of use cases and their relationship to class models in UML.

USE CASE FUNDAMENTALS

The term "use case" was introduced by Jacobson (1987) to refer to "a complete course of events in the system, seen from a user's perspective" (Jacobson, Christerson, Jonsson, & Overgaard, 1992, p. 157). The concept resembles others being introduced around the same time. Rumbaugh, Blaha, Premerlani, Eddy, and Lorensen (1991); Wirfs-Brock, Wilkerson, and Wiener (1990); and Rubin and Goldberg (1992) used scenarios or scripts in a similar way. But, despite concerns about the awkwardness of the name, the use case has become an important part of most object-oriented analysis and design methodologies. Use cases were incorporated into UML in late 1995, after Ivar Jacobson joined forces with Grady Booch and James Rumbaugh.

The use case differs from typical structured requirements analysis tools that preceded it in two important ways. First, the use case is largely text-based. Structured analysis emphasized the importance of graphical tools, such as Work Flow and Data Flow Diagrams. The rationale for preferring diagrams to text was the oft-cited "a picture is worth a thousand words." In addition, before structured methodologies became available, analysts often generated extensive and unstructured text descriptions of existing and proposed systems that were very difficult to use. UML has not abandoned diagrams; Activity, Sequence and Use Case Diagrams all play important roles during analysis. But use cases are the key communication tool, so that "users and customers no longer have to learn complex notation" (Jacobson et al., 1999, p. 38).

Second, use cases focus on transactions from the user's perspective. In Data Flow Diagrams, transaction sequences were often not explicitly articulated. All the steps needed to, for example, sell goods to a customer would be there, but the connections between taking orders, checking inventory levels, determining payment types and authorizations, printing receipts, and other activities were not always clear. The focus on complete transactions shares some important similarities with the concept of a "process" in Business Process Reengineering, "a collection of activities that takes one or more kinds of input and creates an output that is of value to the customer" (Hammer & Champy, 1993, p. 35). Both emphasize complete transactions viewed from a customer or user perspective, although the terms "user" and "customer" imply a different level of analysis. Jacobson, Ericsson, and Jacobson (1994) deal extensively with using use cases to support reengineering, suggesting the similarity is not coincidental.

Use cases have been all but universally embraced in object-oriented systems analysis and development books written since Jacobson et al. (1992). There are a few exceptions, but their alternatives still share some common features. For example, Coad (1995) refers to "scenarios" that seem more detailed or lower level than use cases (e.g., a sale calculating its total (p. 61)). Nevertheless, Norman (1996, p. 165) suggests that Jacobson's use cases and Coad's scenarios are "similar concepts." Kilov and Ross (1994, pp. 9-10) use the notion of a "contract" that states "what has to be true before and what will be true after the operation." Contracts focus more on pre- and post-conditions rather than the steps in between, but again there are similarities.

USE CASE INTERNAL STRUCTURE
Analysis Versus Design Focus

Despite the strong endorsement of the general use case concept, there are many variations on Jacobson's original theme. Not all use cases are created equal. First, there is a difference in content. Use cases, at least during the analysis phase, are generally viewed as a conceptual tool. The use case should emphasize 'what' and not "how" (Jacobson et al., 1994, p. 146). This suggests use cases shouldn't mention technology (e.g., Evans, 1999).

A review of use case examples shows that determining when the "what" ends and the "how" begins is not always easy. Brown (1997) interprets "what" to mean what the system will do rather than the internal implementation. Thus, his use cases include references to screen designs. So do those of Satzinger and Orvik (1996, p. 126). Harmon and Watson (1998, p. 121) go further in their example and refer to the salesperson's laptop. And even Jacobson et al. (1992, p. 162) refer to a display "panel," "receipt button" and "printer" in one of their examples. Some use cases also include more detail on business rules. For example, the IBM Object-Oriented Technology Center (1997, p. 489) video store example includes the condition that customers who are not members pay a deposit of $60.

However, as Larman (1998, p. 10) notes, use cases are not tied to object-oriented methodologies and thus are technology-independent in that sense. The same cannot be said for Data Flow Diagrams, which were designed to produce a basic module structure for a COBOL program. Object-oriented systems can be built without use cases and, conversely, use cases could be used in non-OO projects.

A second issue in use case structure is the variety of formats that have been proposed. Some, such as whether use case titles should begin with gerunds (e.g., "Adding a Customer") or action verbs (e.g., "Add a Customer"), are not serious. More interesting is the format of the text itself. While the first use cases in Jacobson et al. (1992) were written as a paragraph of text, most others have adopted numbered steps. More recently, Jacobson et al. (1994, p. 109) have done so as well. This may not appear to be a serious issue, but sequenced and numbered steps are an invitation to write about 'how.' While the underlying technology need not be mentioned, use cases have become very process oriented. In most cases, they go much further than simply documenting requirements to providing a suggested solution.

Third, the comprehensiveness of use cases also varies. Some take a minimalist approach. Jacobson et al. (1994, p. 105) suggest that use cases should offer "measurable value to an individual actor." MacMaster (1997) argues that use cases be used only for main system functions. But White (1994, p. 7) states that "the collected use cases specify the complete functionality of the system." While Dewitz (1996) uses 11 use cases in her video store example, the IBM Object-Oriented Technology Center (1997) has 24.

Fourth, the level of detail within each use case also varies. Constantine and Lockwood (2000) distinguish between "essential" use cases, containing few if any references to technology and user interface implementation, and "concrete" use cases that specify the actual interactions. Clearly, use cases could move from essential to concrete as the development process proceeds. But not everyone agrees that concrete use cases should ever be used (e.g., Evans, 1999). There are alternative mechanisms that can be used to document screen design choices and similar decisions.

Jacobson et al. (1999) advocate an iterative development approach in which both the number of uses cases and their level of detail increase as the life cycle progresses. They suggest that only the most critical use cases (less than 10%) be detailed in the first (inception) phase. As analysis progresses and requirements become firmer, additional use cases can be added and each can be expanded to include considerably more detail. The analyst could move toward concrete use cases or simply expand the detail within essential use cases. However, knowing where to start, how far to go at each phase, and when to stop, are clearly critical issues not easily resolved.

To further complicate the issue, some of those who favor fewer or less detailed use cases supplement them with "scenarios." Booch (1994, p. 158) defines scenarios as examples of what can happen within a use case. 'Add a customer' is a use case. Adding a specified customer with a particular name, address, etc. is a scenario. A well-chosen set of scenarios provides further detail on exception handling and other special cases (e.g., customers with missing, improbable, or unusual data (Lockheed Martin, 1996)). The same scenarios can later be used in testing. A minimalist approach to use cases combined with extensive scenarios may still result in a large and very detailed set of specifications.

Fifth, and perhaps most important, the role of use cases varies among methodologies. Earlier work on UML focused on the language itself, and was largely agnostic on issues of methodology. But the Unified Process (Jacobson et al., 1999, p. 34) makes clear what was always implicit – use cases "drive the whole development process." In particular, they provide "major input when finding and specifying the classes, subsystems and interfaces." Rosenberg and Scott (1999), however, suggest that "domain modeling" precede use case development. Their domain model is a "glossary of terms" (p. 16), intended to evolve into the objects, attributes, operations and associations. This glossary is based on "available relevant material" (p. 16). From this, a skeletal class diagram is constructed. They warn, "Don't try to write use cases until you know what the users will actually be doing"

(p. 45). Thus, use cases will drive design, but not problem solving. Schneider and Winters (1998) begin with a written project description and risk analysis, before defining the system boundary and the actors. Then, use cases are identified. Blaha and Premerlani (1998, p. 49) state that, "Once you have a sound object model, you should specify use cases" and warn that early use cases must be regarded as "tentative and subject to revision" (p. 150).

In summary, review of the literature shows extensive differences in how use cases are defined and used. These differences certainly exceed the basically cosmetic variations in Data Flow Diagram and Entity Relationship Diagram formats found in standard structured analysis books. The existence of different use case formats and roles is not surprising, given UML's relatively short history. Moreover, UML brings together many analysis and design constructs because of its roots. While this is a notable achievement, the end product is loosely defined, complex (perhaps overly so), lacks a strong theoretical foundation, and thus is very difficult to test in a definitive way.

Determining Appropriate Use Case Focus

The use case variations are real. Despite a general consensus that use cases are intended for conceptual modeling of system requirements, many versions of use cases incorporate significant design and implementation details (e.g., at the level of the user interface). One potential way to resolve this apparent inconsistency is to adopt a contingency perspective. Different approaches may be useful under different circumstances, with the best approach in a specific situation depending on the analysts, the task, the users, and other situational variables.

However, we believe a stronger basis can be adopted to predict a most appropriate form for use cases that is applicable across a wide range of circumstances. The key to this proposal is implied by the general idea outlined earlier that use cases are requirements analysis and modeling tools that should describe what a system does (or should do), rather than how the system works (or should work).

Within this context, detailed use cases that specify low-level actor interactions with a system (e.g., down to the point of screen designs) essentially embed certain design choices. Introducing such considerations during analysis may prematurely guide the developers to specific implementation decisions. This is particularly a concern when the development process is intended to support the reengineering of existing processes, an endeavor for which Jacobson et al. (1994) strongly advocate the application of use case-driven methodology.

The potential impact on systems development of use cases that embed design decisions can be understood in the context of a well-known phenomenon in psychology – *anchoring and adjustment* (Tversky & Kahnemann, 1974). Experiments have shown that, when people are given a problem and an initial estimate of its solution, and then asked to find a final solution to a problem, they tend to anchor to the initial estimate (Plous, 1993). That is, they tend to provide solutions close to the initial estimate (anchor), even when those estimates are severely flawed. Anchoring is a useful heuristic that helps humans simplify problem solving in a complex situation. Unfortunately, people tend to rely on anchoring too much, resulting in an adjustment bias, in which people fail to make adequate modifications to an initial solution.

The concepts of anchoring and adjustment, although originally proposed in the context of activities such as subjective probability estimation, have a natural application to use cases. To the extent that use cases include design or implementation details that reflect current ways of doing things, reengineering or process innovation are likely to be inhibited. Consequently, we postulate that the level of innovation that can be achieved through use case-driven process design is inversely related to the level of design or implementation detail embodied in the use cases.

FROM USE CASES TO A CLASS MODEL
Finding Objects in Use Cases

In addition to modeling systems requirements from a user perspective, use cases and use case diagrams specify the behavior of the objects in a system. Some developers use them to identify the object classes required in the implementation, and the behavior of objects. In this way, use cases feed the development of subsequent models in UML: particularly the class model, but also sequence, activity and statechart diagrams and other UML artifacts.

In this context, it is useful to examine prescriptions in the UML literature for proceeding to the development of a class model from use cases. Booch et al. (1999) advocate applying "use case-based analysis to help find these abstractions" (p. 55), and describe this as an "excellent" way to identify classes. This view has subsequently been echoed in the Unified Process. According to Jacobson et al. (1999, p. 34), "use cases provide major input when finding and specifying classes." They further go on to assert "classes are harvested from the use case descriptions as the developers read them looking for classes that are suitable for realizing the use cases." However, they do not offer specific prescriptions for finding classes of objects in use cases.

Jacobson et al. (1994) provide a more detailed description of the role of use cases in finding classes of domain objects:

When you have a first proposal for the most obvious entity objects, you continue to work with the use cases. You identify objects by traversing one use-case description at a time to ensure that there is an object responsible for each part of the use case's course of events. ... When you work through the use case's course of events in this way, it is probable that you will identify further object entities. (pp. 184-185)

"Noun/verb analysis" is also applied to use cases (e.g., Holland & Lieberherr, 1996). Nouns, particularly things, persons or roles, events, places and interactions, are possible classes. But Jacobson et al. (1994, p. 105) state: "when we say that we identify and describe a use case, we mean that we identify and describe the class." This suggests that whoever is writing use cases should have a reasonable understanding of what classes are and what ones are likely to emerge during analysis. Interestingly, using nouns to identify classes of objects or entities for an application predates UML by a large period, and has been advocated for data modeling for many years. In contrast, some others have suggested the class model (or at least an initial attempt) ought to precede the creation of use cases. Pooley and Stevens (1999), for example, offer a detailed description of methods for identifying classes. They describe a process of identifying nouns in a systems requirement document as a mechanism for identifying candidate classes for an application (p. 58). These nouns may come from use case descriptions or other requirements documents, although Pooley and Stevens are silent on the source and nature of these documents. Rosenberg and Scott (1999, p. 16-17) search for nouns and verbs in "available relevant material," which includes the "problem statement, lower-level requirements, and expert knowledge," along with other sources such as marketing literature. They also identify classes before writing use cases. Booch (1994) similarly advocates the use of noun analysis to identify classes.

Indeed, Pooley and Stevens (1999) indicate a potential problem with use cases as a component of UML:

Use case modeling should be used with caution, however, since ... [t]here is a danger of building a system which is not object-oriented. Focusing on use cases may encourage developers to lose sight of the architecture of the system and of the static object structure. (p. 101)

Moreover, they go on to state "we do not believe that examination of the use cases is *on its own* a good way to find objects and classes" (p. 102, emphasis at source).

Meyer (1997, p. 738) also states that, "use cases are not a good tool for finding classes." One reason is that use cases emphasize procedural sequences and this is at best irrelevant to class modeling and could even be dangerous to the process. Other concerns are that users will either tend to develop use cases around what is happening now, thus failing to consider reengineering of the process, or will simply revert to functional design. However, Meyer believes that use cases can be effectively employed as a validation tool and implementation guide. The final system must be capable of handling the scenarios identified by users, although perhaps not in the same way as they originally envisioned.

Another approach to modeling classes is the use of CRC cards (Beck & Cunningham, 1989; Pooley & Stevens, 1999). While not specifically part of UML, they can be used to model the required functionality responsibilities and association collaborations of classes once the classes that are needed have been identified.

In summary, the process for moving forward from the use case model to identify classes is neither universally accepted, even among use case adherents, nor does it appear to be clearly defined or articulated. Proposed techniques, such as noun identification, are rooted in older techniques from data modeling. The lack of integration between use cases and class models raises questions about the value of use cases in an object-oriented modeling approach.

Objects Versus Processes

A use case is inherently task focused. It describes a sequence of activities, from start to finish, involved in completing a well-defined task or transaction. As in any task, many participants may be involved in the successful completion of a use case. These participants are candidates for objects that will be important to the system. A task or process focus, however, involves participants only to the extent that they contribute to the task. Hence, a use case involves objects only peripherally and only as needed for the task being modeled. Therefore, a complete use case model may not offer a cohesive picture of the structural and behavioral characteristics of the objects in the domain. Instead, these characteristics may be spread over several use cases.

The fragmentation across use cases of information needed to construct class definitions conceptually violates the principle of *encapsulation*, widely recognized as one of the cornerstones of object orientation. As a result, it can create a significant amount of work for analysts and developers in "defragmentation," or reconstructing classes from a potentially large number of narrowly focused views that might be embedded in many different use cases. Although we are not aware of empirical research, or even anecdotal reports, on the extent of this problem, a case can be made that the task can be daunting. The problem is analogous to the issue of *view integration* in database design (Navathe, Elmasri, & Larson, 1986). There, the issue is one of developing a global conceptual schema from a set of diverse user views of the kinds of entities about which data need to be kept. Since different users have different needs, they generally have a different perspective on which entities are important, and how they are defined in terms of attributes and relationships. Problems to be resolved include identifying synonyms (entities, attributes, and/or relationships with the same meaning that have different names in different views) and homonyms (entities, attributes, and/or relationships with different meanings that have the same name in different views).

Similar problems are possible when identifying object classes, their attributes, and their operations from a series of use cases. Given that different use cases are likely to be relevant to different users of a system, it is reasonable to expect that resolving synonyms and homonyms will impede the comprehensive and consistent identification of objects from use cases. Consequently, we propose that identifying a comprehensive and consistent class model from use cases alone will be very difficult, if not practically impossible.

USE CASES AS A COMMUNICATION MECHANISM
Isolating Users from the Class Model

In view of the apparent lack of "object" focus in use cases and the potential problems that can arise in deriving a class model from a use case model, it is natural to question the rationale for including use cases in UML. This is particularly interesting since use cases are a relatively recent addition to UML. Much of the rationale for adopting use case modeling in UML focuses on their simplicity and the fact that they are "comparatively easy to understand intuitively, even without knowing the notation. This is an important strength, since the use case model can sensibly be discussed with a customer who need not be familiar with the UML" (Pooley & Stevens, 1999, p. 93). This view suggests that other UML models, in particular the class model, are too technical for end users to understand or be capable of verifying.

Communication with the system's intended users is clearly an important, if not always explicitly articulated, goal of use cases. A use case model provides an inventory of the kinds of interactions that can occur between users and a system, providing "a forum for your domain experts, end users, and developers to communicate to one another" (Booch et al., 1999, p. 229). Use cases are thus oriented towards interaction with end users for the purpose of verifying the developers' understanding of how a system works or will work.

This understanding is essential for effective system development, and also helps create a "shared understanding" among team members that is a critical part of the trust building process (Ring & Van de Ven, 1989). Text may be easier to understand than diagrams, at least to an untrained user. Thus, use cases could contribute both to the accuracy of the requirements specification and also to its apparent openness. The analyst does not appear to be hiding behind diagrams that only IS professionals can understand.

In discussing the value of use cases in reengineering business processes, Jacobson et al. (1994) similarly explain the role of the use case in communicating with users or those responsible for a business process:

Use cases are best described using simple language to facilitate understanding. … The rightful owner, that is, the defined business process

owner for the use case, will thereafter validate each use case's compliance with the established corporate objectives. (p. 178)

Here, use cases are clearly established as a tool for communicating and verifying with users the developers' understanding of how tasks are performed. In contrast, they clearly see the verification of class or object models as the purview of developers:

The reviewers are normally people in the reengineering team. It is unusual to communicate the object models to the employees in general, which means that the only people who are really involved and competent to review these models are in the reengineering team. (p. 190)

Taken together, these statements suggest that use cases are an appropriate mechanism to 'shield' users from the underlying technical UML models that are the basis for systems design and implementation.

The need to exclude users from direct exposure to the class model in particular highlights an interesting contradiction in UML. One of the main arguments offered for developing object-oriented approaches to systems analysis and design is that objects provide a "natural" way of thinking about a problem domain. In this regard, Booch (1996, p. 39) notes that "in a quality object-oriented software system, you will find many classes that speak the language of the domain expert" and "(e)very class in an object-oriented system should map to some tangible or conceptual abstraction in the domain of the end user or the implementer." Jacobson et al. (1992) make the case more directly:

People regard their environment in terms of objects. Therefore it is simple to think in the same way when designing a model. A model which is designed using an object-oriented technology is often easy to understand, as it can be directly related to reality. Thus, with such a design method, only a small **semantic gap** (emphasis at source) will exist between reality and the model. (p. 42, emphasis at source)

The previous discussion shows that, despite this avowal of the naturalness and ease of understanding of UML models, the developers of the language explicitly introduce use cases as the primary mechanism for communicating with users to verify understanding of system functionality.

Use Cases Versus Class Models for Communication

The contradiction highlighted above can be dealt with in at least two ways. First, there is significant literature in cognitive psychology to support the contention that people think about the world in terms of things that are classified in particular categories (e.g., Medin & Smith, 1984). Lakoff (1987) views such category structures as vital for human survival, arguing that "(w)ithout the ability to categorize, we could not function at all" (p. 1). Parsons and Wand (1997) apply categorization research to analyze those aspects of object orientation that are meaningful from a systems analysis perspective, and conclude that classification is a vital element for object-oriented analysis.

From a cognitive perspective, one would expect that users should be able to handle class models as a mechanism for communicating with developers in verifying the conceptual structure of the domain being modeled. Of course, issues such as the difficulty of learning the notation associated with a particular class modeling technique can negatively influence communication. Nevertheless, the fundamental idea that a domain can be described in terms of the kinds of objects in it, the attributes of the objects, the behavior the objects can exhibit, and the associations among kinds of objects, is highly consistent with research on the nature of categories that people use to structure their knowledge about things in the world. Consequently, we hypothesize that end users will be able to interact directly with class models in verifying the structure of a domain.

Cognitive psychology also provides a second basis for understanding the contradiction inherent in advocating use cases as the primary mechanism for communicating and verifying system requirements with users. Advocates of use cases point to the ease with which they can be understood, as they describe a process from start to finish. Not surprisingly, a significant body of research in cognitive science deals with how people think procedurally. For example, Schank and Abelson's (1977) work on scripts deals with the sequencing of ordinary and exceptional events involved in a goal-oriented activity. Scripts provide a mechanism by which people can understand the temporal relationship in a list of events, including inferences about events that are not explicitly stated in a description (Bower, Black, & Turner, 1979).

Since people can think in either process-oriented or object-oriented modes, we postulate that both process-oriented and object-oriented models can be understood by users and are appropriate for verifying different aspects of application requirements. This suggests that advocating use cases for work with users, while isolating users from the class models that are the primary basis for the design of an object-oriented architecture, is not necessary. Moreover, the peripheral and diffuse role of objects in use cases is a potential source of difficulty in developing class models from use cases and verifying whether they are a good model of the domain's category structure as understood by users. It may be more appropriate to use class models directly as a mechanism for communicating and verifying the structure of the application domain with users.

CALL FOR RESEARCH

The analysis presented above is purely theoretical. As far as we are aware, advocates of use cases do not offer empirical evidence that they are a "good" mechanism for communicating with users. "Goodness" of use cases could be ascertained by developing a standard of effective communication against which use cases can be evaluated. Alternatively, "goodness" could be established in a relative sense by comparing them to other mechanisms for communicating the same information with users. At present, the value of use cases has not been established empirically in either of these senses.

Similarly, although we have presented an argument that use cases may be inadequate for developing class models, such inadequacy has not been demonstrated empirically. In addition, although research on classification points to the naturalness of category structures in organizing information about things in the world, there are few empirical studies addressing the ability of users to understand class models. The few studies that have addressed this were conducted prior to the development of the particular class modeling technique that is part of UML. For example, Vessey and Conger (1994) found that novice analysts were better able to specify requirements using process- and data-oriented methodologies than using object-oriented methodologies.

In addition, we have identified the growing tendency for use cases to include design or implementation decisions that could be a possible impediment to effective process design in systems development. Despite the attention paid by some to the role of use cases in process reengineering, there is reason to believe that popular use case structures may anchor developers to particular solution approaches and thereby narrow the scope of possible solutions considered. However, there is no empirical evidence that such adjustment biases occur in practice.

In view of the movement toward UML as a standard modeling language in practice, the paucity of empirical research on the effectiveness of various modeling techniques and prescriptions in UML is troubling. We have offered a theoretical framework for studying three issues: premature inclusion of design decisions, the adequacy of use cases for extracting class models, and the justification for choosing use cases as the primary mechanism for developer interaction with users. From these perspectives, we think it is important to conduct a range of empirical studies to evaluate the various modeling components of UML.

First, research is needed to examine whether including design and implementation details in use cases leads to anchoring and adjustment problems with respect to effective process redesign. This question can be addressed directly through lab experiments in which developers design a system starting from either abstract use cases or use cases in which design or implementation decisions are stated. In each group, the "innovativeness" of the resulting designs relative to existing processes can be measured. To measure the external validity of such results, correlational field studies of object-oriented development using UML can also be undertaken to measure the relationship between the structure of use cases used and the extent to which implementations achieve effective redesign.

Second, research is needed to test the assertion that, since use cases do not focus on objects, it will be difficult to extract a class model from a set of use cases. Although it may be possible to test this in a controlled laboratory experiment, it would be difficult to avoid biases in the development of use cases that might influence the ability to extract class models. Consequently, an appropriate method for examining the degree to which use cases support the development of class models (and, more generally, how class models are developed and verified) would be surveys and/or case studies of the progression from use case models to class models in projects that use UML. Among the variables to measure are: the extent to which use cases are the exclusive mechanism for communication and verification of requirements with users; the extent to which use cases drive the development of the class model; problems encountered in using use cases to develop the class model; perceptions about the causes of such problems; and approaches that are used to deal with these problems.

Third, research is needed to examine whether users are capable of directly reading and understanding class models, as well as other UML models. In addition, there is a need to study whether use cases add value (e.g., in ease of understanding or ability to capture additional information relative to other models in UML). For this type of study, laboratory experiments offer the ability to enforce necessary control to permit useful comparisons across groups. Several issues need to be resolved in conducting this kind of study. For example, use cases include process or task information, while class diagrams do not. Hence, comparisons between use cases and class models must be restricted to object/attribute/relationship identification, or class models must be used in conjunction with other UML models to conduct comprehensive comparisons with use cases.

Table 1 summarizes a research framework for studying the need for, and effectiveness of, use cases in UML.

CONCLUSIONS

UML is a modeling language for object-oriented development that grew out of the combination of three distinct approaches developed in the early 1990s. Much of the conceptual foundation of the language comes out of issues in object-oriented programming (Booch, 1994), and there is little evidence about the extent to which it is appropriate as a language for modeling an application domain or system requirements. In short, we feel there is a strong need for academic research to evaluate the usefulness of UML and determine its limitations for modeling requirements. Here, we have offered a framework for evaluating the roles of, and relationships between, use cases and class models in the UML. Similar research is needed to understand the capabilities and limitations of the other models in the language.

Table 1: A Framework for Empirical Research on Use Cases

Research Question	Primary Independent Variable	Primary Dependent Variable	Methodology
Do design/implementation details in use cases impede process redesign efforts?	Use case structure	Process innovation	Experiment; Case study
Can class models be effectively extracted from use cases?	Use cases	Class model completeness	Case study; Developer surveys
Do use cases facilitate communication between developers and users?	Communication medium (use cases or class models)	User understanding Domain coverage	Experiments; User surveys

ENDNOTE

[1] This research was supported in part by a research grant from the Social Sciences and Humanities Research Council of Canada to Jeffrey Parsons.

REFERENCES

Beck, K. and Cunningham, W. (1989). A laboratory for teaching object-oriented thinking. *ACM SIGPLAN Notices*, 24(10), 1-6.

Blaha, M. and Premerlani, W. (1998). *Object-Oriented Modeling and Design for Database Applications*. Upper Saddle River, NJ: Prentice Hall.

Booch, G. (1994). *Object-Oriented Analysis and Design with Applications* (2nd ed.). Redwood City, CA: Benjamin/Cummings.

Booch, G. (1996). *Object Solutions: Managing the Object-Oriented Project*. Reading, MA: Addison-Wesley.

Booch, G., Jacobson, I. and Rumbaugh, J. (1999). *The Unified Modeling Language User Guide*. Reading, MA: Addison-Wesley.

Bower, G., Black, J. and Turner, T. (1979). Scripts in memory for text. *Cognitive Psychology*, 11, 177-220.

Brown, D. (1997). *An Introduction to Object-Oriented Analysis: Objects in Plain English*. New York: John Wiley & Sons.

Coad, P. (1995). *Object Models: Strategies, Patterns, and Applications*. Englewood Cliffs, NJ: Yourdon Press.

Constantine, L. L. and Lockwood, L. A. D. (2000). Structure and style in use cases for user interface design. In Van Harmelen, M. and Wilson, S. (Eds.), *Object Modeling User Interface Design*. Reading, MA: Addison-Wesley. Available: http://www.foruse.com. (June 12, 2000).

Dewitz, S. (1996). *Systems Analysis and Design and the Transition to Objects*. New York: McGraw-Hill.

Evans, G. (1999). Why are use cases so painful? *Thinking Objects,* [on line serial], *1*(2). Available: http://evanetics.com/TONewsletters/thinking-v1n2.htm. (June 12, 2000).

Hammer, M. and Champy, J. (1993). *Reengineering the Corporation: A Manifesto for Business Revolution*. New York: Harper-Collins.

Harmon, P. and Watson, M. (1998). *Understanding UML: The Developer's Guide*. San Francisco, CA: Morgan Kaufmann.

Holland, I. and Lieberherr, K. (1996). Object-Oriented Design. *ACM Computing Surveys*, 28, 273-275.

IBM Object-Oriented Technology Center. (1997). *Developing Object-Oriented Software*. Upper Saddle River, NJ: Prentice Hall.

Jacobson, I. (1987). Object-oriented development in an industrial environment.

OOPSLA'87 Conference Proceedings, SIGPLAN Notices, 22(12), 183-191.

Jacobson, I., Booch, G. and Rumbaugh, J. (1999). *The Unified Software Development Process.* Reading, MA: Addison-Wesley.

Jacobson, I., Christerson, M., Jonsson, P. and Overgaard G. (1992). *Object-Oriented Software Engineering: A Use Case Driven Approach.* Reading, MA: Addison-Wesley.

Jacobson, I., Ericsson, M. and Jacobson, A. (1994). *The Object Advantage: Business Process Reengineering with Object Technology.* Reading, MA: Addison-Wesley.

Kilov, H. and Ross, J. (1994). *Information Modeling: An Object-Oriented Approach.* Englewood Cliffs, NJ: Prentice Hall.

Lakoff, G. (1987). *Women, Fire, and Dangerous Things: What Categories Reveal about the Mind.* Chicago, IL: University of Chicago Press.

Larman, C. (1998). *Applying UML And Patterns: An Introduction to Object-Oriented Analysis and Design.* Upper Saddle River, NJ: Prentice Hall.

Lockheed Martin Advanced Concepts Center and Rational Software Group. (1996). *Succeeding With The Booch And OMT Methods: A Practical Approach.* Menlo Park, CA: Addison-Wesley.

MacMaster, B. (1997). Saving time with "use cases." *Computing Canada,* 23(21), 52.

Medin, D. and Smith, E. (1984). Concepts and concept formation. *Annual Review of Psychology,* 35, 113-138.

Meyer, B. (1997). *Object-Oriented Software Construction.* Upper Saddle River, NJ: Prentice Hall.

Navathe, S., Elmasri, E. and Larson, J. (1986). Integrating user views in database design. *IEEE Computer,* 19, 50-62.

Norman, R. (1996). *Object-Oriented Systems Analysis And Design.* Upper Saddle River, NJ: Prentice Hall.

Parsons, J. and Wand, Y. (1997). Using objects in systems analysis. *Communications of the ACM,* 40(12), 104-110.

Plous, S. (1993). *The Psychology of Judgment and Decision Making.* New York: McGraw-Hill.

Pooley, R. and Stevens, P. (1999). *Using UML: Software Engineering with Objects and Components.* Reading, MA: Addison-Wesley.

Ring, P. S. and Van de Ven, A. H. (1989). Formal and informal dimensions of transactions. In Van de Ven, A. H., Angle, H. L. and Poole, M. S. (Eds.), *Research on the Management of Innovation: The Minnesota Studies,* 171-192. New York: Harper & Row.

Rosenberg, D. and Scott, K. (1999). *Use Case Driven Object Modeling with UML.* Reading, MA: Addison-Wesley.

Rubin, K. and Goldberg, A. (1992). Object behavior analysis. *Communications of the ACM*, 35(9), 48.

Rumbaugh, J., Blaha, M., Premerlani, W., Eddy, F. and W. Lorensen (1991). *Object-Oriented Modeling and Design.* Englewood Cliffs, NJ: Prentice Hall.

Satzinger, J. and Orvik, T. (1996). *Object-Oriented Approach: Concepts, Modeling, and System Development.* Danvers, MA: Boyd & Fraser.

Schank, R. and Abelson, R. (1977). *Scripts, Plans, Goals, and Understanding.* Hillsdale, NJ: Erlbaum.

Schneider, G. and Winters, J. P. (1998). *Applying Use Cases: A Practical Guide.* Reading, MA: Addison-Wesley.

Tversky. A. and Kahneman, D. (1974). Judgment under uncertainty: Heuristics and biases. *Science*, 185, 1124-1131.

Vessey, I. and Conger, S. (1994). Requirements specification: Learning object, process, and data methodologies. *Communications of the ACM*, 37(5), 102-113.

White, I. (1994). *Rational Rose Essentials: Using the Booch Method.* Redwood City, CA: Benjamin/Cummings.

Wirfs-Brock, R., Wilkerson, B. and Wiener, L. (1990). *Designing Object-Oriented Software.* Englewood Cliffs, NJ: Prentice Hall.

Chapter 9

Enhancing a Rigorous Reuse Process with Natural Language Requirement Specifications

Laura Felice, Carmen Leonardi, Liliana Favre, and Maria Virginia Mauco
Universidad Nacional del Centro de la Pcia. de Buenos Aires, Argentina

Reusability is the ability to use the same software elements for constructing many different applications. Formal specifications can help to semiautomatic design processes based on reusable components. However, during the first stages of development, when the interaction with the stakeholders is crucial, the use of client-oriented requirements engineering techniques seems to be necessary in order to enhance the communication between the stakeholders and the software engineers. In this chapter, we propose a systematic reuse approach that integrates natural language requirement specifications with formal specifications in RSL (RAISE Specification Language). On the one hand, some heuristics are described to develop a formal specification in RSL starting from models belonging to the Requirements Baseline. On the other hand, we have defined a reusable component model that integrates RSL specifications at different levels of abstraction, as well as presented a process with reuse based on the model.

INTRODUCTION

The challenge of the software engineering is to satisfy the increasing demand of software systems in an economic and rapid way. Reusability software techniques based on component library provide a great potential to face it.

Previously published in *Managing Information Technology in a Global Economy*, edited by Mehdi Khosrow-Pour. Copyright © 2001, Idea Group Publishing.

The main problems associated with reusability techniques are:
- How to define reusable components library
- How to identify reusable components in a library
- How to integrate "implementation pieces" in a consistent system implementation

Our work hypothesis is that the formal specification of reusable components and the development of rigorous methods for their systematic reuse can help building "correct" and efficient software. "If, instead of being developed for just one project, a software element has the potential of serving again and again for many projects, it becomes economically attractive to submit it to the best possible quality techniques, such as formal specifications of components" (Meyer, 1997). There are many works which prove that software reusability can be addressed from formal descriptions (Krueger, 1992; Mili et al., 1995; Zaremski & Wing, 1997). Besides, formal descriptions are only accessible to specialists. If we want to construct a new software system we need other kind of techniques to represent the domain in which the software will be inserted. Those representations may be familiar to the stakeholder, whose participation in the first stages of development is crucial.

This work integrates and extends previous results from our research (Favre et al., 2000; Mauco, 2000). We propose a reuse strategy that integrates informal specifications with a reusable component library. In particular we use natural language-oriented models belonging to Requirements Baseline (Leite et al., 1997). These models are used to produce incomplete algebraic specifications in RSL (George et al., 1992), the formal specification language used in RAISE method. Those specifications are the input for the second part of the strategy, the reuse process, whose final result is a complete imperative specification in RSL, directly connected to code through the RAISE method. The reuse process is based on the RC model which integrates specifications at different levels of abstraction. The manipulation of RC components by means of reuse operators is the basis for the reusability. An essential step in the reuse process is component identification, not only because of its complexity, but also because is the key to the success of the overall process.

THE REQUIREMENTS BASELINE

The Requirements Baseline (Leite, 1997) is a structure which incorporates descriptions about a desired system in a given macrosystem. It is composed of five views, but in this paper we will deal only with the Lexicon Model View and the Scenario View.

The Lexicon Model View

It is implemented by the LEL (Language Extended Lexicon). The LEL is a structure that allows the representation of significant terms in the studied macrosystem. It delimits external language and enriches the internal one by providing each symbol with semantics. For each symbol we have a name and a set of synonyms, notions, describing its denotation, and behavioral responses, that describe its connotation.

LEL terms define objects (passive entities), subjects (active entities), phrasal verbs and states. Figure 1 shows two terms of the LEL for a Credit Card System. The underlined terms correspond to other LEL entries.

Figure 1: Examples of LEL terms

BANK CARD / CREDIT CARD / CARD:
Notions:
- Card to carry out bank operations in teller machines and shops.
- It has a PIN
- It belongs to a holder
- It may have additional cards.
- It has an expiration date.
Behavioral responses:
- It can be stolen, lost, cancelled or invalid.
- It may be renewed.
PIN
Notions:
- It is a secret number that uniquely identifies a credit card.
Behavioral responses:
- It is required for any bank operation in a teller machine.
- It may be modified by the holder.

The Scenario View

Scenarios describe macrosystem situations using natural language description as their basic representation. They are naturally connected to the LEL. In Figure 2 the components of a scenario are described.

Figure 2: Components of a scenario

Title: identifies a scenario.
Objective: describes the purpose of a scenario.
Context: defines geographical and temporal locations and preconditions.
Resources: identify passive entities with which actors work.
Actors: define entities actively involved in a scenario, generally a person or an organization.
Set of episodes: a number of related episodes which represent actions performed by actors to fulfill the *objective* using resources. An episode may be explained as a scenario.

Figure 3: Partial Description of a Scenario

TITLE: **Carry out a common withdrawal**
OBJECTIVE: A holder wants to carry out a withdrawal in a teller machine with a card
CONTEXT: The holder is operating the Credit Card System in a teller machine. Precondition: The holder has a valid card.
ACTORS: Holder
RESOURCES: Bank Account
EPISODES:
The holder chooses the option withdrawal and an amount to extract.
IF the bank account has enough funds
THEN the amount is debited from the bank account
IF the bank account has not got enough funds
THEN the teller machine cancels the operation.
...

Constraints (non-functional requirements) may be applied to Context, Resources or Episodes. Exceptions, applied to episodes, cause serious disruptions in a scenario, asking for a different set of actions. Figure 3 shows a partial description of a scenario for the Credit Card System. Underlined terms represent LEL symbols connecting both models.

THE RSL LANGUAGE

The aim of the project RAISE (Rigorous Approach to Industrial Software Engineering), was to develop a language, techniques and tools that would enable industrial use of formal methods. The results of this project include the RSL Language which allows us to write formal specifications. In addition to this, a method to carry out developments based on such specifications, and a set of tools to assist in edition, checking, transforming and reasoning about specifications (Bjorner, 2000) are provided.

A development in RAISE begins with an abstract specification and gradually evolves to concrete implementations. The first specification is usually an abstract applicative one, for example functional or algebraic. A first algebraic specification should have:
- A hierarchy of modules whose root is the system module.
- A module containing types and attributes for the non-dynamic identified entities.
- The signatures of the necessary functions associated with types. These func-

Figure 4. Card Scheme

```
scheme GLOBAL_TYPES =
class
  type
    Date,
    Card_id,
end

T
scheme CARD =
class
 object
    H: HOLDER,
type
    Card :: Pin: Nat  Holder: H.Holder  AddCards: T.Card_id-set  ExpDate: T.Date
CardState: State,
    State == Valid | Stolen | Invalid | Lost | Cancelled
  value
    RenewCard: Card x T.Date → Card

      ...
      pre is_valid(acard),
    ChangeCardState: Card x State→ Card,
      ...
end
```

tions should be categorized as generators and as observers. Besides, preconditions should be formulated for partial functions by means of functions, called guards.
- The specification may contain invariants expressed as functions.

In Figure 4 a specification in an algebraic style is shown.

THE RC MODEL

The Reusable Component model (RC) describes object classes at three different conceptual levels: specialization, realization and implementation.

The specialization level describes a hierarchy of incomplete algebraic specifications in RSL as an acyclic graph. Specialization relations relate the nodes. In this context, it must be verified that if $P(x)$ is a provable property about objects x of type T, then $P(y)$ must be verified for every object y of type S, where S is a specialization of T.

Every leaf in the specialization level is associated with a subcomponent at the realization level. A realization subcomponent is a tree of complete specifications in RSL; where the root is the most abstract definition; the internal nodes correspond to different realizations of the root and finally, the leaves correspond to subcomponents at the implementation level.

If E1 and E2 are specifications, E1 can be realized by E2 if E1 and E2 have the same signature and every model of E2 is a model of E1 (Hennicker & Wirsing, 1992).

The realization level allows us to distinguish the design decisions related to the choice of physical data structure. Every specification at the realization level is linked to subcomponents at the implementation level.

The implementation level groups a set of imperative schemes in RSL associated with code. RAISE method provides translation processes which start with a final RSL specification and produce a program in some executable language, for example Ada and C.

Transforming RC Components

The transformation operators on RSL algebraic specifications are informally described as follows:

Rename: changes the name of sorts or operations.

Hide: forgets parts of a specification.

Extend: adds sorts, operations or axioms to a specification.

Combine: combines two or more specifications in only one.

Building operators on specifications can be extended to manipulate subcomponents in the realization level. Informally, this implies simultaneous application of an operator to every node of the subcomponent. The subcomponents are inductively defined by the operator: $realize(S, \{RS_1, RS_2, ...\})$ where S is a specification and $RS_1, RS_2, ...$ are reusable specifications (these roots are realizations of S). rename_r, hide_r, extend_r, combine_r operators were defined in the realization level. For example, Rename-r operator is inductively defined by

$Rename\_r(realize(SP, \{SP_1, SP_2, ...SP_n\}), \rho) =$
$realize(rename(SP, \rho), \{rename\_r(SP_1, \rho), rename\_r(SP_2, \rho), ..., rename\_r(SP_n, \rho)\})$

Given a specification SP with signature $\Sigma = sig(SP)$, a signature Σ' and a morphism signature $\rho: \Sigma \rightarrow \Sigma'$ that represents a rename; $rename(SP, \rho)$ is a specification with signature Σ'. Rename_ρ is defined as a renaming of its root and, recursively, all its children.

Building operators for specifications are extended to manipulate subcomponents at the implementation level. Informally, this implies application of an operator to every scheme of a subcomponent. Subcomponents are inductively defined by the operator: $implement(E, \{ESQ_1, ESQ_2, ... ESQ_n\})$, where E is a specification and $ESQ_1, ESQ_2, ... ESQ_n$ are schemes of imperative versions in RSL. rename_i, hide_i, extend_i and combine_i operators are defined inductively, for example rename_i is defined by

$rename\_i(implement(E, \{ESQ_1, ... ESQ_n\}), \rho) =$
$implement(rename(E, \rho), \{rename\_i(ESQ1, \rho),$
$, ... rename\_i(ESQn, \rho)\})$

Figure 5: Overall Process

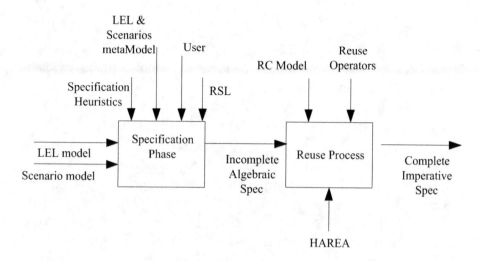

FROM REQUIREMENTS MODELS TO RSL IMPERATIVE SPECIFICATIONS

As it was mentioned in the introduction, our objective is to construct imperative specifications starting from natural language-oriented models. Therefore, in
our proposal two essential phases are distinguished: Specification and Reuse. In
the Specification phase an incomplete algebraic RSL specification (IAS) is built
starting from the LEL and Scenario models. IAS is then used as input for the
Reuse phase, applying the operators presented previously. to match RC components with IAS. The final specification is an imperative complete RSL Specification (ICS). A prototype HAREA assists in the retrieval and adaptation of RC
components (Fariña & Reale, 1999). It implements not just exact matching between components, but many kinds of relaxed matches. In Figure 5 the strategy
through like-SADT (Ross, 1980) is shown, followed by a detailed description of
its different phases.

Once we obtain the imperative specification in RSL, a code for the implementation in a programming language can be produced by RAISE method in a
semi-automatically way.

Specification Phase

In this phase we present some heuristics to define a first specification in
RSL starting from the LEL and scenarios models. The main tasks of the proposal
are Types Identification and Functions Definition. However these steps are not
sequential, they can be overlapped or carried out in cycles.

Types Identification

The following heuristics are used for the Identification of types.

- Model the subjects in the LEL as types in RSL. These subjects are the actors in the scenarios; so they always have a significant and "complex" behavior which justifies their modelization as a type.
- Analyze the relevance of each term which corresponds to an object in the LEL (a resource in the scenarios), in order to define it as a type or to include it as an attribute of a type. For example, the term Card (Figure 1) that represents an object in the LEL is defined as a type. Mean while the term PIN (Figure 1), also an object in the LEL, becomes an attribute of the type Card.
- Determine the attributes for each identified type by analyzing the notions of the corresponding term in the LEL, in order to find out the properties that characterize it. It is important to analyze the behavioral responses of the terms which correspond to the LEL objects and were modeled as types; due to some possible appearances of attributes as a result of operations applied to that object. When defining attributes in general, two cases have to be considered:

  - The property is directly modeled as an attribute of the type since it represents the property name. For example, for the term Card the properties Holder, Expiration Date, Additional Cards and PIN, are individually modeled as an attribute.

  - The term has several properties that model its different states or concrete values. In this case, there are two alternatives depending on the software developer. The first one is to model only one attribute whose domain is the set of values which appeared in the term and the second one is to define a Boolean attribute for each property. Taking into account that in the term Card four possible states appear stolen, invalid, lost or canceled; we have decided to define a attribute called CardState containing five possible values, the four previous and a ValidState. The last one appears implicitly in the requirement models, but it is convenient to define it in a solution model.

Functions Definition

In this section, we describe the heuristics related to the definition of functions.

- Define the functions considering the classification of the LEL terms that were modeled as classes:

- if the term is a subject, define each behavioral response as a function, choosing a name that summarizes it. To determine its input values and the output value it is necessary to analyze in detail the scenarios in which this behavioral response appears.

- if the term is an object, analyze the definition of each behavioral response.

Several behavioral responses may modify or access the same attribute. It is the software engineer's decision either to define one function for each behavioral response or to define a single function managing the different variants through the function parameters. For example, for the type Card it is possible to define five functions (SetStolen, SetLost, SetInvalid, SetValid, Set Cancelled) or a single one ChangeCardState(card, state).

- Determine if the functions are partial or total. For each function, the scenarios in which it appears should be analyzed in order to find possible restrictions, exceptions to the clause If Then. If some of these components do exist, the function is defined as partial and the associated sentence becomes the precondition, modeled as a guard. For example, for the function CommonWithdrawal of the type BankAccount we analyzed the scenario "Carry out a common withdrawal" (Figure 3) and we found a clause If Then to verify the account balance. Therefore, CommonWithdrawal is a partial function with precondition defined by the guard EnoughFunds(account).
- Complete the definition by adding functions to return the value of each attribute of the corresponding type, in case they had not been defined in the previous analysis.

After all the types are identified, they are analyzed to re-design the specification from a global perspective. For example, if a particular type is used in several types of the system, then it is modeled as global. A typical example is the type Date.

Figure 4 shows an example of one incomplete algebraic specification obtained by applying the heuristics presented before in the Credit Card System.

The Reuse Process

The next phase is to transform the incomplete algebraic specification into complete imperative specification by reusing existing components. The steps of the method are depicted in Figure 6:

Figure 6: Reuse Process

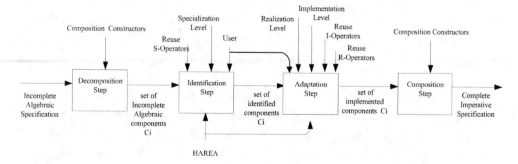

In Decomposition step the decomposition of a goal specification E_g into sub-specifications $E_1, E_2, ... E_n$ is formalized.

In Identification step (described in detail in next section), it must be identified, for each specification E_i a component C_i (in the specialization level) and a sequence $s_1, s_2, ..., s_n$ of RSL specifications, verifying specialization relations. It must be selected a leaf in Ci as a candidate to be transformed. The identification of a component is correct if rename, hide and extend operators can modify it to match the query E_i.

In Adaptation step, not only a leaf in the subcomponent associated in the realization level but also a sequence of operators used in the previous steps are applied. Then, a scheme in the implementation level is selected and the same operators in the selected leaf are applied. Finally, in Composition step, the sub-specifications E_i and their implementations are composed.

RC Component Identification

In this section, the use of specification matching to identify RC components are described. In the identification process, we search for all RC-components that satisfy a given query. This process has two essential steps: signature matching and semantic matching. The signature matching enables a syntactic comparison of a query specification with specifications existing in RC reusable components. The semantic matching compares the specifications dynamic behavior. The bases of the signature matching come from Zaremski and Wing (1997), even though they were adapted to the identification of RC components.

The signature of a specification consists of a set of sorts and a set of operations, each operation being equipped with a particular functionality.

Let $L=<S_L, F_L>$ be the signature of a library specification and $Q=<S_Q, F_Q>$ the signature of a query specification where S_L and S_Q are set of sorts and F_L and F_Q are set of operation symbols, the signature matching is defined as follows:

This means that given a query specification Q, a RC library C and a predicate P, it gives back the RC components that satisfy P. The signature matching is based on operations matching. Different kinds of operation matching are described bellow:

Let $O_L: T_{L1} \times T_{L2} \times ..... \to T_{Lm}$ and $O_Q: T_{Q1} \times T_{Q2} \times ..... \to T_{Qm}$, be two operations, the exact matching of them is defined as follows:

The exact matching is a good starting point but it is very restrictive. There may be useful functions in the library, which may be more specific or more general and after being found can be adapted by means of the application of reuse operators. Two relaxed matchings, the specialized and the generalized matchings, that

Figure 7: R-Credit_Card Specification

```
scheme GLOBAL_TYPES =
  class
    type
        Date,
        CR_CID,
 end

T
scheme
R-CREDIT_CARD=
     class
       type
          R-Credit_Card :: CrCId: T.CR_CID  Additonal: Card-set  Pin: String
              ValidDate: T.Date  State: StateCard  Type: TypeCard  Bank: String Limit:
        Real
           StateCard == Valid | Invalid | Stolen | Lost | Cancelled
           TypeCard == International | National | Gold | Platinum

       value
           GetExpDate: R-Credit_Card → T.Date,
           GetState: R-Credit_Card → StateCard,
           GetPIN :R-Credit_Card → Pin,
           GetBank: R-Credit_Card → String,
           GetType: R-Credit_Card → TypeCard,
           Cr_Card?: R-Credit_Card x T.CR_CID → Bool
           ChangeState: R-Credit_Card x State → R-Credit_Card,
           Additional: R-Credit_Card → Card-set,
           NewPIN: R-Credit_Card x Pin→ R-Credit_Card,
           Valid_Cr_Card: R-Credit_Card → Bool
           DateExp: T.Date x R-Credit_Card → Bool
           LimitCard: R-Credit_Card → Real
        axioms
   ........
  end
```

enable operations identification in these case are defined as follows:

$$\text{Generalized Matching}: \quad \text{Match}_G(O_L, O_Q) = O_L \geq O_Q$$

where "$O_L \geq O_Q$" expresses that O_L is "more general" than O_Q. This means that the argument types in O_Q are specializations of the types associated in O_L.

$$\text{Specialized Matching}: \text{MatchS}(O_L, O_Q) = O_L \leq O_Q$$

where "$O_L \leq O_Q$" expresses that O_L is "more specific" than O_Q. This means that the argument types in O_L are specializations of the types associated in O_Q.

The exact, generalized and specialized matchings of operations have been extended for signatures of RSL specifications:

S-Exact Matching

$\text{S-Match}_E(L, Q) = \exists$ a mapping $A_F : F_Q \rightarrow F_L$ such that A_F is one-to-one and onto

and $\forall O_Q \in F_Q: \text{Match}_f(A_F(O_Q), O_L)$

S-Generalized Matching

$\text{S-Match}_E(L,Q) = \exists$ a mapping $A_F : F_Q \rightarrow F_L$ such that A_F is onto

and $\forall O_Q \in F_Q: \text{Matchf}(A_F(O_Q), O_L)$

S-Specialized Matching

$\text{S-Match}_S(L,Q) = \text{S-Match}_G(Q,L)$

Signature acts as a "filter" that eliminates obvious non-matches before trying the semantic match. Hence, for the correct reuse of a component it remains to check that the semantic requirements of the goal specification, expressed by the axioms, are satisfied by a component. The RAISE tools can help to the semantic matching.

AN EXAMPLE

In this section we describe a simple example in order to show the reuse process.

Supposing that a RC component has to be adapted to match the specification given in Figure 4, let R-Credit_Card (Reusable Credit Card) be a specification belonging to a reusable component R_Card_System (Reusable Card System)(Figure 7).

When identifying R-Credit_Card as a candidate to be modified to match the query CARD, the following aspects are taken into account. There are more types involved in the R_Credit-Card definition, such as Bank and Type of Card. Besides, some of its functions are linked with controls for validation that were not derived from the initial requirements. For example the validation of a card (Valid_Cr_Card), the existence of a credit card (Cr_Card?) and so on. Thus, we say that the arguments of the R_Credit-Card functions are 'more specific' than the arguments of Cards functions.

For this reason the matching selected for operations and signature matching is the 'Specialized Matching'. The R_Credit-Card signature is a sub-signature of the CARD signature, under the following renaming ρ and restriction r.

ρtypes = {R-Credit_Card: Cards; CR_CID: HOLDER; Additional: AddCards; Card-set:

Card-collection; ValidDate: ExpDate; State:CardState}

ρoperations = {NewCard:RenewCard; Additional:AddCards; GetPIN: PIN?; ChangeState: ChangeCardState}

r= {GetExpDate: undefined; Cr_Card?: undefined; GetState: undefined; NewPIN: undefined; Valid_Cr_Card: undefined; DateExp:undefined; GetBank: undefined;

GetType: undefined}

CONCLUSIONS

We have described a reuse process based on the integration of requirements engineering and reuse techniques with the RAISE method; hoping that our approach may be integrated with other rigorous methods. As regards the possible contributions of our work the following concepts may be considered:

• The definition of heuristics to obtain RSL incomplete algebraic specifications from LEL and Scenario models.

• The definition of the RC model.

• The definition of a rigorous reuse process to transform RSL algebraic specifications into RSL imperative versions.

Besides, it is worth mentioning that Requirements acquisition as well as modelization are not deeply addressed by RAISE METHOD; meanwhile Requirements Baseline, more specifically LEL and Scenario Models, are techniques accepted and used by the requirements community. Those specifications not only model the behavior, the vocabulary of the system and its environment, but also are easily validated by the stakeholders. Therefore, we think the integration of requirement techniques with formal RSL specifications could enhance the overall process.

We would like to mention that our proposal has been partially implemented by one prototype, HAREA, that assists in the identification step of the reuse process. Finally, we will focus on the refinement of the heuristics by applying them in real and more complex systems.

REFERENCES

Bjorner, D. (2000) Software engineering: A new approach. *Lecture Notes*, Technical University of Denmark.

Fariña and Reale. (1999). Object-oriented reusability through formal specifications. *Undergraduate Thesis*. Universidad Nacional del Centro. Argentina.

Favre, Felice, Mauco and Leonardi. (2000). From RAISE specifications to object-oriented code: A reusable component model. *Proc. Intersymp'2000*. Germany.

George, C., Haff, P., Havelund, K., Haxthausen, A., Milne, R., Nielsen, C., Prehn, S. and Ritter, K. (1992). *The RAISE Specification Language*. Englewood Cliffs, NJ: Prentice Hall.

George, C., Haxthausen, A., Hughes, S., Milne, R., Prehn, S. and Pedersen, J. (1995). *The RAISE Development Method*. Englewood Cliffs, NJ: Prentice Hall.

Hennicker, R. and Wirsing, M. (1992). A formal method for the systematic reuse of specifications components. *Lecture Notes in Computer Science 544*, Springer-Verlag.

Krueger, C. (1992). Software reuse. *ACM Computing Surveys*, 24(2), June.

Leite, J., Rossi, G., Balaguer, F., Maiorano, V., Kaplan, G., Hadad, G. and Oliveros, A. (1997). Enhancing a requirement baseline with scenarios. *Requirement Engineering Journal*, 2(4), 187-198.

Mauco, Leonardi, Favre and Felice. (2000). Enhancing formal techniques with requirements engineering models. *Proc. Intersymp'2000*, Germany.

Meyer, B. (1997). *Object-Oriented Software Construction (Second Edition)*. Englewood Cliffs, NJ: Prentice Hall.

Mili, H., Mili, F. and Mili, A. (1995). Reusing software: Issues and research directions. *IEEE Transactions on Software Engineering*, June, 528-562.

Ross, D. (1980). Structured analysis (SA): A language for communicating ideas. In Freeman and Wasserman. (Eds.), *Tutorial on Design Techniques*, 107-125. IEEE Computer Society Press.

Zaremski, A. and Wing, J. (1997). Specification matching of software components. *ACM Transactions on Software Engineering and Methodology (TOSEM)*, 6(4), 333-369.

Chapter 10

Extended Spatiotemporal UML: Motivations, Requirements, and Constructs

Rosanne Price
Monash University, Australia

Nectaria Tryfona and Christian S. Jensen
Aalborg University, Denmark

This chapter presents a conceptual modeling language for spatiotemporal applications that offers built-in support for capturing spatially referenced, time-varying information. More specifically, the well-known object-oriented Unified Modeling Language (UML) is extended to capture the semantics of spatiotemporal data. The extension, Extended Spatiotemporal UML, maintains language clarity and simplicity by introducing a small base set of fundamental modeling constructs: spatial, temporal, and thematic. These constructs can then be combined and applied at attribute, attribute group, association, and/ or class levels of the object-oriented model; where the attribute group is an additional construct introduced for attributes with the same spatiotemporal properties. A formal functional specification of the semantic modeling constructs and their symbolic combinations is given and an example is used to illustrate the simplicity and flexibility of this approach.

INTRODUCTION

Spatiotemporal applications have been the focus of considerable attention recently. The need for a temporal dimension in traditional spatial information systems and for high-level models useful for the conceptual design of the resulting spatiotemporal systems has become clear. Although having in common a need to manage *spatial data* and their

Previously published in the *Journal of Database Management*, *vol.11, no.4,* Copyright © 2000, Idea Group Publishing.

changes over time, various spatiotemporal applications may manage different types of spatiotemporal data and may be based on very different models of space, time, and change. For example, the term *spatiotemporal data* is used to refer both to *temporal changes in spatial extents*, such as redrawing the boundaries of a voting precinct or land deed, and to *changes in the value of thematic* (i.e., alphanumeric) *data across time or space*, such as variation in soil acidity measurements depending on the measurement location and date. A spatiotemporal application may be concerned with either or both types of data. This, in turn, is likely to influence the underlying model of space employed, e.g. the two types of spatiotemporal data generally correspond to an object-versus a field-based spatial model. For either type of spatiotemporal data, change may occur in discrete steps, e.g., changes in land deed boundaries, or in a continuous process, e.g., changes in the position of a moving object such as a car. Another type of spatiotemporal data is *composite data whose components vary depending on time or location*. An example is the minimum combination of equipment and wards required in a certain category of hospital (e.g., general, maternity, psychiatric), where the relevant regulations determining the applicable base standards vary by locality and time period.

A conceptual data modeling language for such applications should provide a clear, simple, and consistent notation to capture alternative semantics for time, space, and change processes. These include point- and interval-based time semantics; object- and field-based spatial models; and instantaneous, discrete, and continuous views of change processes. Multiple dimensions for time (e.g., valid, transaction) and space should also be supported.

Although there has been considerable work in conceptual data models for time and space separately, interest in providing an integrated spatiotemporal model is much more recent. Spatiotemporal data models are surveyed in Abraham (1999), including lower-level logical models (Claramunt, 1995; Langran, 1993; Pequet, 1995). Those models that deal with the integration of spatial, temporal, and thematic data at the conceptual level are the most relevant to this work and are reviewed here.

Several conceptual frameworks have been designed to integrate spatial, temporal, and thematic data based on Object-Oriented (OO) or Entity-Relationship (ER) data models that include a high-level query language capable of specifying spatiotemporal entity types. The data definition component of these query languages thus has some potential for use in modeling spatiotemporal applications.

Becker (1996) and Faria (1998) propose OO models based on extensions of ObjectStore and O2 respectively. Becker (1996) considers both object- and field-based spatial models, defining a hierarchy of elementary spatial classes with both geometric and parameterized thematic attributes. Temporal properties are incorporated by adding instant and interval timestamp keywords to the query language. In Faria (1998), spatial and temporal properties are added to an object class definition by associating it with pre-defined temporal and spatial object classes. This solution is not suitable for representing temporal or spatial variation at the attribute level, as the timestamp and spatial locations are defined only at the object component level. In addition, both Becker (1996) and Faria (1998) offer text-based query languages; the non-graphical query languages of these models reduce their suitability as conceptual modeling languages.

A few papers specifically address the need for a graphical modeling language to support conceptual design of applications dealing with space and time. The MADS model (Parent, 1999) extends an object-based model with pre-defined hierarchies of spatial and temporal abstract data types and special complex data types to describe all of an attribute's properties, i.e. name, cardinality, domain, and temporal or spatial dimensions. The use of a non-standard, hybrid ER/OO model and the definition of new composite data structures for spatiotemporal properties, rather than exploiting existing features of the ER or OO models, increases the complexity of the model syntax. A thematic attribute value can be associated with a spatial extent describing where it is valid; however, there is no provision for attributes having a spatial domain. This reduces the flexibility of the model since any data element associated directly with several different spatial extents must be modeled as an association of spatial objects rather than as a single object with several spatial attributes.

Tryfona (1999) proposes the SpatioTemporal ER model (STER) that adds temporal and spatial icons to entities, attributes, and relationships to support timestamped spatial objects and layers. Composite data whose components vary over space and relationships associated with spatial extents are not considered. Instead, spatial relationships are used to represent explicit geometric or topological relationships between associated spatial objects, which could otherwise be derived on demand. Therefore, temporal relationships describe model structure (i.e., timestamps), whereas spatial relationships describe model integrity (i.e., constraints).

None of the models described above provide explicit support for modeling a group of thematic properties measured at the same times and locations, consider interpolation, or support alternative time models (i.e., periodic versus aperiodic recording of data values). An earlier spatiotemporal extension to the Unified Modeling Language (UML) proposed in Price (1999) defines an attribute group within the OO model and then defines constructs that provide support for modeling spatiotemporal properties at the object, association, attribute, and attribute group levels. However, neither the syntax nor the semantics of the symbols introduced in Price (1999) are presented formally.

In this paper, we propose an extension of UML intended to address the goals outlined earlier, i.e. to support a range of spatiotemporal models and data types using a clear, simple, and consistent notation. Extending the OMG standard for OO modeling was selected as the best approach given its high level of acceptance, tool support, understandability, and extensibility. Although the applicability of the proposed model is not necessarily limited to the Geographic Information System (GIS) domain, the focus is primarily on GIS concerns and application examples in this paper. We introduce a small base set of modeling constructs for spatiotemporal data that can be combined and applied to different levels of the object-oriented model in a consistent manner, guided by the same simple principles. The result is the *Extended Spatiotemporal UML*. A formal functional specification of the semantic modeling constructs and symbolic combinations is given.

The rest of the paper is organized as follows. The next section illustrates the problems with using UML to model spatiotemporal data and considers possible solutions. Then we describe the syntax and semantics of the fundamental new constructs introduced—the spatial, temporal, and thematic symbols—for the solution (i.e. UML extension) proposed in this paper. This is followed by a section that discusses three other symbols: the attribute group symbol, the existence-dependent symbol, and the specification box (used to specify the details of the spatiotemporal semantics). The section "Using Extended Spatiotemporal UML" shows how the previous example presented would be modeled using the proposed UML extension. Finally, conclusions and future directions are pesented.

USING UML FOR SPATIOTEMPORAL DATA

In this section, we evaluate the core constructs and extension mechanisms defined in UML (Booch, 1999; Rumbaugh, 1999; OMG 1999) in terms of their suitability for modeling spatiotemporal data and defining a UML extension to facilitate such modeling respectively. The UML usage and notation used is based on Rumbaugh (1999), except that we use informal textual descriptions for complex attribute domains and constraints for the sake of readability. We use Backus-Naur Form (BNF) for specific explanations of syntax or terminology. The next section uses an application example to demonstrate some of the problems associated with modeling spatiotemporal data using only the core model of UML. We then evaluate alternative approaches to extending a conceptual modeling language and evaluate UML's extension mechanisms.

Using UML: An Example

The following regional health application will be used to illustrate the use of UML to model spatiotemporal data. Assume an application measuring health statistics of different provinces, in terms of average lifespan, as related to the location (i.e. a point in 2D space), number of beds, accessibility (i.e. a half-hour travel zone around the hospital), and surrounding population densities of a province's hospitals. A hospital is classified by category, where a given category is required to have a minimum number of beds in specific kinds of wards. However, category definitions may differ between regions due to local regulations.

For properties dependent on time and/or location, we want to record information about when (using time intervals unless otherwise specified) and/or where a given value is valid (i.e. valid time) or current (i.e. transaction time). For example, a province's population densities and average lifespans can vary and are recorded yearly at the same time instants (values are averaged between yearly measurements) and for the same regions. The number of beds, the half-hour travel zone, a hospital's category, and the regional definition of hospital categories may change over time as well. We want to record existence and transaction time for hospitals, valid time and transaction time for a hospital's category, and valid time for all of the other time dependent properties. The time unit for the half-hour travel zone is not yet specified, demonstrating incremental design specification. Time elements are used to model hospital existence time since hospitals may sometimes be closed and later re-opened based on changes in local population density. Note that the number of beds, half-hour travel zone, and hospital category are only defined when the hospital is open.

Representation of spatiotemporal concepts using the core constructs of UML is not straightforward, as is illustrated using the regional health example in Figure 1. Figure 1 uses the following BNF definitions:

spatial-extent := { point | line | region | volume }^{n}

timestamp := { instant | interval | element }

Attributes with spatial and/or temporal properties (e.g. the half-hour travel zone or number of hospital beds) can be modeled (e.g. *halfHourZone* or *numBeds* attributes, respectively) using composite attribute domains consisting of a set of tuples, where each tuple consists of a thematic value, spatial extent, and/or timestamp(s). Alternatively, an attribute with spatial and/or temporal properties (e.g. population density or average lifespan) could be promoted to a separate but associated class with the same information added to the new class. Although not required by the semantics of the example application, we must also create an artificial *identifier* attribute for this class because its instances must be uniquely identified (see Rumbaugh, 1999, pp. 304, 307). Of more concern, this approach will lead to redundancy whenever the same attribute value is repeated for different object instances, times, and/or spatial extents. This is especially significant for spatial data because of their size.

A more correct approach, in general, would be to promote the association to an association class (e.g., *Has*) with spatial data in the *associated* class (e.g.,

Figure 1: Regional Health Application in UML

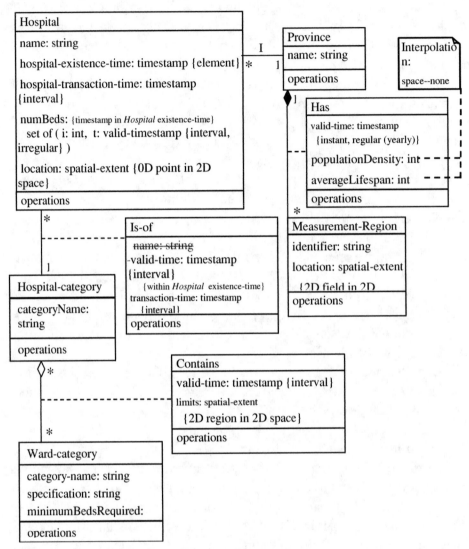

Measurement-Region) and thematic and/or timestamp data (e.g., *populationDensity, averageLifespan*, and *valid-time*) in the *association* class. This still does not solve the problem of the artificial identifier or the extra complexity introduced for adding classes. However, this approach is preferred when (1) the same spatial extent is associated with different object instances or timestamps or (2) several attributes are associated with the same timestamps or spatial extents. Classes and associations with temporal and/or spatial properties (e.g. *Hospital* and hospital *Is-of* category respectively) can be treated similarly by adding timestamp and/or spatial attributes, after promoting the association to an association class in the latter case.

Constraints are used to indicate the time units for timestamps, the time model, the dimensions of spatial extents, and the existence-dependencies described for the application example. Notes are used to show interpolation semantics. Association, rather than generalization, is used to represent hospital category since its definition varies regionally and does not affect the properties defined for the hospital class.

Figure 1 shows that a new association class must be created for each association with spatial or temporal properties. As can be seen, this leads to the creation of a host of artificial constructs that significantly complicate the schema diagram. Furthermore, there is no single, easily visible notation to represent spatiotemporal properties. This violates the requirement that the notation be simple, clear, and consistent. A better approach is to extend the fundamental characteristics of the existing UML elements to meet the spatiotemporal requirements. Next, we consider several alternative methods of extending UML and discuss the advantages and disadvantages of each approach.

Alternative Approaches to Extending UML

Gregersen (1999) discusses three different ways of extending the ER model to incorporate semantics: (1) implicit extension by redefining the semantics of existing notation, (2) explicit extension by representing the additional semantics using existing constructs, i.e., essentially defining standard patterns in the style of Fowler (1997b), or (3) explicit extension by adding additional constructs to the modeling language. Another explicit approach would be to define new data types (or abstract data types) incorporating the semantics that could then be used to describe attribute domains as needed. While the implicit approach may require less initial training for users than the explicit approaches, it results in problems of incompatibility with the original model (i.e., pre-existing schemas now have different semantics) and lack of flexibility (i.e. since the new extended model is no longer suitable for applications not requiring the additional semantic support).

With respect to the explicit approaches, we can see that the pattern-based approach, illustrated in Figure 1, has the disadvantage of producing awkward and overloaded schemas, whereas the other two options add to the constructs or data types that must be learned by the user. Essentially, the additional complexity introduced by the new semantics is evident at the level of the schema for the pattern approach and at the level of the modeling language for the other two approaches. This essentially involves a trade-off between ease of initial use versus regular use.

It is our contention that (1) the priority should be for facilitating regular use and that (2) new constructs and/or data types can be designed to minimize learning time by taking advantage of orthogonality. Furthermore, conversion of new constructs that have equivalents in the original model can be automated for implementation or reference purposes. In the OO context, if the additional semantics impact the object or association levels, then the definition of new abstract data types for attribute domains is not sufficient: some new constructs will be required. As objects and associations can also have spatiotemporal semantics, we adopt the approach of defining new constructs. Next, we examine the potential use of existing UML extension mechanisms to define such constructs.

Using UML Extension Mechanisms

Stereotypes, tagged values, and constraints are advanced features of UML intended to support extensions to the UML meta-model; therefore, they provide a potential basis for defining a spatiotemporal extension. One problem with these mechanisms, as with some other aspects of UML such as aggregation and composition, is that they are inconsistently described in the main sources for UML (Booch, 1999; Rumbaugh, 1999; OMG, 1999). A detailed discussion of some inconsistencies in UML is described in Henderson (1999).

Stereotypes are used to indicate a variation in usage or meaning for an existing UML model element. Tagged values and constraints can be attached to the stereotype to define its additional properties and semantics respectively. A set of standard stereotypes has been defined for UML (Booch, 1999, pp. 442), but none is defined as applying both to attributes and composite model elements having identity (i.e., classes and associations versus composite attribute domains) or used for both spatial and temporal properties. Fowler (1997a) suggests using a *history* stereotype to model historical associations between classes by adding a temporal subtype to one of the classes. But this seems to imply that a new stereotype should be added for each different level of granularity and does not account for spatial or spatiotemporal attribute variation.

Even if we introduce new stereotypes for spatiotemporal semantics, a strict adherence to the definition of UML extension mechanisms can be problematic. According to Rumbaugh (1999, p. 450), a model element can have at most one stereotype. Instead of defining a model element with multiple stereotypes, a new composite stereotype should be defined using generalization and multiple inheritance, e.g. one for each meaningful combination of spatial, temporal, and thematic data semantics. However, this leads to a proliferation of modeling constructs and a less intuitive representation. Defining a small set of basic constructs that can be combined in a simple and semantically meaningful manner is a much more elegant way to add expressive power to a modeling language without sacrificing understandability or simplicity. Therefore, there are strong arguments for allowing a spatiotemporal extension to violate the strict definition of UML stereotypes by allowing model elements to have more than one stereotype.

Furthermore, Rumbaugh (1999) states that "stereotypes may extend the semantics but not the structure of pre-existing metamodel classes" (p. 449), with the exception that tagged values can be used to change the structure of a model element (but not its instantiations). Thus, they do not allow specification of types or domains (all tagged values are text strings) and are not intended for "serious semantic extensions to the modeling language itself" (Rumbaugh, 1999, p. 469). However, spatiotemporal semantics require a change in the structure of model elements to allow relevant time periods and/or spatial extents to be associated with the model element's instances or values. Based on this discussion, it is clear that constructs added to extend UML with spatiotemporal semantics will necessarily go beyond the extension mechanisms defined for UML.

EXTENDED SPATIOTEMPORAL UML

The proposed extension to UML is based on the addition of five new symbols, illustrated in Figure 2, and a *specification box* describing the detailed semantics of the spatiotemporal data represented using the five symbols. The basic approach is to extend UML by adding a minimal set of constructs for spatial, temporal, and thematic data, represented respectively by *spatial, temporal,* and *thematic* symbols. These constructs can then be applied at different levels of the UML class diagram and in different combinations to add spatiotemporal semantics to a UML model element. In addition, the *group* symbol is used to group attributes with common spatiotemporal properties or inter-attribute constraints and the *existence-dependent* symbol is used to describe attributes and associations dependent on object existence.

As discussed previously, although these new symbols can be roughly described as stereotypes; they do not adhere strictly to the UML definition. For improved readability, we use the alternative graphical notation for stereotypes described in Rumbaugh (1999, pp. 451). These symbols can be annotated with a unique label used to reference the associated specification box. The first four symbols can optionally be used without the abbreviations shown in the figure (i.e., *S, T, Th,* and *G* respectively). The specific alphanumeric domain can be optionally indicated, e.g., *Th: int.*

The *group* symbol, *existence-dependent* symbol, and *specification box* are discussed in the section, "Specificaton Box, Existence Time and Groups." The

Figure 2: Extended Spatiotemporal UML Symbols

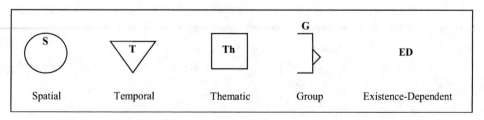

spatial, temporal, and *thematic* symbols are described in this section. A general overview of the meaning and use of these three symbols is given. Then we explain the use and associated semantics of these symbols at the attribute (and attribute group), object class, and association levels respectively.

Spatial, Temporal, and Thematic Constructs

These constructs can be used to model spatial extents, object existence or transaction time, and the three different types of spatiotemporal data previously discussed (i.e. *temporal changes in spatial extents*; *changes in the values of thematic data across time or space*; and *composite data whose components vary depending on time or location*). To understand the use and semantics of the *spatial, temporal,* and *thematic* constructs, we first discuss the interpretation of each individual symbol separately.

The *spatial* symbol represents a spatial extent, which consists of an arbitrary set of points, lines, regions, or volumes. The spatial extent may be associated with thematic or composite data, or may be used to define an attribute domain. The *temporal* symbol represents a temporal extent, or timestamp, which may be associated with thematic, spatial, or composite data. Timestamps may represent existence time for objects, valid time for associations and attributes, and transaction time for objects, associations, and attributes. The *thematic* symbol represents thematic data.

The *thematic* symbol can only be used at the attribute level and only in conjunction with one of the other two symbols to describe an attribute with temporal or spatial properties. A thematic attribute domain with no spatial or temporal properties uses standard UML notation, i.e. *<attribute-name>: <domain>*. When there are such properties, either this notation can be used or the specific thematic domain can be indicated inside the *thematic* symbol. Figure 3 illustrates the four possible cases for a thematic attribute: attributes with a thematic domain and (a) no spatial or temporal properties, (b) temporal properties, (c) spatial properties, or (d) spatiotemporal properties. Adjectives are used to describe the attribute domain (e.g., *thematic* attribute) and adverbs with the word *dependent* to describe additional attribute properties for composite attribute domains (e.g., *temporally dependent* thematic attribute). Therefore, the four possible cases for thematic attributes are called (a) thematic, (b) temporally dependent thematic, (c) spatially dependent thematic, or (d) spatiotemporally dependent thematic attributes respectively.

The semantics of Extended Spatiotemporal UML depend on three factors: (a) the symbol used, (b) the model element described by the symbol (i.e., object, association, or attribute), and (c) whether the symbol is combined with other symbols. The general rules for combining symbols can be summarized as follows:

Figure 3: Thematic Attribute Examples

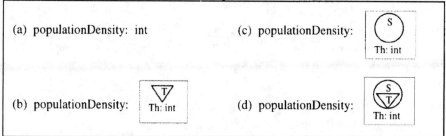

(a) populationDensity: int

(c) populationDensity:

(b) populationDensity:

(d) populationDensity:

- *Nesting one symbol inside another* represents mathematically a function from the domain represented by the inner symbol to the domain represented by the outer symbol. Therefore, different orders of nesting symbols correspond to different functional expressions and represent different perspectives of the data.

    For example, Figure 3(b) represents a function from the time to the integer domain for a given object or association instance. If we reverse the order of the symbol nesting, this would represent the inverse function from the integer to the time domain. However, from the conceptual design and schema perspective, both represent the same semantic modeling category and would result in the same conceptual and logical schema, i.e., a temporally dependent, thematic attribute.

    Rather than arbitrarily restricting the representation of a semantic modeling category to one order of nesting, we prefer to allow the users to select the order of nesting that best matches their perspective of the application data. Although not explored in the current paper, the different orders of nesting could be exploited for a graphical query language or to indicate preferred clustering patterns to the database management system in generating the physical schema.

    Note also that in Figure 3(b), only one integer value is associated with each timestamp; however, several different timestamps may be associated with the same integer value. In Figure 3(d), several integer values will be associated with each timestamp, one for each spatial location.

- *Placing one symbol next to another* symbol represents mathematically two separate functions, one for each symbol. The order in which the two symbols are written is not significant.

    We now give the *rule* for which symbolic combinations are legal at each model level, the *semantic modeling constructs* defined at each level, and a *mapping* between the two. For a given semantic modeling construct, the textual and mathematical definitions are given for each possible symbol nesting that represents that construct.

    Note that any reference to a timestamp, timestamps, a time point, or time validity in the definitions for a given symbol nesting could be for any time dimension, i.e., transaction and/or either valid (for attributes and associations) or existence (for objects) time dimensions. The first symbol nesting given for each semantic modeling construct is used in the examples.

We first summarize the *primitives* used in this section to denote various time, space, and model elements.

<T>	::= domain of time instants
$<2^T>$	::= arbitrary set of time instants, i.e., a timestamp or set of timestamps
<S>	::= domain of points in space
$<2^S>$	::= arbitrary set of points in space, i.e., a spatial extent or set of spatial extents
<oid>	::= domain of object-identifiers
<aid>	::= domain of association-instance identifiers, essentially { <oid> }^{n}
<id>	::= domain of object and association identifiers, essentially { <oid> | <aid> }
<D>	::= thematic, i.e. alphanumeric, domain (e.g., integer, string)
<d>	::= thematic attribute symbol
<t>	::= temporal symbol
<s>	::= spatial symbol
<s&t>	::= any nested combination of a spatial and a temporal symbol
<s&d>	::= any nested combination of a spatial and a thematic symbol
<t&d>	::= any nested combination of a temporal and a thematic symbol
<s&t&d>	::= any nested combination of a spatial, a temporal, and a thematic symbol
<ED>	::= existence-dependent symbol

The Attribute (and Attribute Group) Level

At the attribute level, we can model *temporal changes in spatial extents*, where the spatial extent represents a property of an object (i.e., spatial attribute), and *changes in the value of thematic data across time and/or space* (i.e., spatially and/or temporally dependent thematic attributes).

Legal combinations of symbols at the attribute level are any nested combination of a spatial symbol, a temporal symbol, and/or a thematic symbol. The only exception is that the temporal symbol cannot be used alone. An attribute with a temporal domain is treated as thematic data since temporal data types are predefined for popular standard query languages such as SQL. The attribute domain can optionally be followed by an *existence-dependent* symbol (discussed later). The rule for notation at this level can be defined using BNF notation and the *primitives* defined previously: *attribName:* [<D> \| <s&d> \| <t&d> \| <s&t&d> \| <s> \| <s&t>] [<ED>]

Six different attribute domains are possible, corresponding to the semantic categories of attributes (i.e., modeling constructs). Reading the domain symbols left to right, we have: *thematic attributes; spatially, temporally, and spatiotemporally dependent thematic attributes; spatial attributes*; and *temporally dependent spatial attributes*. Except for thematic attributes, these domains represent extensions for spatiotemporal data modeling.

For each of the semantic categories, a general textual description, symbolic representation(s), mathematical definition(s), and textual definition(s) are given below. Note that each one of the definitions below applies to the identified object or association instance: therefore, we do not state this explicitly in the definitions.

- *Thematic Attribute:* This is an attribute with thematic values.

  <D>   f: <id> ➜ <D>

  Returns the thematic attribute value.

- *Spatially Dependent Thematic Attribute:* This is a set of thematic attribute values, each associated with a spatial extent representing the location where that attribute value is valid. This implies that the attribute values may change over space and their changed values may be retained.

  ◯   f: <id> ➜ (<S> ➜ <D>)

  Returns a set of spatial points, each with its associated thematic attribute value (valid for that spatial point).

  ▢   f: <id> ➜ (<D> ➜ $<2^S>$)

  Returns a set of thematic attribute values, each with its associated spatial extents (where that thematic attribute value is valid).

- *Temporally Dependent Thematic Attribute:* This is a set of thematic attribute values, each associated with one or more timestamps, representing the attribute value's valid and/or transaction time. This implies that the attribute values may change over time and their changed values may be retained.

  ▽   f: <id> ➜ (<T> ➜ <D>)

  Returns a set of time points, each with its associated thematic attribute value (i.e. valid for that time point).

  ▽   f: <id> ➜ (<D> ➜ $<2^T>$)

  Returns a set of thematic attribute values, each with its associated timestamps (i.e. when that thematic attribute value is valid).

- *Spatiotemporally Dependent Thematic Attribute:* This is a combination of spatially and temporally dependent thematic attributes as defined above, i.e. a set of thematic attribute values, each associated with a spatial extent and one or more timestamps.

f: <id> → (<T> → (<S> → <D>))

Returns a set of time points, each with its associated set of spatial points, and, for each spatial point, its associated thematic attribute value (i.e., valid for that time and spatial point).

   f: <id> → (<D> → (<T> → $<2^S>$))

Returns a set of thematic attribute values, each with its associated set of time points, and, for each time point, its associated spatial extents (i.e., where that thematic value is valid for that time point).

   f: <id> → (<S> → (<D> → $<2^T>$))

Returns a set of spatial points, each with its associated set of thematic attribute values, and, for each thematic attribute value, its associated timestamps (i.e., when that thematic attribute value is valid for that spatial point).

   f: <id> → (<S> → (<T> → <D>))

Returns a set of spatial points, each with its associated set of timepoints, and, for each time point, its associated thematic attribute value (i.e., valid for that spatial and time point).

   f: <id> → (<T> → (<D> → $<2^S>$))

Returns a set of time points, each with its associated a set of thematic attribute values, and, for each thematic attribute value, its associated spatial extents (i.e., where that thematic attribute value is valid for that time point).

   f: <id> → (<D> → (<S> → $<2^T>$))

Returns a set of thematic attribute values, each with its associated set of spatial points, and, for each spatial point, its associated timestamps (i.e., when that thematic attribute value is valid for that spatial point).

- *Spatial Attribute:* This is an attribute with a spatial domain, i.e., the attribute value is a spatial extent.

   f: <id> → $<2^S>$

Returns the spatial attribute value.

- *Temporally Dependent Spatial Attribute:* A spatial attribute is associated with one or more timestamps, representing the spatial extent's valid and/or transaction time.

   f: <id> → (<T> → $<2^S>$)

Returns a set of time points, each with its associated spatial attribute value (i.e., spatial extent).

▽   f: <id> → (<S> → <2ᵀ>)

Returns a set of spatial points, each with its associated timestamps (i.e. when the spatial attribute value, i.e., spatial extent, intersects that spatial point).

The use of these symbols at the attribute level is illustrated in Figure 4. The difference between (a) thematic attributes, (b) temporally dependent thematic attributes, (c) spatiotemporally dependent thematic attributes, (d) spatial attributes, and (e) temporally dependent spatial attributes is illustrated by (a) *name (for Hospital and Province)*, (b) *numBeds*, (c) *populationDensity*, (d) *location*, and (e) *halfHourZone* respectively.

A thematic attribute domain is indicated as a string after the attribute or—if that attribute also has temporal or spatial properties—by the use of a thematic symbol. If no domain is explicitly specified for an attribute, then the use of the spatial symbol indicates that the attribute has a spatial domain. Thus, the *Hospital location* and *halfHourZone* attributes represent spatial data. The nested temporal symbol used for *halfHourZone* indicates that the spatial extent associated with this attribute may change over time and thus should be timestamped. Therefore, an attribute marked by a spatiotemporal symbol (and no thematic domain) represents a spatial extent that changes over time. In this case, as transport networks change, the geometry of the half-hour travel zone must be updated.

In contrast, an attribute that has a thematic domain and a spatial and/or temporal symbol represents a spatially and/or temporally dependent thematic attribute. This is indicated graphically by using the thematic symbol; thus this symbol

Figure 4: Using Extended Spatiotemporal UML at the Attribute Level

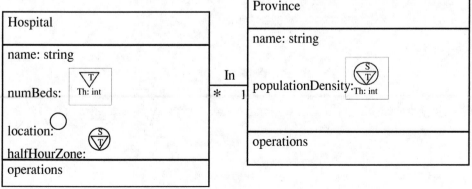

is used to differentiate two different types of spatiotemporal data: *temporal changes in spatial extents* and *changes in the value of thematic data across time and space*. Therefore, the fact that *numBeds* has an integer domain associated with a temporal symbol indicates that the integer value of *numBeds* may change over time and should be timestamped. Analogously, the integer value of *populationDensity* may change over time or space and thus each value is associated with a timestamp and spatial extent.

The Object Class Level

At the object class level, we can model *temporal changes in spatial extents*, where the spatial extent is associated with an object instance. We can also model the time an object exists in the real world (i.e., existence time) or is part of the current database state (i.e., transaction time).

An object class can be marked by a temporal symbol, a spatial symbol, or any nested combination of these. In addition, this is the only level where the symbols can be paired; i.e., a temporal symbol can be paired with either a spatial symbol or a nested combination of the two symbols. The separate temporal symbol represents the existence or transaction time of the object. The spatial symbol represents the spatial extent associated with that object. If the spatial symbol is combined with a nested temporal symbol, then the spatial extent is timestamped to show the valid or transaction time of the spatial extent. Since the object can exist or be current even when not actually associated with a spatial extent, separate timestamps are required for the object instance and for the object instance's spatial extent. The rule for object level notation can be given in BNF as follows:

  className [<s> | <s&t>] [<t>]

Corresponding to the five possible instantiations of this rule, <s>; <s&t>; <t>; <s><t>; and <s&t><t>, there are five different categories of object classes as defined below.

- *Spatial Object (Class):* An object is associated with a spatial extent. This is equivalent to an object having a single spatial attribute except that there is no separate identifier for the spatial extent.

  ◯ f: <oid> → <2^s>

Returns the spatial extent of the identified object.

- *Temporally dependent Spatial Object (Class):* The spatial extent associated with a spatial object is also associated with one or more timestamps, representing the spatial extent's valid and/or transaction time.

  ▽ f: <oid> → (<T> → <2^s>)

Returns a set of timepoints, each associated with the spatial extent of the identified object at that timepoint.

▽ (inverted triangle with line)   f: <oid> → (<S> → <2^T>)

Returns a set of spatial points, each with its associated timestamps (i.e., when the object's spatial extent intersects that spatial point), for the identified object.

- *Temporal Object (Class):* An object is associated with one or more timestamps, representing the object's existence and/or transaction time.

▽   f: <oid> → <2^T>

Returns the timestamp of the identified object.

- *Spatiotemporal Object (Class):* This is a combination of a spatial and temporal object as defined above, i.e., each object instance is associated with a spatial extent and one or more timestamps representing the object's existence and/or transaction time.

▽ ○   f: <oid> → <2^T> and   f: <oid> → <2^S>

Returns the timestamp and the spatial extent of the identified object.

- *Temporally Dependent Spatiotemporal Object (Class):* This is a combination of a temporally dependent spatial object and a temporal object as defined above, i.e., an object is associated with a spatial extent, one or more timestamps representing the spatial extent's valid and/or transaction time, and one or more timestamps representing the object's existence and/or transaction time.

▽ ▽ (with line inside)   f: <oid> → <2^T> and f: <oid> → (<T> → <2^S>)

Returns the timestamp of the identified object and a set of timepoints, each with its associated spatial extent (i.e., valid at that timepoint), for the identified object.

▽ ▽ (with line)   f: <oid> → <2^T> and f: <oid> → (<S> → <2^T>)

Returns the timestamp of the identified object and a set of spatial points, each with its associated timestamps (i.e., when the object's spatial extent intersects that spatial point), for the identified object.

The use of symbols at the object class level is illustrated in Figure 5. In Figure 5(a), the temporal symbol at the *Hospital* object level represents a temporal object class with existence and transaction time. In Figure 5(b), we give an example of a temporally dependent spatial object. This example assumes that there is no need to represent hospital location separately from the half-hour travel zone. Instead, a hospital object is treated as a spatial object with a single associated spatial extent, showing the half-hour travel zone around that hospital. The temporal symbol indicates that the spatial extent should be timestamped, since the half-hour travel zone can change over time. Finally, Figure 5(c) combines (a) and (b), illustrating a

*Figure 5: Using Extended Spatiotemporal UML at the Object Class
Level*

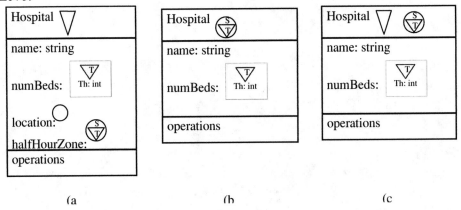

(a   (b   (c

temporally dependent spatiotemporal object. The object is *spatiotemporal* because it has a timestamp and a spatial extent; and it is *temporally dependent* because the spatial extent also has a timestamp.

The Association Level

At the association level, we can model *temporal changes in spatial extents*, where the spatial extent is associated with a relationship between object instances (i.e., spatiotemporal association), and *composite data whose components vary depending on time or location* (i.e., spatiotemporal aggregation or composition). The following discussion applies to any type of association, including aggregation and composition.

At the association level, any nested combination of a spatial and/or a temporal symbol represents a legal combination describing spatiotemporal properties of the association. Except for the omission of the *thematic* symbol, the association level is similar to the attribute level. The association spatiotemporal properties can optionally be followed by an *existence-dependent* symbol (discussed later). The rule for the association level notation can be given in BNF as follows:

assoc-line [<s> | <t> | <s&t>] [<ED>]

Reading the BNF rule from left to right, three different categories of associations are possible, as defined below.

• *Spatially Dependent Association:* An association instance is associated with a spatial extent representing the location where the association instance is valid. This implies that the association instances may change over space and their changed instances may be retained.

⃝   f: <aid> ➜ <2^s >

Returns the spatial extent of the identified association.

- *Temporally Dependent Association:* An association instance is associated with one or more timestamps, representing the association's valid and/or transaction time. This implies that association instances may change over time and the changed instances may be retained.

$$\triangledown \qquad f: <aid> \rightarrow <2^T>$$

Returns the timestamp of the identified association.

- *Spatiotemporally dependent Association:* This is a combination of spatially and temporally dependent associations as defined above, i.e., an association is associated with a spatial extent and one or more timestamps.

$$\ominus \qquad f: <aid> \rightarrow (<T> \rightarrow <2^S>)$$

Returns a set of time points, each with the associated spatial extent for the identified association at that time point.

$$\triangledown \qquad f: <aid> \rightarrow (<S> \rightarrow <2^T>)$$

Returns a set of spatial points, each with its associated timestamps (i.e., when the association instance's spatial extent intersects that spatial point), for the identified association.

The use of these symbols at the association level is shown in Figure 6. Marking the *Is-of* association with a temporal symbol signifies that the category of a hospital may change over time, as local health needs change and wards are opened or closed. Therefore, association instances should be timestamped.

A spatially dependent association is one where an association instance is associated with a spatial extent to show where that instance is valid. For

Figure 6: Using Extended Spatiotemporal UML at the Association Level

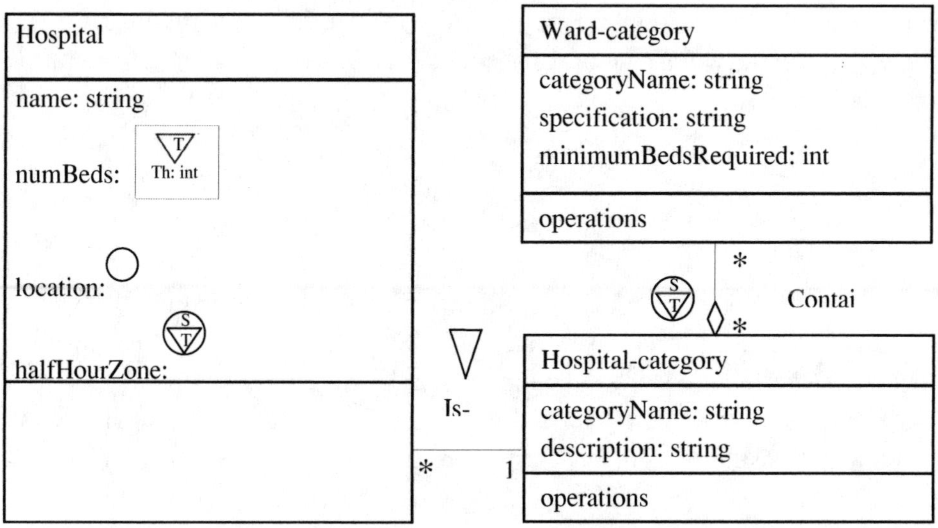

example, the same category of hospital may require different categories of wards in different areas depending on local regulations. Therefore, the *Contains* aggregation association must be spatially dependent. In fact, since the local categories may also change over time, the *Contains* aggregation association is actually spatiotemporally dependent. In this case, both of the associated object classes are purely conceptual. An association between two physical object classes can also be spatiotemporally dependent; e.g. a consultation of a ward doctor with a specialist is scheduled for a specific location and period of time in the hospital.

It is important to consider whether any constraints should be implicitly assumed between the timestamps or spatial extents of participating objects with those of a temporally and/or spatially dependent association, especially in the case of aggregation and composition. The specific constraints that are appropriate depend on the semantics of the particular association. As an illustration, consider a grandparent/grandchild association between two people. Such an association can be defined even outside the existence time of the grandparent. Similarly, the *aggregation* of particular types of car components (i.e., *component class*) in the design of a given car model (i.e., *model class*) may vary regionally. For example, special anti-polluting devices may need to be added to the car model in certain states. However, there are no implied constraints between the spatial extents of the classes and the aggregation.

These examples show that such constraints are application dependent; therefore, they should not be incorporated as implicit defaults in the modeling language but should be specified explicitly. This can be done either on an ad hoc basis as required using UML constraints or by defining explicit modeling constructs for commonly used constraint patterns. The latter approach is illustrated by the introduction of the existence-dependent symbol to support the semantics of temporal dependency between associations and their participating objects or between objects or associations and their attributes. Explicit modeling constructs for common spatial constraints have been defined in Price (2000).

SPECIFICATION BOX, EXISTENCE TIME, AND GROUPS

The previous section described the different types of timestamps that can be associated with an attribute, association, or object class: but where do we specify which types are required for a given application? Detailed spatiotemporal semantics are specified in a *specification box*, which can be associated with any of the icons or combinations using a unique naming convention (used in this paper) or label. A specification box was adopted instead of standard UML mechanisms such as tagged values or constraints for the reasons discussed previously. The specification box includes information on the time units and the time and space dimensions, models, and interpolation. Users can specify regular (recorded at regular intervals) or irregular time models and object- or field-based space models. Interpolation functions can be specified to derive values between recorded spatial locations or timestamps for spatially and/or temporally dependent thematic attributes. The time dimensions and units (i.e., instant, interval, element) used are defined in Jensen (1998). Specification boxes can be inherited from parent classes as with any other class property. The *specification box* syntax is illustrated in Figure 7.

Time dimensions include existence time (for objects), valid time (for attributes and associations), and transaction time (for objects, attributes, or associations), as defined in Jensen (1998). However, object existence time is more precisely defined as the time during which existence-dependent attributes and associations can be defined (i.e., have legal values) for that object. In other words, existence-dependent attributes and associations are those that are defined only when the related object(s) exist. This implies that attributes and associations that are not existence-dependent (e.g., an employee's social-security number) may be defined even when the related object(s) no longer exist. Other attributes, e.g. work-phone number, are defined only while the related object(s) exist (e.g., the employee works at the company) and are therefore existence-dependent.

Note that existence time is not necessarily equivalent to biological lifespan. The exact meaning will be dependent on the application; therefore, individual applications define which attributes and associations are existence-dependent. Object identifiers are never existence-dependent, as they can be used to refer to historical objects. Any other attribute or association can be defined as being existence-dependent.

Figure 7: Specification Box Syntax in Extended Spatiotemporal UML

SPECIFICATION BOX <Identifier>:

TimeDimen. ::= [existence | valid] [transaction]

TimeInterpolation ::= discrete | step | min | max | avg | linear | spline | <user-defined>

TimeModel ::= irregular | (regular {<frequency> [,<beginning>,<end>]})

TimeUnit [(<TimeDimen.>)] ::= instant | interval | element

SpaceInterpolation ::= <same as TimeInterpolation>

SpaceModel ::= '(' <max object/field dim>, <max search space dim> ')': object | field

Group ::= independent | (dependent (formula)*)]

If existence time is associated with a given object, the existence-dependent attributes and associations for that object class must be explicitly marked as such by adding the superscript *ED* to the attribute or association name. Conversely, existence-dependent attributes and associations can only be defined for objects having existence time specified. In the case of an existence-dependent association, existence time must be defined for at least one of the participating objects.

If an existence-dependent attribute is temporally dependent, then every valid-time timestamp for the attribute's instance data must be included within the existence time of the corresponding object instance. If an existence-dependent association is temporally dependent, then every valid-time timestamp for the association's instance data must be included in the intersection of the existence times for those participating object instances that have existence time defined. An existence-dependent attribute is undefined outside the existence time of the corresponding object instance. Similarly, an existence-dependent association is undefined outside the intersection of the existence times for those participating object instances that have existence time defined.

Note that the time model and interpolation specification apply only to valid time, whereas the time unit specification is used both for valid or existence time and transaction time. Therefore, the dimension must be specified for time unit whenever a model element is associated with both valid or existence time and transaction time. In addition, time interpolation is normally used for temporally dependent thematic attributes. Time interpolation of spatial attributes (i.e., spatial extents) must be discrete (i.e., no interpolation) or user defined.

Space dimensions include the dimensions of the spatial extent(s) being specified, followed by the dimensions of the underlying search space. The object-based spatial model is used for a spatial attribute, i.e., the attribute instance for a single object instance consists of a single spatial extent. The field-based spatial model is used for a spatially dependent, thematic attribute; where a single object instance has a set of thematic values, each associated with a different spatial extent. Space interpolation applies only to spatially dependent thematic attributes using the field-based spatial model.

The specification box can also be used to specify spatiotemporal constraints, including constraints within an attribute group. The group symbol is used to group attributes sharing the same timestamps or spatial extents, that then only need to be specified once for the group. Thus, the group symbol graphically illustrates associated sets of attributes and avoids the possibility of redundantly specifying the same spatial extents and timestamps. Note that a group's attributes never share thematic values, even if the thematic symbol is used in the group specification. If the group's attributes have different thematic domains, then these can be indicated next to each attribute using standard UML text notation.

Following UML convention, another compartment is added to the object class to accommodate the *specification boxes* for that class, i.e., the *specification* compartment. The *specification* compartment can be used to specify spatiotemporal semantics for the object, the attributes of the object class, and any associations in which the object class participates. Alternatively, a *specification* compartment can be added to an association class to specify spatiotemporal semantics for that association and its attributes. A detailed discussion of the specification compartment and box can be found in Price (1999).

USING EXTENDED SPATIOTEMPORAL UML: THE REGIONAL HEALTH CARE EXAMPLE

Figure 8 shows the full regional health application described earlier as it would be represented using the proposed extension and illustrates the use of the specification box, group symbol, and existence-dependent symbol.

For example, *Hospital location* is specified as a single point in 2D space. *Hospital halfHourZone* and *Contains* are specified as a region in 2D space. In contrast, the *Province populationDensity* and *averageLifespan* group is associated with a 2D field in 2D space. This means that, for a single object instance, the two attributes in the group are associated with a set of regions and have a separate attribute value for each region for a given point in time. Since these two attributes share common timestamps and spatial extents, they are grouped. Since both attributes are integers, we can specify the thematic domain in the group symbol. If the attributes had different thematic domains, then we would specify them for each attribute rather than for the group.

The group is then associated with a single symbol and *specification box*. Here we specify that any attribute in the group uses average interpolation in time and no interpolation in space, has a valid time dimension using *instant* as the time unit, and is measured yearly (i.e. a new set of values is recorded for the attribute each year). This means that the population density and average lifespan between recorded time instants is assumed to be the average of the values at the two nearest time instants and undefined outside of recorded spatial regions. No inter-attribute constraints are defined for the group, as shown by the keyword *independent*.

The temporal symbol at the *Hospital* object level is used to indicate existence time and transaction time. Existence time is used to model the periods when the hospital is open, i.e., when the existence-dependent attributes *numBeds* and *halfHourZone* and the existence-dependent association *Is-of* are defined. Since these model elements are temporally dependent, the valid timestamps of all their instances must be included within the *Hospital* existence time. Attribute *numBeds* is specified as irregular because this attribute is not recorded periodically: whenever it changes the new value is recorded.

Figure 8: Regional Health Application in Extended Spatiotemporal UML

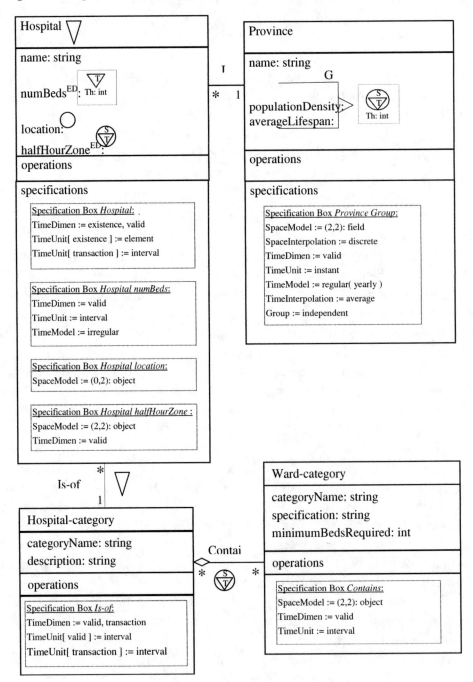

The specification box for an association (e.g., *Is-of*) can be placed in the specification compartment of either of its participating object classes (e.g., *Hospital* or *Hospital-category*). Note that since *Hospital-category* is not temporal and therefore does not have existence time defined, the only constraint on the valid-time timestamps of the *Is-of* association comes from the *Hospital class* existence time.

DISCUSSION AND CONCLUSION

Comparing the schemas of the regional health application from Figure 8 and Figure 1, it is clear that the schema that uses Extended Spatiotemporal UML is much simpler than the corresponding UML schema. The use of UML in Figure 1 results in the creation of a host of artificial constructs to represent spatiotemporal semantics, obscuring the schema design. We can see that far fewer object classes are required in Figure 8 to describe the same application example. Modeling representative excerpts of actual spatiotemporal applications showed a similar pattern, e.g., 50% and 30% fewer object classes were required using the proposed extension to model a cadastral application (Tryfona, 1999) and medical multimedia application (Dionisio, 1998), respectively. In particular, fewer object classes were required to model spatiotemporal associations or attribute groups. Fewer attributes were required, since graphical symbols and specification boxes were used instead of extra attributes (e.g. for time dimensions or identification) to provide a compact, distinct, and consistent representation of spatiotemporal properties.

By incorporating spatiotemporal semantics in the modeling language itself, Extended Spatiotemporal UML reduces the complexity of the resulting schemas. The level of detail is reduced without sacrificing understandability. This allows the application developer to concentrate on the characteristics of the specific application domain of interest. The modular specification of spatiotemporal properties also facilitates schema reuse and extension.

For example, if we want to reuse the schema from Figure 8 for the same application but without historical records, we can simply delete all of the temporal symbols and specifications. Similarly, if hospital definitions do not vary regionally, one need only remove the spatial symbol from the *Contains* icon and specification box. In contrast, the modifications required to reuse the schema from Figure 1 are not nearly so obvious or modular. Each schema element would have to be examined to determine which model elements would need to be modified or deleted.

If, on the other hand, we want to extend the existing application with another group of spatiotemporally dependent thematic attributes with shared properties; we simply add another group to the definition of the *Province* object class (or alternatively define a sub-class of *Province* containing this additional group). The same extension would be much more complicated in Figure 1, involving the creation of a new object class and association for the additional spatial extents and their associated timestamped thematic attributes respectively. This process substantially complicates the extended schema and reduces its readability.

The specification box aids readability by providing a clear and consistent framework for the detailed specification of spatiotemporal semantics. These semantics are represented in UML using constraints and notes that are unlikely to be standardized among users, making the diagram more difficult to read. The specification box can serve as a guideline for application developers, highlighting generally relevant semantics to be considered when modeling spatiotemporal data. This facilitates effective communication and consistent design documentation.

In summary, this paper proposes a UML extension to support applications requiring a range of spatiotemporal models and types. A clean technique is introduced for modeling *composite data whose components vary depending on time or location, temporal changes in spatial extents*, and *changes in the value of thematic data across time and space*. Alternative models of time and change processes are also supported, as well as valid, transaction, and existence time dimensions. By introducing a small base set of modeling constructs that can be combined and applied at different levels of the UML model (including attribute groups), language clarity and simplicity is maintained without sacrificing expressive power or flexibility.

The introduction of a thematic symbol and formal rules for combining spatial, temporal, and thematic symbols provides a consistent and well-defined notation for representing spatiotemporal semantics. Temporal and spatial associations are treated in a parallel manner, i.e. to describe model structure.

In addition, we have proposed a definition of object existence time based on application-defined dependencies of individual object properties and introduced modeling constructs to reflect these semantics. This allows users to differentiate between those properties that *are* still defined when the object does not exist (e.g., employee social security number) and other properties that *are not* (e.g., work phone number).

Future directions include the classification and specification of spatiotemporal aggregation constructs and exploiting the behavioral features of UML to describe operations on spatiotemporal data.

ACKNOWLEDGEMENTS

We thank B. Srinivasan and K. Ramamohanarao for their insightful comments. This research was conducted in part while the first author visited Aalborg University and supported in part by the Danish Technical Research Council (grant 9700780), the Chorochronos project (EC contract FMRX-CT96-0056), and Nykredit Corporation.

REFERENCES

Abraham, T. and Roddick, J.F. (1999). Survey of spatio-temporal databases. *GeoInformatica*, 3(1), 61-99.

Becker, L., Voigtmann, A. and Hinrichs, K. (1996). Temporal support for geo-data in object-oriented databases. *Proceedings of Database and Expert Systems Applications*, 79-93.

Booch, G., Rumbaugh, J. and Jacobson, I. (1999). *The Unified Modeling Language User Guide*. Reading, MA.: Addison-Wesley.

Claramunt, C. (1995). Managing Time in GIS An Event-Oriented Approach. *Proceedings of the International Workshop on Temporal Databases*, 23-42.

Dionisio, J.D.N. and Cardenas, A.F. (1998). A unified data model for representing multimedia, timeline, and simulation data. *IEEE Transactions on Knowledge and Data Engineering*, 10(5), 746-767.

Faria, G., Medeiros, C.B. and Nascimento., M.A. (1998). An extensible framework for spatio-temporal database applications. *Time Center Technical Report* TR-27, 1-15.

Fowler, M. (1997b). *Analysis Patterns: Reusable Object Models*. Menlo Park, CA: Addison-Wesley.

Fowler, M. and Scott, K. (1997a). *UML Distilled*. Reading, MA.: Addison-Wesley.

Gregersen, H. and Jensen, C.S. (1999). Temporal entity-relationship models—A survey. *IEEE Transactions on Knowledge and Data Engineering*, 11(3), 464-497.

Henderson-Sellers, B. and Barbier, F. (1999). Black and white diamonds. *Proceedings of Unified Modeling Language*, 550-565.

Jensen, C.S. and Dyreson, C.E. (Eds.). (1998). The consensus glossary of temporal database concepts. *Temporal Databases: Research and Practice*, 367-405. Berlin: Springer-Verlag.

Langran, G. (1993). *Time in Geographic Information Systems*. London: Taylor & Francis.

OMG Unified Modeling Language Specifications, version 1.3. (1999, June). Needham, MA: Object Management Group, 1-808. Retrieved May 19, 2000 from World Wide Web: http://www.ftp.omg.org/pub/docs/ad/99-06-08.pdf.

Parent, C., Spaccapietra, S. and Zimanyi, E. (1999). Spatio-temporal conceptual models: Data structures + space + time. *Proceedings of the 7th ACM Symposium on Advances in Geographic Information Systems*.

Pequet, D.J. and Duan, N. (1995). An event-based spatiotemporal data model (ESTDM) for temporal analysis of geographical data. *International Journal of Geographic Information Systems*, 9(1), 7-24.

Price, R., Srinivasan, B. and Ramamohanarao, K. (1999). Extending the unified modeling language to support spatiotemporal applications. *Asia Technology of Object Oriented Languages and Systems*, 163-174.

Price, R., Tryfona, N. and Jensen, C.S. (2000). Supporting conceptual modeling of complex spatial relationships. *Chorochronos Technical Report # CH-00-5*, 1-31 (in process).

Rumbaugh, J., Jacobson, I. and Booch, G. (1999). *The Unified Modeling Language Reference Manual*. Reading, MA.: Addison-Wesley.

Tryfona, N. and Jensen, C.S. (1999). Conceptual data modeling for spatiotemporal applications. *Geoinformatica*, 3(3), 245-268.

Chapter 11

A Design Method for Real-Time Object-Oriented Systems Using Communicating Real-Time State Machines

Eduardo B. Fernandez, Jie Wu, and Debera R. Hancock
Florida Atlantic University, USA

Many methodologies for software modeling and design include some form of static and dynamic modeling to describe the structural and behavioral views respectively. Modeling and design of complex real-time software systems requires notations for describing concurrency, asynchronous event handling, communication between independent machines, timing properties. Dynamic modeling of real time systems using object-oriented methodologies requires extensions to the traditional state machine notations in order to convey the real-time system characteristics and constraints. This chapter proposes an object-oriented analysis and design methodology that augments the traditional UML (Unified Modeling Language) dynamic model with real-time extensions based on high-level parallel machines and communication notations from CRSM (Communicating Real-Time State Machines). An example of the proposed methodology is provided using a realistic example of an automated passenger train system.

INTRODUCTION

Real-time systems are characterized by their response requirements (deadlines) and underlying concurrency of functions. These time-critical systems often have stringent safety requirements, necessitating that they be highly reliable and

Previously published in *Managing Information Technology in a Global Economy*, edited by Mehdi Khosrow-Pour. Copyright © 2001, Idea Group Publishing.

that their functions be predictable when subjected to real-time, concurrent events. Although the systems may be quite complex, good analysis and design methodologies must be simple and understandable while conveying accurately the design and its real-time aspects. Methodologies for specifying system requirements and designs typically include some form of requirements specification and notations for modeling the static, dynamic, and functional aspects of the system. This specification is often a textual description of the functional characteristics of the system and alone may not serve to accurately and unambiguously define the requirements. Formal languages are required to clearly specify and validate critical system requirements such as timing and safety constraints (Heitmeyer & Mandrioli, 1996). For real-time systems where there are often critical timing requirements or safety considerations, verification of the design and implementation with respect to formally specified critical requirements is necessary.

Once the requirements are specified, a series of analysis and design steps are performed that refine and map the requirements to a complete design. With object-oriented methods, the analysis step includes a representation of the real-world problem as a static class diagram. This modeling of the real-world problem into independent, data-encapsulated classes maps conceptually into the system as a collection of concurrently active communicating components. In a good methodology, the mapping of the problem information described in the requirements specification to the objects in the static class diagram should be consistent and visibly intuitive.

In practice, the complete system design is typically derived through a series of refinements from the static analysis model. It is often difficult to pinpoint when analysis ends and design starts. A series of iterations of lower level analysis and design steps is performed. Many notations and methodologies have been used for these steps. With any good methodology, some form of dynamic modeling is required to model and design the behavior of the system elements over time. State machines and variations on state machine notations are popular modeling tools for both object-oriented and functional methodologies. High-level state machines are often decomposed and refined into lower-level state machines. Sequence diagrams and scenario descriptions are examples of design approaches that are used to refine the operations and states of the lower level state machines.

Many real-time method extensions for function-oriented methodologies have been proposed and applied to real system development (Gomaa, 1986; Harel et al., 1990; Leveson & Heimdahl, 1994). Object-oriented design has recently become popular as an alternative for designing complex software systems. It is clear that the popularity and inherent concurrency of object-oriented designs makes it a highly desirable approach for producing real-time systems. Methodologies that map closely to object-oriented methodologies and programming languages have been developed such as O-Charts (Harel & Gary, 1996), Real-Time Object-

Oriented Modeling (ROOM) (Selic et al., 1992), Octopus (Awad, 1996), RT UML (Douglass, 1998), SOMT (Telelogic), and ObjectGEODE (Verilog). The Unified Modeling Language,UML, is a comprehensive methodology, encompassing the entire analysis and design life cycle with modeling of the static, dynamic, and functional views of the system (Rational, Inc.). Extending UML for real-time system preserves the well-understood and readable approach of UML while introducing extensions necessary for clearly modeling real-time systems.

The dynamic modeling in the standard UML does not provide a mechanism for visibly distinguishing the physical system concurrency and external events from the concurrency introduced by the underlying object design. UML also does not clearly distinguish external communication mechanisms from internal design-oriented communication. This paper proposes modifications to the standard UML dynamic modeling to include a hierarchical system design based on concurrent high-level communicating state machines. The notations for UML state diagrams are modified and extended to include concepts from Communicating Real-Time State Machines (CRSMs) (Selic & Rumbaugh) and OMT extensions proposed by M. Chonoles and C. Gilliam (Chonoles & Gilliam).

Section 2 provides an overview of the proposed object-oriented modeling and design methodology. Sections 3 to 5 use the proposed methodology to model and design a hypothetical automated Passenger Train System (PTS). This example contains specification elements, analysis model, dynamic model, design refinements, and some implementation considerations. The last section provides conclusions.

A DESIGN METHODOLOGY

A seamless development approach is utilized from analysis through design in (Rumbaugh et al., 1991) and this approach is typical of object-oriented methodologies. From the specification of the requirements, the problem progresses from model to detailed design through a series of refinements that use the same or consistent notations, syntax, and constructs. Details, optimizations, and implementation considerations are added iteratively. From each step to the next, there is a clear mapping of the higher level requirements or design elements to the lower level refinements. This is essential in order to verify that the resulting design and implementation are correct.

The following steps are used in our methodology:

Requirements Specification: The approach used for specifying the system functional requirements is a combined formal and informal specification. These can be expressed also as Use Cases.

Object Oriented Analysis (OOA): The analysis phase used is identical to the UML analysis phase.

Dynamic Modeling with Communicating Real-Time State Machines: We propose that the traditional dynamic modeling step from UML be augmented with a multilevel communicating state machine hierarchy (Shaw, 1992).

Iterative Design Refinement with Sequence Diagrams: Sequence diagrams provide a mechanism for illustrating a particular scenario and the associated events between objects from that scenario.

Communicating real-time state machines (CRSMs) are a notation for specifying concurrent, real-time systems including monitoring and controlling functions (Shaw, 1992). CRSMs have the notion of synchronous communication between state machines instead of the UML notation for external events. CRSMs also have added notations and facilities for describing timing properties and for accessing real time.

CRSMs are specified in two levels. The first level is the machine level. The machine level concept is similar to the UML notion of concurrent subsystems and interaction between subsystems. CRSM machines at the machine level execute concurrently and independently of one another, except when they directly communicate. Machines are distributed (they do not share variables other than the notion of real time). Machines communicate over channels that connect pairs of machines. Channels are also uniquely identified with an event or message. A separate channel is associated with each different communication type between machines. The channel notation provides a mechanism for arguments or message components that are the content of the communication.

Each machine from the first level is further refined in the second level as a serialized finite state machine. These state machines are conceptually similar to UML state machines although the notations for event transitions differ. The CRSM state machines have guarded internal commands instead of constrained event transitions. The CRSM guards are equivalent to the UML constraints.

CRSM commands can be internal or external commands. External commands are I/O commands where "<command> ?" is an input command and "<command> !" is an output command. These external commands are conceptually similar to external events in UML notation although the notations for input and output in CRSM more crisply identify the type of communication than in UML (where the event name implies the type of communication). CRSM internal commands are equivalent to transition events and operations in UML.

CRSM provides notations for specifying real-time functions and properties. An external real-time clock command of "RT(x)?[y]" results in a state transition and generates a timeout at relative time y, setting to the real time at the time of the timeout. When the timeout notation is omitted, "RT(x)?[0] or RT(x)?", the result is that x is set to the current real time. When the time argument is omitted, "RT?[y]"

a pure timeout is generated at relative time y. The CRSM real-time notations are useful for specifying periodic events and timeouts for real-time constraints.

PASSENGER TRAIN SYSTEMS (PTS) REQUIREMENTS

This section provides the requirements specification elements for an example problem that is used to illustrate the proposed methodology. The Passenger Train System (PTS) example is hypothetical but realistic and was invented for this purpose.

Problem Statement

An amusement park has a passenger train system that allows passengers to travel from one section of the park to another (Figure 1). Several trains can operate at one time. The trains all run in the same direction on a track consisting of one large loop. Passengers embark and disembark the trains at any of several stations along the track. All trains stop at all stations, regardless of whether or not there are passengers waiting to board. There is one siding that leads to a storage and maintenance depot. Similarly, trains can enter the main track or be returned to operation by switching them back onto the main track from this siding.

The trains are powered by electric current from a power rail carried in the tracks. Power to the power rail is managed by a power control system. Each yard section of track can be powered on and off independently by the power control system. When no power is applied to a section of track, a train running in that section cannot accelerate or maintain its speed. As a fail-safe mechanism, a train's braking system requires power to be disengaged. This ensures that when a train loses power, the brakes automatically engage and the train comes to a fast and smooth stop.

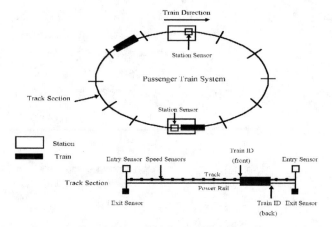

Figure 1: Passenger Train System(PTS) Configuration

The automatic movement and speed of each train is controlled remotely via transmitted communication signals. Each train is equipped with a receiver and an automatic movement control system. The movement control system translates signals such as "brake," "accelerate," and "decelerate" into signals to the train's motor and brakes. Each train is also equipped with manual override controls to move and stop the train. When the manual override is in use, the automatic control is disabled.

The position of each train is monitored with sensors. Each track section contains entry and exit sensors that detect when a train enters and leaves a section of track. In addition to detecting the presence of a train, the entry and exit sensors scan a train's unique identifier (train ID). The train ID is used by the movement control system to track the location of each train and to transmit movement control signals to a particular train.

The speed of each train is continually monitored and managed by a speed controller. Many speed sensors are placed throughout the main track. The speed sensors are used to detect the passing of a train at a particular point in time to determine its current traveling speed.

A special station sensor exists in each station at precisely the point at which the train is expected to brake for a station stop. Once stopped in a station, a station operator must manually restart the train upon successful disembarking of passengers.

The most important design issue is safety of operation. System failures must result in safe actions. Trains must maintain a safe distance between each other of at least 1000 yards (two track sections). Trains must never exceed a speed of 45 MPH and should normally travel at a safe speed of 40 MPH. Trains within 500 yards of a station must not exceed a safe station approach speed of 20 MPH. A traffic controller manages the position of trains. Trains can be automatically slowed, sped up, stopped, and restarted to handle the traffic flow.

In addition to being safe, the train system should be convenient for passengers. Trains should depart within 10 minutes of arrival at a station. A station stop exceeding this time results in warning messages to the station operator and automatic slowing of any train approaching the station. Trains should travel as quickly as possible (within the safety parameters) between stations to maintain passenger satisfaction.

Problem Focus

The system development example here focuses primarily on the major control functions of the Passenger Train System (PTS). Particular emphasis is placed on the modeling of the interaction and behavior of the traffic and speed controllers and their lower-level components. To ensure focus on the key controllers, the

Figure 2: Illustration of Traffic Regions

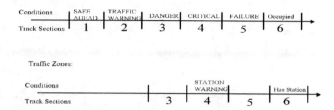

following simplifying assumptions have been made: (1) Only the interaction between the power controller and the other controllers of the PTS are included in the design; (2) The switches and track sections that are part of the storage and maintenance depot are included in the problem description to indicate that a variable number of trains can be running in the PTS at one time. The siding elements are not included in the PTS design; (3) Interactions between the automatic controller on a train and its motor and brake systems are included in the design; (4) The focus of this work is on the object-oriented model and design and its real-time characteristics. Specific algorithms for computing train speed and managing tables of data are not included; (5) The physical configuration of stations and track sections is known in advance (it is part of the PTS setup program). This permits the use of attributes such as "section number," functions such as "Has Station(section number)," and constants such as "MAX SPEED" and "SAFE SPEED" to be used in the design; (6) A separate power mechanism is maintained for powering the sensors. Power to the sensors is not dependent on power in the power rail of that track section.

Naming conventions are used throughout this design example to simplify the figures and specifications. Many of these naming conventions and definitions are used to define the safe behavior of trains traveling in different regions of the PTS track under different traffic conditions. These regions are illustrated in Figure 2. For example, when train A occupies track section 6, the condition for train B in track section 1 is "SAFE AHEAD." If train B gains on train A, and train B moves into track section 2 while track section 6 is occupied, the condition for train B in track section 2 is "TRAFFIC WARNING."

Table 1 provides a list of all of the shorthand naming conventions associated with the initial configuration of the PTS (track and stations) as well as the initial number of trains in the operational track sections. Table 2 provides a list of all of the naming conventions for track conditions that change depending on the position of trains and naming conventions associated with a train's speed.

Where safety and timing issues are critical, formal specifications are required. This section provides property-based specifications for the key areas of train

Table 1: Naming Conventions for PTS Configuration

r	the total number of speed sensors in the PTS
g	the total number of stations in the PTS
n	the total number of operational track sections in the PTS
m	the total number of trains in the PTS
Has Station(section number)	True if there is a station in this section number
MAX STATION TIME	The maximum time a train should remain stopped in a station before departing.
WARNING TIME	The interval of time between operator warning messages when a train has been delayed in a station beyond the MAXSTATIONTIME.
STATION SPEED	The maximum allowable speed a train should travel when approaching a station (20 MPH in the problem description).
MAX SPEED	The maximum allowable speed a train can safely travel on any track section (45 MPH in the problem description)
SAFE SPEED	The safe speed at which a train is normally maintained to ensure that it travels below the MAX SPEED (e.g., a SAFE SPEED of 40 MPH could provide a 5 MPH threshold under the MAX SPEED).
WARNING SPEED	The speed a train should travel when the system has detected that there is either traffic or a delay ahead (WARNING SPEED < SAFE SPEED).

Table 2: Naming Conventions for Track Conditions and Train Speed

HasPower(section number)	True if the power rail in this section number is powered on
Available (section number)	True if any train has entered this section number but not exited this section number.
Occupied (section number)	= NOT (Available(section number))
SAFE AHEAD	True if for all i, i=1 to 4, Available ((sectionnumber+i) mod n) = True
SAFE BEHIND	True if for all i, i=1 to 4, Available ((section numbers) mod n) = True
TRAFFIC WARNING	True if for all i, i=1 to 3, Available ((sectionnumber+i) mod n) AND Occupied((section number + 4) mod n) = True
SECTION WARNING	True if HasStation ((section number + 2) mod n) = True
DANGER	True if Occupied ((section number + 3) mod n) = True
CRITICAL	True if Occupied ((section number + 2) mod n) = True
FAILURE	True if Occupied ((section number + 1) mod n) = True
TRAIN APPROACHING	True if for some i, i=3 to 10, Occupied ((section number+i) mod n) = True
WAITING TRAIN	True if a train has been slowed down as a result of a problem or delay with the current train.
SPEED OK	True if the monitored speed of the current train is less than or equal to the current allowed top speed (SAFESPEED or STATION SPEED)
SPEEDING	True if the monitored speed of the current train is greater than the current allowed top speed (SAFESPEED or STATION SPEED)

location, movement, spacing, and speed as well as the status of the PTS power. Similar property-based specifications are described in (Heitmeyer & Mandrioli, 1996). These specifications can be used in later development of test cases to validate the critical aspects of the design and implementation. Throughout the formal specification, the symbol $\ddagger$ is used for "implies."

Train Location: This section specifies the exact position of a train with respect to a particular track section based upon the entry and exit sensor detection.

The front of a train enters a track section: For some values of i and j, Entered(PT_i,TS_j) = True $\ddagger$ the entry sensor in track section TS_j has detected that passenger train PT_i has entered track section TS_j but the entry sensor in $TS_{(j+1)}$ has not yet detected passenger train PT_i.

The back of a train exits a track section: For some values of i and j, $Exited(PT_i, TS_j)$ = True ‡ the exit sensor in track section TSj has detected that passenger train PTi has exited track section TS_j.

A train is entirely within one track section: For some values of i and j Entered (PT_i, TS_j) AND NOT $Exited(PT_i, TS_j)$ ‡ $Within(PT_i, TS_j)$.

Power Status: This section specifies the enablement and disablement of the PTS with respect to the status of power to the power rails for each track section. It also specifies the effect that removing power from a power rail where a train is traveling will have on the motion of the train.

PTS is enabled: For all i, i = 1 to n, $HasPower(TS_i)$ = True ‡ EnabledPTS = True.

PTS is disabled: DisabledPTS = True ‡ for all i, i = 1 to n, $HasPower(TS_i)$ = False.

Removing power from a track section stops a train that has entered the section: For some time t, and some train PT_i in track section TS_j. i = 1 to m and j = 1 to n, $HasPower(TS_i)$ = False ‡ at time t + d, $Speed(PT_i)$ = 0, where *d is the* time it takes to stop the train when its brakes are fully applied.

Train Movement: This section specifies the direction of movement of trains

Trains travel in the same direction on the track: For some values of i and j, $Within(PT_i, TS_j)$ ‡ $NextTrackSection(PT_i) = TS_{(j+1)}$ (mod n).

Train Spacing: This specifics the minimum safe distance between trains.

Trains always have two track sections between them: For all i, i = 1 to n, $Occupied(TS_i)$ ‡ $Available(TS_{(i-1)}$ (mod n)) AND $Available(TS_{(i-2)}$ (mod n)).

Train Speed: This specifies the safe operating speed of trains.

Trains do not exceed the maximum speed: For all values of time *t*, and all values of i, i = I to m, $Speed(PTi)$ £ MAX SPEED.

Trains approaching stations do not exceed the safe approach speed: For all values of time *t*, and all trains PTi in track section TS_j, i = 1 to m, j = 1 to n, $HasStation(TS_{(j+1)}$ (mod n)) ‡ $Speed(PT_i)$ £ STATION SPEED.

STATIC ANALYSIS OF THE PTS

The class diagram of Figure 3 illustrates the objects from the real world problem and their relationships with each other. Multiplicity is also illustrated for objects that have identical copies (e.g., trains). Behavior and timing are introduced in the dynamic model. Fault tolerance can be introduced as a design refinement although we do not consider it in this paper.

The class diagram depicts the PTS as an aggregation of three main controllers. These controllers (Power Controller, Traffic Controller, and Speed Controller) represent the three main independent control functions required to manage operational functions of the PTS.

Figure 3: OOA Class Diagram

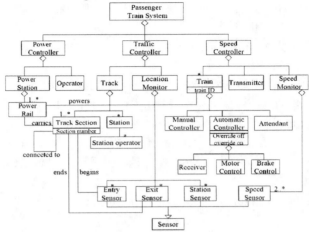

The Power Controller manages the power aspects of the PTS. It contains the power station that provides power to the power rails. The power rails are part of the Power Controller since they are turned on and off by the Power Controller. There is a power station operator. The operator class represents the user interface for the real-world power station operator (e.g., displays and manual operations).

The Traffic Controller manages the position of trains on the track. It contains the track, consisting of multiple connected track sections and multiple stations. An association between a track section and a power rail is included to show the physical configuration of track sections carrying the power rails that power the trains. For each station there are station operators. The station operators are included since they manage the movement of trains once the train is stopped in the station. Trains do not depart the station automatically. When a train is detained in a station (past the expected 10 minute soft deadline), warning messages are displayed on the station operator's display.

The Traffic Controller class also contains a location monitor. The location monitor manages thefeedback from the entry, exit, and station sensors to determine the train locations and appropriate actions for traffic control. Associations are included to indicate that an entry sensor begins a track Section and an exit sensor ends a track section.

The Speed Controller controls the physical movement of trains and manages the speed of trains to maintain safe operating conditions. As such, it accepts and acts on train movement messages from the Traffic Controller. The Speed Controller contains a speed monitor that continually receives events from the speed sensors along the track to determine the measured speed of the trains. The Speed Controller attempts to adjust the train speeds whenever speed limits or thresholds are reached. The Speed Controller also contains a transmitter that is used to send movement signals to the trains. Each train has an automatic control system that is driven by signals received from the transmitter.   An association between the trains and the power rails is shown to indicate that a train gets its power from the power rails.

The four types of sensors in the PTS have basic characteristics and operations in common. They inherit certain of these attributes from the generalized Sensor class.

PTS CONTROL SYSTEM DYNAMIC MODELING AND DESIGN

The high-level communicating machine model is developed from the PTS problem description and class diagram. The events in the low-level state machines are derived and refined using sequence diagrams for normal operational scenarios defined by use cases in the requirements specification (including normal handling of failures). These sequence diagrams are not shown here because of space limitations.

In the proposed augmented methodology, the first dynamic modeling step is to create a high-level model of the concurrent machines of the system. For the PTS, the major concurrent activities are the Power Controller, Traffic Controller, and Speed Controller. Every train in the PTS also runs independently and concurrently, each with its own automatic and manual controller. The sensors are all independent external entities as well. For these high-level machines, external communication is required for event notification, command communication, and synchronization of system states. The high-level communicating state machine model

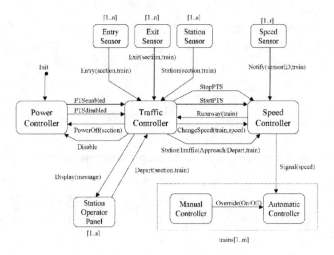

Figure 4: High Level Communicating State Machines

in Figure 4 depicts the physical elements of the system. It is easily derived from the class diagram.

Although it is straightforward to create the high-level machine models from the problem description and the classes in the analysis model, the communication channels themselves are derived through iterative modeling and design of the controller details. After the initial high-level model, each major controller state machine is modeled to determine the key states, activities, and communication requirements. In some cases, each successive refinement of the more detailed state machines indicates necessary modifications to the structure of the high level machines that were not apparent in the initial model. Care should be taken, however, not to introduce implementation-level details into the high-level analysis model. Details such as object creation and destruction associated with programming languages; although required at the implementation level, only introduce complexity and confusion into the high-level model.

The first controller that starts when the PTS system is initiated is the Power Controller. Once good power status of the system has been determined, the Power Controller starts the Traffic Controller with a PTSenabled message. If at any point in the operation of the PTS, power is disabled, the Power Controller will give the Traffic Controller a PTSdisabled message.

Once started, the Traffic Controller starts the Speed Controller with the StartPTS command. Similarly, when the Traffic Controller is given the PTSdisabled message, it also stops the Speed Controller with the StopPTS command.

The Traffic Controller manages the location of trains with respect to each other and also with respect to their proximity to stations. The Traffic Controller can detect certain failure cases when a train does not appear to be responding to normal control signals. To prevent catastrophic events, the Traffic Controller can request that specific track sections be powered off (Poweroff command) or that all track sections in the TS be powered off (Disable command).

There are multiple independent machines modeled for each of the many entry, exit, and station sensors. These machines are all very similar in that they continually scan passing trains, reading the train ID when a train passes. Upon detection, each sensor notifies the Traffic Controller of the event by sending the appropriate event notification message and event data. For all entry, exit, and station events, the Traffic Controller receives two pieces of information; the section number identifying the particular sensor location and the train ID of the passing train.

The Traffic Controller communicates with the Speed Controller to request that the speed of trains be changed (ChangeSpeed message). The Traffic Controller issues these commands to control the flow of traffic in the PTS. For example, when a train is approaching a station, the Traffic Controller requests that the train's speed be reduced to the station approach speed (STATION SPEED) of 20 MPH. When a train departs a station, the Traffic Controller requests that the train's speed be increased to the normal safe speed (SAFE SPEED). The Traffic Controller monitors the position of trains and issues requests to the Speed Controller to adjust the speed (and therefore position) of trains. When the Traffic Controller needs to stop a train under normal operating conditions, it issues a ChangeSpeed message with a speed of zero.

Through the speed sensors, the Speed Controller monitors the externally measured speed of trains and sends speed control signals to trains. There are many speed sensors in the PTS. These speed sensors are very similar in operation to the other sensors in that they scan for the passing of trains and report the event and train ID to the Speed Controller. Since there are many more speed sensors than track sections, the speed sensors must each have a unique identifier that identifies their location to the Speed Controller. Using the speed sensor data, tha Speed Controller can detect when a train may be traveling beyond the safety speeds. When all normal attempts to slow a speeding train have failed, the Speed Controller will give a Runaway train message to the Traffic Controller.

The Traffic Controller also notifies the Speed Controller when a particular train is approaching or departing a station (StationTraffic message). The Speed Controller uses this notification to set the appropriate top speed for the train.

CONCLUSIONS

We have proposed a methodology for the modeling and design of real-time systems and we have shown here the static and dynamic analysis stages. Although based upon UML concepts and process steps, unique process steps enhance the traditional UML for real-time systems. Specifically, we included property-based formal specification to ensure that the system specification accurately describes the critical constraints and behavior; these are useful to verify timing constraints. High-level communicating real-time machine modeling was added as a refinement of the static class diagram; these model concurrency and external communication paths. New notations were introduced to convey the real-time behavior and events of the dynamic model (communicating state machines). We also showed a unique, hypothetical example of a complex real-time system. The example is used to illustrate the process steps of the methodology and to refine the methodology. In a companion paper we show how to extend these ideas to consider fault tolerance (Douglass, 1998). The methodology does not include detailed design or implementation aspects or a way to validate the timing constraints specified. In this sense, this is not a complete real-time methodology, such as ROOM (Selic et al., 1992) or Octopus (Awad et al., 1996), but it could be used to complement one of these approaches.

A strength of our extended CRSMs is that they specify timing aspects and concurrency in a natural way. This is not always true in some real-time methodologies; for example, Gomaa (1986) and Douglass (1998), do not consider time constraints explicitly.

Other related methodologies are:

Harel's O-charts (1996). They are more implementation oriented (to C++) but do not seem to handle communication and concurrency so precisely as our extended CSRMs.

RSML (Leveson & Heimdahl, 1994), emphasizes requirements aspects and uses another type of state model. However, that approach doesn't include data aspects and is not oriented to concurrency.

Telelogic's SOMT and Verilog's ObjectGeode use SDL as dynamic model because of the need for more formalization and explicit concurrency. Our approach is an alternative to using SDL.

REFERENCES

Awad, M., Kuusela, J. and Ziegler, J. (1996). *Object-Oriented Technology for Real-Time Systems*. Englewood Cliffs, NJ: Prentice-Hall.

Chonoles, M. J. and Gilliam, C. C. (1995). Real-time object-oriented system design using the object modeling technique (OMT). *Journal of Object Oriented Programming*, June, 16-24.

Douglass, B. P. (1998). *Real-time UML: Developing Efficient Objects for Embedded Systems*. Reading, MA: Addison-Wesley.

Fernandez, E. B., Wu, J. and Hancock, D. (1999). A design methodology for object-oriented real-time fault-tolerant systems. *Report TR-CSE-99-20*, Dept. of Comp. Science and Eng., FAU.

Gomaa, H. (1986). Software development of real-time systems. *Communications of the ACM*, 29(7), July, 657-668.

Harel, D. and Gery, E. (1996). Executable object modeling with statecharts. *Proceedings of the 18th International Conference on Software Engineering*, 246-257. IEEE Press. March.

Harel, D., Lachover, H., Naamad, A., Pnueli, A., Politi, M., Sherman, R., Shtull-Trauring, A. and Trakhtenbrot, M. (1990). STATEMATE: A working environment for the development of complex reactive systems. *IEEE Transactions on Software Engineering*, 16(4), April, 609-620.

Heitmeyer, C. and Mandrioli, D. (1996). *Formal Methods for Real-Time Computing: An Overview*. New York: John Wiley & Sons.

Leveson, N. G. and Heimdahl, M. P. E. (1994). Requirements specification for process-control systems. *IEEE Transactions on Software Engineering,* 20(9), September, 684-707.

Rational Inc. *Unified Modeling Language* http://www.rational.com/uml.

Rumbaugh, J., Blaha, M., Premerlani, W., Eddy, F. and Lorensen, W. (1991). *Object Oriented Modeling and Design.* Englewood Cliffs, NJ: Prentice Hall.

Rumbaugh, J., Jacobson, I. and Booch, G. (1999). *The Unified Modeling Language Reference Manual.* Reading, MA: Addison-Wesley.

Selic, B., Gullekson, G., McGee, J. and Engelberg, I. (1992). ROOM; An object-oriented methodology for developing real-time systems. *Proceedings on the Fifth International Workshop on Computer-Aided Software Engineering,* 230-240.

Selic, B. and Rumbaugh, J. Using UML for modeling complex real-time systems. http://www.rational.com/products/rosert.

Shaw, A. C. (1992). Communicating real-time state machines. *IEEE Transactions on SoftwareEngineering,* 18(9), September, 805-816.

Telelogic. Combining object-oriented analysis and SDL design, http://www.telelogic.com

Verilog. ObjectGEODE, http://www.csverilog.com/products.

Chapter 12

Java Integrated Development Environments' Support for Reuse-Oriented Software Development

Jenni Ristonmaa, Jarmo Ahonen, and Marko Forsell
University of Jyväskylä, Finland

Component reuse is a promising direction to develop software more efficiently and cost effectively. One part of software development is the actual programming with an integrated development environment (IDE). We studied three Java IDEs and how they support reuse-oriented software development. We derived evaluation criteria from a known reuse model. As a conclusion we suggest that current Java IDEs need to improve their support for the reuse process.

INTRODUCTION

To cope with the current trend to produce quality software in tightening schedules software developers see reuse as one possible answer (e.g., Lim, 1997; McIllroy, 1968). Reuse of components is one approach to handle reuse (Biggerstaff & Richter, 1987). The basic idea in component reuse is to use some results of the development effort more than once (Basili et al., 1992; Krueger, 1992). To be successful, reuse has to be systematic: it has to be planned in advance and it must be acknowledged in every phase of software development cycle (Lim, 1997). One part of this cycle is programming. Here integrated development environments (IDEs) are especially important. Early IDEs included such tools as an editor and a compiler but currently these environments may include, among other things, source code control, library management, support for workgroups, and version control (Kölling & Rosenberg, 1996).

Previously published in *Managing Information Technology in a Global Economy*, edited by Mehdi Khosrow-Pour. Copyright © 2001, Idea Group Publishing.

Java has emerged as one of the most popular programming languages and its advantage is that it closely follows emerging trends in software development. One such trend is the support for component-based development in the form of JavaBeans standard. JavaBeans brings component technology to the Java platform. With JavaBeans you can create reusable, platform-independent components (Sun, 2000).

Our research question is: "Do Java IDEs support the creation and reuse of code components?" As the only components supported by the chosen IDEs are JavaBeans, we limited our study to JavaBeans components.

SELECTION OF JAVA IDEs AND RESEARCH METHOD

We selected three Java IDEs that reflect the current state-of-the-practice in Java programming. We chose the environments considering the market share and how well the supplier is known. Using our criteria we selected:

- Forte for Java Community Edition 1.0 Windows Version by Sun Microsystems Inc.,
- Borland JBuilder 3.0 Professional by Inprise Corporation, and
- VisualAge for Java Enterprise Edition Version 3.0 by IBM.

We planned to use Visual J++ 6.0 Professional Edition from Microsoft but we excluded it for its strong orientation towards ActiveX and Windows.

We wanted to find out how Java IDE supports reuse processes involved in component (JavaBean) reuse. To base our evaluation framework on a well known model we chose Lim's (1997) reuse model over alternatives (e.g., NATO, 1992, Karlson, 1995, see Forsell et al., 2000). Lim's model is not biased toward any specific implementation technology and it includes code components as well as other software development artifacts (assets in Lim's vocabulary). Figure 1 shows Lim's reuse model, its four major activities, and tasks in them.

Figure 1. The Reuse Process (Lim, 1997)

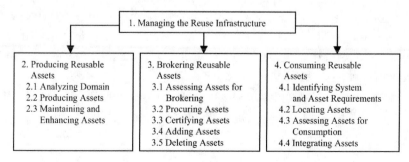

Because Lim's model is not focused solely on the code component reuse it has activities and tasks which are irrelevant for the programming phase. We argue that the following tasks are not and should not be concern for IDE: analyzing domain, component assessing, procuring an asset, certifying an asset, identifying system requirements, and assessing assets. Also, managing the reuse infrastructure as a whole is not a concern for IDE.

RESULTS OF THE EVALUATION

The results of the evaluation are presented below. The main interest is in the differences and interesting features.

Producing a Component

All IDEs have fairly similar tools and techniques. The main tools are wizards and dialogues, but only VisualAge offers dialogs for the creation and addition of methods. Only VisualAge creates the BeanInfo class for the produced component. With JBuilder and Forte users have to add the BeanInfo manually, which is easy. The possibility to create this functionality by using visual tools is present only in VisualAge.

Forte feels slow, which makes it difficult to use, and its structure of menus is not consistent or intuitive. JBuilder offers methods to add comments to the code and its BeanExpress is well thought out. VisualAge offers fairly sophisticated and usable visual tools for the creation of components, it is even possible to create complicated components with minimal programming. In VisualAge a great deal of functionality can be defined by applying the visual tools.

VisualAge is clearly the best tool for producing components. JBuilder has better structure and is more practical than Forte.

Maintaining and Enhancing a Component

Maintenance and enhancement generally means bug removal and feature enhancement. Maintenance is unnecessarily complicated if IDE allows users to save source code components without compilation. VisualAge allows users to save and add source-level components, but it compiles the code before saving the component. Forte allows users to save incorrect components. JBuilder allows only .class- and .JAR-files to be saved as JavaBeans requiring fairly strict conformance from components. Unfortunately all environments allow users to modify components in incorrect ways.

The only IDE of these three to support versioning of components is VisualAge. This feature is important when considering the support offered by IDEs for maintenance and enhancement.

Adding a Component

In Forte and VisualAge it is possible to add source code components to the menu structure. In VisualAge those components are confirmed to be at least syntactically right. JBuilder allows only .class- and .JAR-files to be added to the menu structure.

All IDEs have specific menu structures into which components should be added. Both VisualAge and JBuilder allow users to add their own components to any position in a JavaBeans menu structure. Forte stops working if users try to add a component to any other position than the Beans-sheet. JBuilder and VisualAge offer a straightforward and logical way for adding components. In Forte the technique is more complicated and not so easy to use.

Deleting a Component

The support for removing a component from the menu structure is present in JBuilder and VisualAge, while Forte has no such support. If users want to delete components from Forte, they have to use filesystem tools and remove the files associated with the components.

The deletion of a component is immediately shown in the menu structures of VisualAge. JBuilder and Forte remove the component from the menu structure only after the IDE has been restarted.

Identifying a Component

IDEs do not identify the JavaBeans or Enterprise JavaBeans component requirements correctly. The only requirement identified by every IDE is that the component class must be public. JBuilder often correctly identifies all requirements, but it makes mistakes. VisualAge checks if the component is syntactically right and if it is generated by using the automatic tools of VisualAge it fulfills all requirements.

Locating a Component

The menu structures reserved for components are very similar and they are easy to use. The menu structures do not support classification of components, although every IDE has specific menu sheets or structures for custom components and components shipped with the IDE. The only IDE which offers additional tools for the location of components is VisualAge with its Choose Bean tool.

Integrating a Component

Only VisualAge and Forte have visual tools for the integration of components. Users can either use those tools or do the integration through traditional programming, or users may use a combination of programming and tools. In this respect VisualAge is more sophisticated than Forte.

Table 1: Additional Questions for Ranking.

Criteria	Question	Forte	JBuilder	VisualAge
Producing	Is the BeanInfo class required?	No	No	Yes
Maintaining and enhancing	Is versioning of classes supported?	No	No	Yes
Adding	Is syntactical correctness required?	No	Yes	Yes
Deleting	Are there tools for the deletion of components?	No	Yes	Yes
	Are menus and data structures updated immediately after the deletion?	No	No	Yes
Identifying	Does the IDE prohibit the saving of syntactically erroneous components?	No	No	Yes
Locating	Are there additional tools for the location of components?	No	No	Yes
Integrating	Are there visual tools for the integration of components?	Yes	No	Yes

Table 2: The Ranking of the IDEs

Criteria	Forte	JBuilder	VisualAge
Producing	3	2	1
Maintaining and enhancing	3	2	1
Adding	3	1	2
Deleting	3	2	1
Identifying	3	1	2
Locating	2	3	1
Integrating	2	3	1

The Best Features and Ranking of the Evaluated IDEs

The evaluated IDEs are considered in the perspective of Lim's model. The best features of Forte are its visual tools for component integration and intuitively appealing naming conventions in its menu structures. The best feature of JBuilder is that it allows only .class and .JAR -files to be added as components, and its BeanExpress-tool is a good tool. The best features of VisualAge are the versioning of classes, its visual integration tools, its tool for component location, and its automatic compilation of source code before saving.

The IDEs have been ranked according the results and the answers in table 1. The ranking is shown in Table 2 (1 = best, 3 = worst).

DISCUSSION

We have evaluated Java IDEs from the point of view of how they support reuse process. We based our evaluation on Lim's reuse model and derived evaluation criteria from it. It seems that Java IDEs, in general, still need improvement. IBM's environment shows promising directions for future in keeping with their efforts to provide reuse-oriented features. The support for reuse requires improvement.

Companies can use these results and our approach when they want to choose a Java IDE for themselves. However, this implies that companies know their needs for reuse support and find out which tool fits these needs best. Furthermore, we believe that the evaluation method is not limited to the evaluation of Java IDEs, it can be used to evaluate any programming language specific IDE. Also, Lim's framework as a whole can be used to evaluate software development methods (Forsell et al. 2000), and we believe it can be used to evaluate software engineering environments, i.e. repositories, CASE tools, and project management tools.

Main limitation of the study is that it focuses on Java language and three Java IDEs. We need more research on how to add reuse support in any IDE. Furthermore, IDEs and other tools that support software development should be integrated more closely together and these should support and integrate components in different levels of abstraction from the reuse point of view.

REFERENCES

Basili, V., Caldiera, G. and Cantone, G. (1992). A reference architecture for the component factory. *ACM Transactions on Software Engineering and Methodology*, 1(1), January, 53-80.

Biggerstaff, T. and Richter, C. (1987). Reusability framework, assessment, and directions. *IEEE Software*, March, 41-49.

Forsell, M., Halttunen, V. and Ahonen, J. (2000). Use and identification of components in component-based software development methods. *Software Reuse: Advances in Software Reusability, Proceedings of the 6th International Conference, ICSR-6*, 284-301.

Karlson, E. (Ed.). *Software Reuse: A Holistic Approach*. Chichester: John Wiley & Sons.

Kölling, M. and Rosenberg, J. (1996). An object-oriented program development environment for the first programming course. *Proceedings of the Twenty-Seventh SIGCSE Technical Symposium on Computer Science Education*, 83-87.

Krueger, C. (1992). Software reuse. *ACM Computing Surveys*, 24(2), June, 131-182.

Lim, W. (1997). *Management of Software Reuse*. Reading, MA: Addison-Wesley.

McIlroy, D. (1976). Mass produced software components. Report on a conference by the NATO science committee, Garmish, Germany, October 7-11 1968. In Naur, P., Randel, B. and Buxton, J. (Eds.), *Software Engineering: Concepts and Techniques*, 88-98. New York: Petrocelli/Charter.

NATO. (1992). NATO standard for the development of reusable software components. Volume 1 (of 3 documents). http://www.asset.com/WSRD/abstracts/archived/ABSTRACT_528.html, accessed 1st of June 2000.

Sun. (2000). http://java.sun.com/docs/books/tutorial/javabeans/index.html, accessed 11th of September 2000.

Chapter 13

Information Modeling and Method Engineering: A Psychological Perspective

Keng Siau
University of Nebraska-Lincoln, USA

Information modeling is the cornerstone of information systems analysis and design. Information models, the products of information modeling, not only provide the abstractions required to facilitate communication between the analysts and end users, but they also provide a formal basis for developing tools and techniques used in information systems development. The process of designing, constructing, and adapting information modeling methods for information systems development is known as method engineering. Despite the pivotal role of modeling methods in successful information systems development, most modeling methods are designed based on common sense and intuition of the method designers with little or no theoretical foundation or empirical evidence. Systematic scientific approach is missing! This paper proposes the use of cognitive psychology as a reference discipline for information modeling and method engineering. Theories in cognitive psychology are reviewed in this paper and their application to information modeling and method engineering are also discussed.

Even though research in systems analysis and design has been going on for over 40 years, successful software development is still an art rather than a science. In the 1980s, Jones (1986) observed that a typical project was one year late and 100% over budget. Yourdon (1989) reported application backlogs of four to seven years or more. The maintenance phase typically consumed up to 70% of the programmer's effort, and it was errors, not enhancements, that accounted for 40% of maintenance (Rush, 1985). Page-

Previously published in the *Journal of Database Management, vol.10, no.4*, Copyright © 1999, Idea Group Publishing.

Jones (1988) wrote: "It looks as if traditionally we spend about half of our time making mistakes and the other half of our time fixing them."

We are, however, no better as we move toward the end of this century. The IBM's Consulting Group (Gibbs 1994) released the results of a survey of 24 leading companies that had developed large distributed systems. The numbers were unsettling: 55% of the projects cost more than budgeted, 68% overran their schedules, and 88% had to be substantially redesigned. A recent high-profile failure is the Denver Airport baggage-handling system, responsible for delaying the opening of the airport. The Standish Group research (Chaos 1995) predicted that a staggering 31.1% of projects would be canceled before they ever get completed and 52.7% of projects would cost 189% of their original estimates.

In the early days of computerized information systems, technological failure was the main cause in the failure of business data processing systems (Avison & Fitzgerald 1995). Today, the failure of information systems is rarely due to technology that is on the whole reliable and well tested. Failure is more likely to be caused by miscommunication and misspecification of requirements. Similar sentiments were echoed in the Standish Group's report (Chaos, 1995) which listed incomplete requirements and specifications as the second most important factor that caused projects to be challenged and the top factor that caused projects to be impaired and ultimately canceled (Chaos, 1995). A recent survey of hundreds of Digital's staff and an analysis of the corporate planning database revealed that on average, 40% of the requirements specified in the feasibility and requirements phase of the life cycle were redefined in the later phases. This cost Digital an average of 50% more than the budgeted amount (Hutchings & Knox, 1995).

The process of investigating the problems and requirements of the user community, and building an accurate and correct requirement specification for the desired system is known as information modeling (Siau, 1999; Siau & Rossi, 1998; Siau et al., 1997; Mylopoulos, 1992, Rolland & Cauvet, 1992; Kangassalo, 1990).

INFORMATION MODELING

Information modeling is the process of formally documenting the problem domain for the purpose of understanding and communication among the stakeholders (Siau, 1999; Siau, 1998; Mylopoulos, 1992). Information modeling is central to information systems analysis and design, and takes place in the early phases of the software development life cycle. The product of the information modeling process is one or more information models (e.g., data flow diagrams, entity-relationship diagrams, use cases, activity diagrams, sequence diagrams). Information model provides a conceptual basis for communicating and thinking about information systems (Willumsen, 1993), and a formal basis for tools and techniques used in the design and development of information systems (Kung & Solvberg, 1986).

Information models are constructed using information modeling method, which can be defined as an approach to perform modeling, based on a specific way of thinking, consisting of directions and rules, and structured in a systematic way (Brinkkemper 1996). There is no shortage of information modeling methods in the field. In fact, it is a "methodology jungle" out there (Avison & Fitzgerald, 1995). Olle et al. (1982) and Bubenko (1986) stated that the field was inundated by hundreds of different modeling methods. Recently, Jayaratna (1994) estimated that there were more than a thousand brand name methodologies worldwide. The quest to develop the next modeling method has been wittily termed the YAMA (Yet Another Modeling Approach) syndrome (Oei et al., 1992) and NAMA (Not Another Modeling Approach) hysteria (Siau et al., 1996). Even the new kid on the block, object oriented approach, has more than a dozen variants. Despite the "impressive" number, miscommunication and misspecification continue (Chaos, 1995).

To reduce the chances of misunderstanding and miscommunication during information modeling, the use of natural and intuitive modeling constructs (e.g., entity, relationship, object) in information modeling methods has been stressed and advocated (e.g., Chen, 1976; Coad & Yourdon, 1991). This, they claimed, would enable end-users to better understand the information depicted in the information model and to pinpoint incomplete or incorrect information in the model.

METHOD ENGINEERING AND MODELING CONSTRUCTS

Modeling constructs are semantic primitives that are used to organize and represent knowledge about the domain of interest (Sernades et al., 1989). Modeling constructs form the core of an information modeling method. Method engineering is the process of designing, constructing, and adapting modeling methods for the development of information systems (Siau, 1999; Siau, 1998; Brinkkemper, 1996). To design, construct, and adapt methods, we need to understand the role and value of each modeling construct.

The importance of modeling constructs can be viewed from two perspectives: ontology and epistemology of information systems analysis and design. Ontology is concerned with the essence of things and the nature of the world

(Wand & Weber, 1993; Avison & Fitzgerald, 1995). The nominalist position in ontology argues that "reality is not a given immutable "out there," but is socially constructed. It is the product of human mind" (Hirschheim & Klein, 1989). The choice of modeling constructs, therefore, directly influences what the modeling method regards as important and meaningful versus what it suggests as unimportant and irrelevant. For example, the use of the entity-relationship (ER) approach emphasizes entities and relationships but ignores the processes involved. The use of the object-oriented (OO) approach, on the other hand, emphasizes objects and the behavior of objects.

Epistemology relates to the way in which the world may be legitimately investigated and what may be considered as knowledge (Avison & Fitzgerald, 1995). The choice of modeling constructs constrains how one can know or learn about reality—the basis of one's claim to knowledge (Klein & Lyytinen, 1983; Walsham, 1993). Users of the entity-relationship approach, for example, would focus on identifying entities and relationships whereas users of data-flow diagram (DFD) would emphasize the eliciting of processes, data flows, external entities, and data stores from the problem domain.

Despite the importance of modeling constructs, not much research has been done in this area. Most modeling constructs are introduced based on common sense, superficial observation, and intuition of researchers and practitioners. Theoretical foundation and empirical evidence are either non-existent or considered non-essential. For example, Coad and Yourdon (1991, p. 16) nicely summed up the practitioners' scant concern:

"It would be intellectually satisfying to the authors if we could report that we studied the philosophical ideas behind methods of organization, from Socrates and Aristotle to Descartes and Kant. Then, based on the underlying methods human beings use, we could propose the basic constructs essential to an analysis method. But in truth we cannot say that, nor did we do it. "(emphasis added)

With this laissez-faire attitude, one can not help but cast doubts on the usefulness and importance of some of these modeling constructs. It is probable that some of these constructs are not actually actors in the modeling drama, but merely incidental artifacts, created by researchers to help them categorize their observations. These artifacts may play no significant role whatsoever in modeling the real world. A reference discipline to guide the design, construction, and adaptation of modeling constructs for information modeling methods is needed!

In this paper, we propose the use of cognitive psychology as a reference discipline in the engineering of methods and the studying of information modeling. Card et al. (1983, p. 1) wrote "advances in cognitive psychology and related sciences lead us to the conclusion that knowledge of human cognitive behavior is sufficiently advanced to enable its applications in computer science and other practical domains." Moray (1984) also argued for the use of knowledge accumulated in cognitive psychology to understand and solve applied problems. Researchers in human-computer interaction have demonstrated that such an effort is valuable and essential in building a scientific understanding of the human factors involved in end-users interaction with computers. We believe that similar effort will be useful in information modeling and method engineering.

HUMAN INFORMATION-PROCESSING SYSTEM

To understand the representation and use of knowledge by humans, we need to approach it from a human information-processing perspective. The information-processing paradigm views thinking as a symbol-manipulating process and uses computer simulation as a way to build theories of thinking (Simon, 1979). It attempts to map the flow of information that a human is using in a defined situation (Gagne et al., 1993) and tries to understand the general changes of human behavior brought about by learning (Anderson 1995).

According to Newell and Simon (1972), all humans are information-processing systems (IPS) and hence come equipped with certain common basic features. Although some of the processes used by the system may be performed faster or better by some than by others, the nature of the system is the same. One of the popular and most well-known human information-processing model is the Adaptive Control of Thought (ACT) proposed by Anderson (1983, 1995) (see Figure 1).

Figure 1: The ACT Architecture

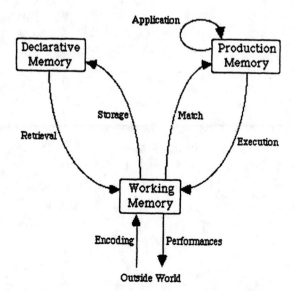

An ACT production system consists of three memories: working, declarative, and production. Working memory contains the information that the system can currently access, consisting of information retrieved from long-term declarative memory as well as temporary structures deposited by encoding processes and the action of productions (Anderson, 1983). Declarative and production are long-term memory. The former is the facts and the latter is the processes or procedures that operate on facts to solve problems. Declarative knowledge is knowing that something is the case whereas procedural knowledge is knowing how to do something (Gagne et al., 1993).

Encoding deposits information about the outside world into working memory whereas performance converts commands in working memory into behavior. The storage process can create permanent records in declarative memory of the contents of working memory and can increase the strength of existing records in declarative memory. The retrieval process retrieves information from declarative memory into working memory. During the match process, data in working memory are put into correspondence with the conditions of productions. The execution process deposits the actions of matched productions into working memory. The whole process of production matching followed by execution is known as production application.

Working Memory

The working memory is activation based; it contains the activated portion of the declarative memory plus declarative structures generated by production firings and perception. Working memory is a temporary memory that cannot hold data over any extended duration. Information in this memory store decays within about 10 seconds (Murdock, 1961) unless it is rehearsed. In addition to its limited duration, working memory is also of limited capacity. Miller (1956) claimed that working memory holds 7 ± 2 units of information while Simon (1974) claimed that it holds only about 5 units. Whatever the actual number, the important point is that it is small. Because of its small size, working memory is often referred to as the "bottleneck" of the human information-processing system.

Declarative Knowledge

There are two types of long-term memory — declarative and procedural. The long-term declarative memory is represented in the form of a semantic net. A basic unit of declarative knowledge in the human information-processing system is proposition and is defined as the smallest unit of knowledge that can possess a truth value (Anderson, 1983). Complex units of knowledge are broken down into propositions. Propositions have at least two parts. The first is called the relation. Verbs and adjectives typically make up the relations of a proposition. The second part of the proposition is called the argument, which is determined by the nouns in the proposition. Arguments are given different names depending on their role in the proposition. Arguments may be subjects, objects, goals (destination), instruments (means), and recipients.

The declarative knowledge for the ER approach can be represented as propositions as shown below. Each proposition comprises a relation, followed by a list of arguments:

(i)   represent, entity, rectangle
(ii) represent, relationship, diamond
(iii) comprise, ER, entity
(iv) comprise, ER, relationship

These four propositions can be depicted diagrammatically using Kintsch's system as shown in Figure 2.

In ACT, individual propositions can be combined into networks of propositions. The nodes of the propositional network stand for ideas, and the linkages represent associations among the ideas (Anderson, 1983). Figure 3 shows the network of propositions for the ER approach.

Figure 2: Diagrammatic Representation of Propositions for ER Approach

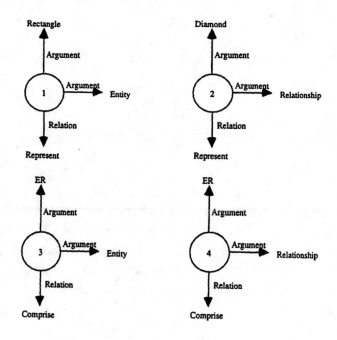

Figure 3: Network of Propositions for ER Approach

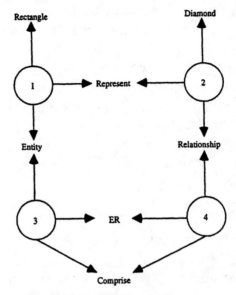

Procedural Knowledge

Unlike declarative knowledge, which is static, procedural knowledge is represented in the form of productions. Each piece of knowledge is called a production because it "produces" some bit of mental or physical behavior. Productions are formally represented as IF-THEN contingency statements in which the IF part of the statements contains the conditions that must exist for the rule to be fired and the THEN part contains the action that will be executed when the conditions are met. The productions are also known as condition-action pairs and are very similar to the IF-THEN statement in programming languages. For example, the following is the production rule for identifying a relationship construct in the ER model.

    IF   Figure is a diamond shape
    THEN   Figure represents a relationship construct

Productions can be combined to form a set. A production system, or production set, represents all of the steps in a mental or physical procedure. The productions in the production systems are related to one another by the goal structure. In other words, each production contributes in some way to achieve the final goal behavior. The use of goals and subgoals in productions creates a goal hierarchy that interrelates the productions into an organized set. For example, Table 1 shows a production system to understand an ER diagram.

Table 1: A Production System to Understand an ER Diagram

			P1
IF	Goal is to understand ER diagram		
	THEN	Set subgoal of identifying meaningful chunks of information in ER diagram	
P2	IF	Subgoal is to identify meaningful chunks of information in ER diagram	
	THEN	Set subgoal of identifying entity in ER diagram and set subgoal of identifying relationship in ER diagram	
P3	IF	Subgoal is to identify entity in ER diagram and symbol is a rectangle	
	THEN	Symbol represents an entity	
P4	IF	Subgoal is to identify relationship in ER diagram and symbol is a diamond	
	THEN	Symbol represents a relationship	

Domain-General Versus Domain-Specific. Procedural knowledge can be discussed from two dimensions. The first dimension refers to the degree to which procedural knowledge is tied to a specific domain, with the anchor points of the continuum being termed as domain-general and domain-specific (Gagne et al,. 1993). Domain-general knowledge is knowledge that is applicable across domains and domain-specific knowledge is specialized because it is specific to a particular domain. The term domain refers to any defined area of content and can vary in its breadth.

Degree of Automation. The second dimension can be labeled as "degree of automation" with the end points of the continuum being called automated and controlled (or conscious) (Gagne et al., 1993). An automated process or procedure is one that consumes none or very few of the cognitive resources of the information-processing system. Controlled process, on the other hand, is knowledge that underlies deliberate thinking because it is under the conscious control of the thinker.

Implication on Information Modeling and Method Engineering

Researchers develop methods, and methods can be reengineered. By contrast, we cannot change the design of human information-processing system. Although the human subsystem is intelligent and adaptive, we cannot change the basic properties that define its strengths and weaknesses. If an information model is to be easy to understand and to function as an effective communication tool, the information modeling method must be compatible with our information processing characteristics. It is, therefore, important for us to consider this constraint when engineering methods and modeling information.

Limitation of Working Memory

The magic number 7 ± 2 has important implication on information modeling and method engineering. Firstly, if there are more than seven chunks of information required to be absorbed by the readers at any one time, the working memory capacity might be exceeded which means that some information might not be acquired. This is consistent with the recommendations by researchers and practitioners (e.g., Hawryszkiewycz, 1991) that there should be no more than seven processes on a data flow diagram. If this is true, some sort of leveling technique, similar to the one employed by data flow diagram, might be needed to limit the amount of information to an information model. Alternatively, the information model should be designed and laid out in such a way that at any time no more than seven pieces of information need to be processed together.

Secondly, if an information modeling method has more than seven modeling constructs, cognitive overload might occur. For instance, it would be difficult for a novice user to remember what each of the construct means if there are more than seven of them. The capacity of working memory serves as a threshold on the number of modeling constructs that can be incorporated into a modeling method. As such, the complexity of Unified Modeling Language (UML) and the number of different diagrams used in UML are causes for concern.

Declarative Knowledge

Declarative knowledge deals with facts. With respect to method engineering, declarative knowledge will consist of facts about the modeling constructs - what they are and what they represent. Since declarative knowledge is one type of long term memory, the larger the number of constructs in a modeling method, the more time is required to learn them. Training time is something that end-users are very reluctant to invest in. One of the reasons for the popularity of entity-relationship (ER) and object-oriented (OO) approaches is that a very small number of constructs is involved and that results in their simplicity. Also, using constructs that tap into existing declarative knowledge facilitates the transfer of knowledge and reduces the training time. For example, many researchers and practitioners claimed that entity-relationship and object-oriented approaches are intuitive and natural. Although research results vary, the constructs used by entity-relationship and object-oriented are undeniably simpler than a modeling method based on algebra or predicate logic, especially from the end-users' perspective.

Procedural Knowledge

Procedural knowledge is knowledge about how to do something. This is one of the most problematic areas in information modeling. For example, the most common criticism of object-oriented approach is the difficulty in identifying objects (e.g., Wand & Woo, 1993). The fuzziness of constructs is also a problem with entity-relationship modeling where one is often not sure when to use relationship, attribute, or even entity to represent something in the real world. For example, Goldstein and Storey (1990) found that users of an automated database design tool had difficulty distinguishing between relationships and attributes. Codd (1990) wrote "one person's entity is another person's relationship." It is, therefore, vital that when engineering methods, we need to precisely define the constructs and specify when and how to use a construct. Saying that the world is made up of objects does not help the analysts or the end-users in information modeling. Metamodeling, which describes the procedural and representational aspects of modeling methods, is a good way of documenting the procedural knowledge of a method. Forcing method engineers to perform metamodeling ensures that they think through and sort out the details involved in using a construct.

Domain-Specific Versus Domain-General Knowledge

Research has shown that experts in a specific domain have more and better conceptual or functional understanding of the domain, automated basic skills in the domain, and domain-specific problem-solving strategies. Domain experts, in contrast to novices, have the ability to perceive large meaningful patterns; highly procedural and goal oriented knowledge; less need for memory search and general processing; and specialized schema which drive performance. The possession of domain specific knowledge, however, is a problem during information modeling. To facilitate end-users' understanding of information model, it is important to use intuitive constructs that the end-users can relate to and recall easily. This has been the argument put forth for the goodness of ER and OO approaches.

Another aspect that is related to method engineering is the advantages of using domain-general constructs in methods. Domain-general constructs facilitate the transfer of knowledge from one method to another. As the degree of overlap of the modeling constructs that underlie two methods increases, transfer also increases. Situation method, which is an information system development method tuned to the situation of the project at hand, might be a problem from this perspective unless it makes use of well-known and easy to understand modeling constructs.

Degree of Automation

Working memory limitation impacts end-users much more significantly than analysts . For analysts, the meaning of each construct is in the long term memory, not the working memory. The knowledge has been internalized and automated by the analysts. Automated skills require little cognitive effort and allow the problem solver to perform necessary, routine mental operations without thinking much about them. On the other hand, remembering what each of the construct stands for would be a controlled process for the end-users. They need to consciously and deliberately think about them. Controlled process requires cognitive effort and is subjected to the limitation of working memory. Thus, when engineering methods, we need to consider the effect on end-users that are not at the automated stage in using modeling methods and will probably never attain the automated stage. Modeling methods, which are convoluted and highly technical, might be an excellent tool for analysts at automatic stage but will be a poor communication vehicle between analysts and end-users.

CONCLUSION

This research attempts to bring the wealth of knowledge in cognitive psychology to bear on the practical problems of information modeling and method engineering. The goal is to apply and adapt cognitive psychology theories and techniques for information modeling and method engineering research and help to span the gap between science and the practice of information modeling. In this paper, we look at some cognitive psychology theories and a popular cognitive architecture, Adaptive Control of Thoughts, and discuss their implication on information modeling and method engineering.

ACKNOWLEDGMENT

This research is supported by a Research Grant-In-Aid funding from the University of Nebraska-Lincoln (LWT/06-185-92501).

REFERENCES

Anderson, J. R. (1995). *Learning and Memory: An Integrated Approach.* New York: John Wiley & Sons.

Anderson, J. R. (1983). *The Architecture of Cognition.* Cambridge, MA: Harvard University Press.

Avison, D. E. and Fitzgerald, G. (1995). *Information Systems Development: Methodologies, Techniques, and Tools*. (second ed.). McGraw-Hill, London.

Brinkkemper, S. (1996). Method engineering: Engineering of information systems development methods and tools. *Information & Software Technology*, 38, 275-280.

Bubenko, J. A. (1986). Information systems methodologies—A research review. In Olle, T. W., Sol, H. G. and Verrijn-Stuart, A. A. (Eds.), *Information Systems Design Methodologies: Improving the Practice*, 289-318. North-Holland: Elsevier Science Publishers.

Card, S. K., Moran, T. P. and Newell, A. (1983). *The Psychology of Human-Computer Interaction*. Hillsdale, NJ: Erlbaum.

Chaos. (1995). *Standish Group Report on Information System Development*. http://www.standishgroup.com/chaos.html.

Chen, P. P. (1976). The entity-relationship model: Toward a unified view of data. *ACM Transactions on Database Systems*, 1(1), 9-36.

Coad, P. and Yourdon, E. (1991). *Object-Oriented Analysis* (second edition). Englewood Cliffs, NJ: Prentice Hall.

Codd, E. F. (1990). *The Relational Model for Database Management: Version 2*. Reading, MA: Addison-Wesley.

Gagne, E. D., Yekovich, C. W. and Yekovich, F. R. (1993). *The Cognitive Psychology of School Learning*. New York: Harper Colins.

Gibbs, W. (1994). Software's chronic crisis. *Scientific American*, September, 86-95.

Goldstein, R. C. and Storey, V. (1990). Some findings on the intuitiveness of entity-relationship concepts. In Lochovsky, F. H. (Ed.), *Entity-Relationship Approach to Database Design*, 9-23. ER Institute.

Hawryszkiewycz, L. T. (1991). *Introduction to Systems Analysis and Design*. (second edition). Englewood Cliffs, NJ: Prentice Hall.

Hirschheim, R. and Klein, H. K (1989). Four paradigms of information systems development. *Communications of the ACM*, 32, 10.

Hutchings, A. F. and Knox, S. T. (1995). Creating products—Customers demand. *Communications of the ACM*, 38(5), 72-80.

Jayaratna, N. (1994). *Understanding and Evaluating Methodologies, NIMSAD: A Systemic Framework*. Maidenhead: McGraw-Hill.

Jones, C. (1986). *Programming Productivity*. New York: McGraw-Hill.

Kangassalo, H. (1990). Foundations of conceptual modeling: A theory construction view. In *Information Modeling and Knowledge Bases*, 20-29. Amsterdam: IOS Press.

Klein, H. K. and Lyytinen, K. (1983). The poverty of scientism in information systems. In Mumford, E. (Eds.). *Research Methods in Information Systems*. North Holland: Amsterdam.

Kung, C. H. and Solvberg, A. (1986). Activity modeling and behavior modeling. In Olle, T. W., Sol, H. G. and Verrijn-Staut, A. A. (Eds.), *Information Systems Design Methodologies: Improving the Practice*, 145-171. North-Holland: Amsterdam.

Miller, G. (1956). The magical number seven, plus or minus two: Some limits on our capacity for processing information. *Psychological Review*, 63, 81-97.

Moray, N. (1984). The usefulness of experimental psychology. In Lagerspetz, K. and Niemi, P. (Eds.), *Psychology in the 1990s*, 225-235. North Holland.

Murdock, Jr., B. B. (1961). The retention of individual items. *Journal of Experimental Psychology,* 62, 618-625.

Mylopoulos, J. (1992). Conceptual modeling and telos. In Loucopoulos, P. and Zicari, R. (Eds.), *Conceptual Modeling, Databases and Case*, 49-68. New York: John Wiley & Sons.

Newell, A. and Simon, H. A. (1972). *Human Problem Solving*. Englewood Cliffs, NJ: Prentice Hall.

Oei, J. L. H., van Hemmen, L. J. G. T., Falkenberg, E. D. and Brinkkemper, S. (1992). *The Meta Model Hierarchy: A Framework for Information Systems Concepts and Techniques*. Katholieke Universiteit Nijmegen, Department of Informatics, Faculty of Mathematics and Informatics, *Technical Report No. 92-17*, 1-30.

Olle, T. W., Sol., H. G. and Verrijn-Stuart (1982). Information systems design methodologies: A comparative review. *Proceedings of the CRIS 82 Conference*. North-Holland, Amsterdam.

Page-Jones, M. (1988). *The Practical Guide to Structured Systems Design* (second edition). Englewood Cliffs, NJ: Prentice Hall.

Rolland, C. and Cauvet, C. (1992). Trends and perspectives in conceptual modeling. In Loucopoulos, P. and Zicari, R. (Eds.), *Conceptual Modeling, Databases and Case*, 27-32. New York: John Wiley & Sons.

Rush, G. (1985). A fast way to define system requirements. *Computerworld*, 19, 40.

Sernades, C., Fiadeiro, J., Meersman, R. and Sernadas, A. (1989). Proof-theoretic conceptual modeling: The NIAM case study. In Falkenberg, E. D. and Lindgreen, P. (Eds.), *Information System Concepts: An In-depth Analysis*, 1-30. Elsevier Science Publishers B.V., North-Holland.

Siau, K. (1997). Using GOMS for evaluating information modeling methods. *Second CAiSE/IFIP8.1 International Workshop on Evaluation of Modeling Methods in Systems Analysis and Design* (EMMSAD'97). Barcelona, Spain, June 16-17, P1-P12.

Siau, K. (1998). Method engineering for Web information systems development–Challenges and issues. *Association for Information Systems 1998 Americas Conference (AIS'98)*. Maryland, USA, August 14-16, 1017-1019.

Siau, K. (1998). The psychology of method engineering. *Third CAiSE/ IFIP8.1 International Workshop on Evaluation of Modeling Methods in Systems Analysis and Design* (EMMSAD'98). Pisa, Italy, June 8-9, P1-P12.

Siau, K. (1999). Method engineering: An empirical approach. *Fourth CAiSE/ IFIP8.1 International Workshop on Evaluation of Modeling Methods in Systems Analysis and Design* (EMMSAD'99). Heidelberg, Germany, June 14-15, I1-I12.

Siau, K. and Rossi, M. (1998). Evaluating information modeling methods–Evaluation techniques. *Thirty-first Hawaii International Conference on System Sciences* (HICSS-31). Big Island of Hawaii, January 6-9, Vol. V, 312-314.

Siau, K., Wand, Y. and Benbasat, I. (1995). A psychological study on the use of relationship concept—Some preliminary findings. *Lecture Notes in Computer Science — Advanced Information Systems Engineering*, 932, 341-354.

Siau, K., Wand, Y. and Benbasat, I. (1996). Evaluating information modeling methods—A cognitive perspective. *Workshop on Evaluation of Modeling Methods in Systems Analysis and Design.* Crete, Greece, M1-M13.

Siau, K., Wand, Y. and Benbasat, I. (1997). Information modeling and cognitive biases–An empirical study on modeling experts. *Information Systems,* 22(2-3), 155-170.

Siau, K.L., Wand, Y. and Benbasat, I. (1996). When parents need not have children—Cognitive biases in information modeling. *Lecture Notes in Computer Science—Advanced Information Systems Engineering,* 1080, 402-420.

Simon, H. A. (1974). How big is a chunk? *Science,* 183, 482-488.

Simon, H. A. (1979). *Models of Thought.* New Haven, CT: Yale University Press.

Walsham, G. (1993). *Interpreting Information Systems in Organizations.* New York: John Wiley & Sons.

Wand, Y. and Weber, R. (1993). On the ontological expressiveness of information systems analysis and design grammars. *Journal of Information Systems,* 3, 217-237.

Wand, Y. and Woo, C. (1993). Object-oriented analysis—Is it really that simple? *Proceedings of the Workshop on Information Technologies and Systems.* Orlando, FL.

Willumsen, G. (1993). Conceptual modeling in IS engineering. In *Executable Conceptual Models in Information Systems Engineering*, 11-21. Trondheim.

Yourdon, E. (1989). *Modern Structured Analysis*, 29. Englewood Cliffs,NJ: Prentice Hall.

Chapter 14

Load-Testing of Web Site Applications: Analysis and Recommendations

Vijay V. Raghavan
Northern Kentucky University, USA

INTRODUCTION

The growth in e-commerce has been accompanied by an enormous need to host robust web sites. Electronic Commerce has changed the role of Information Technology (IT) function from its elementary business support to providing key competitive advantages. Rapid changes in several technologies, while improving the ability to develop and deliver web sites quickly, have also increased the complexity of designing and managing them. It is easy for a consumer or business partner to change to a different supplier if an in-house or outsourced E-Commerce site does not perform up to expectations. Implementing an appropriate web-application testing program is critical in an environment where barriers to switching suppliers of web sites are minimal. Developing robust web sites that perform well under varying loads can be ensured only by a rigorous testing of these web sites before launching them in a production environment.

An ideal e-commerce application testing should enable organizations to predict, measure and improve their e-commerce solutions. Figure 1 shows a simplified e-commerce architecture. This architecture is considerably more complex than an average client/server architecture. This architecture does not include complex network details and load balancing hardware. Complexity of an E-commerce architecture demands application testing that is much more complex than the testing of other types of applications. While there are different types of soft-

Previously published in *Managing Information Technology in a Global Economy*, edited by Mehdi Khosrow-Pour. Copyright © 2001, Idea Group Publishing.

Figure 1. A Simplified Model of E-Commerce Architecture

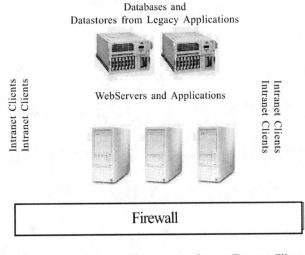

ware testing, this study focuses on load testing especially in the context of web site development.

NEED FOR LOAD-TESTING

"Slashdot Effect" refers to a web site becoming virtually unreachable after being mentioned in another popular web site such as http://www.slashdot.org/. Web marketing is capable of creating sudden surges of interest on web site and sites should be designed to withstand slashdot effects. There are many types of testing commonly used, such as usability testing, functional testing, regression testing, load testing, performance testing and stress testing. Among these, load testing can help an organization guard against slashdot effects. The focus on load testing in this paper does not mean that other types of testing are not applicable to the e-commerce environment. A site that can withstand loads but is hardly usable is obviously worthless. Although other types of testing such as "usability testing" are necessary, the present study focuses on load testing, to withstand sudden surges in demand that are common in a web environment.

BENEFITS OF LOAD-TESTING:

Load testing can elicit information of the expected number of users an application can support, and the time taken by an application to recover from an over-load state. Load testing attempts to simulate real-world interactions of the site. These interactions are then gradually loaded (increased in number) with a view to analyze the system under varying loads to elicit the cutoff point at which the performance becomes unacceptable. Rosenberg and Hyatt (1997) have highlighted the guidelines for developing a successful metrics program that can be applied to a load-testing context. As an example, the Goal/Question/Metric (GQM) paradigm provides a framework for characterization, planning, construction, analysis, learning and feedback. GQM paradigm consists of three steps: generating a set of goals, derive a set of question and develop a set of metrics (Basil & Rambach 1988).

METRICS FOR A LOAD-TESTING PROGRAM

The model proposes criteria for developing a metrics program for load-testing web site applications. Each criterion and its relevance to implementation in web site applications are discussed.

Support for Operational Environments: To be accurate, a load-testing tool must support all operational environments that are commonly used in web site. The load testing tool must support these even if they are not currently used in a given web site design. Some of the operational environment differences could be in client browsers, protocols used, scripting languages and so on. A full verification strategy is effective if it is (a) efficient — load tests can take days — (b) not prone to "false positives" — that is, reporting an error over less-meaningful dynamic content — and (c) configurable.

Database Connections: A production web site almost invariable involves retrieval of data from one or more database. Connecting to the database often involves use of ODBC drivers or other software developed outside of the focal organization. A testing plan must hence include the performance of this software under varying load conditions. For example, proprietary software may have number of user restriction that may not be readily apparent during the development stage.

A much desired capability is for a test tool to generate a test plan automatically based on available data (from server logs to usage patterns, geographic access patterns to domain access logs). No testing tool does this today (with the singular exception of Microsoft, whose free Web Application Stress Tool can generate stress testing from IIS Server logs. Users, as they struggle with ever more complex and large sites, have been crying out for greater site-mapping capabilities in a testing tool. While the vendors have made strides in manageability, developing the test plans and procedures is still a very manual and time-consuming process.

Analysis/Reporting: E-commerce sites within an organization are highly visible. Hence, the ability to generate meaningful reports quickly is important. A Load testing program must convince managers that a web site can generate accurate and timely reports. The ability of a web site application to generate real time reports must be tested under actual load conditions. For less important reports, Real-time monitoring of report generation at later stages of a site's life cycle may be acceptable.

Breadth: A load-testing program must be broad. This breadth refers to the number of different protocols, application server vendors, languages, and client/server integration — the width of Figure 1 — which are supported by a testing program. Benefits of analyzing on HTTP requests and responses and API-level recording by accessing Windows API or Windows messaging traffic must be clearly evaluated.

Depth: Referring back to Figure 1, depth covers how well a testing program addresses concerns moving from the top of the figure to the bottom. If a given request from a web site application takes x seconds to process, how much of it is spent in different components of Figure1. Breaking down the total time taken for requests to different components of the architectures is critical to implementing a successful load-testing program.

Life-Cycle Support: This criterion addresses how well the testing programs and tools are integrated with functional and regression testing methods and performance monitoring methods being used in an organization. Testing does not occur in a vacuum. Support for other parts of development process and tracking of defects become critical for ensuring application reliability. A load-testing plan must work well with other test plan that are currently implemented or being contemplated.

RECOMMENDATIONS

It is critical for organizations deploying web sites to develop a load-testing plan that includes all aspects of site development. Since return on investment (ROI) calculations can be difficult for any test plan, organizations should assume that the costs of implementing a valid testing tool program as a necessary cost of business in the e-commerce space. While the costs of these testing programs can be high, an organization can expect that these costs to be offset by reduced costs of training and maintenance and increased gains by deploying a web site that is fully functional.

REFERENCES

Basil, V. and Rambach H. (1988). *The TAME Project: Towards Improvement-Oriented Software Environments*. University of Maryland, UMIACS-TR-88-8.

Beizer, B. (1995) *Black-Box Testing : Techniques for Functional Testing of Software and Systems*. New York: John Wiley & Sons.

Hetzel, W. (1993). *The Complete Guide to Software Testing* (second edition). New York: John Wiley & Sons.

Kaner, C. and Falk, J. (1993) Coriolis group. *Testing Computer Software (second edition)*.

Kit, E. and Finzi, S. (1995). *Software Testing in the Real World*. Reading, MA: Addison Wesley.

Myers, G. J. (1979). *Art of Software Testing*. New York: John Wiley & Sons.

Rosenberg, L., Hammer, T. and Shaw, J. (1998). Software metrics and reliability. *9th International Symposium on Software Reliability Engineering*, Germany, November. The paper is available at http://satc.gsfc.nasa.gov/support/ISSRE_NOV98/software metrics and_reliability.PDF.

Rosenberg, L. and Hyatt, L. (1997). Developing a successful metrics program. *International Conference on Software Engineering*, San Francisco, CA.

Rubin, J. (1994). *Handbook of Usability Testing: How to Plan, Design, and Conduct Effective Tests* (Wiley Technical Communication Library). New York: John Wiley & Sons.

Chapter 15

Component-based ERP Design in a Distributed Object Environment

Bonn-Oh Kim
Seattle University, USA

Ted Lee
Memphis State University, USA

ERP (Enterprise Resource Planning) vendors have seen a dramatic increase in their sales this decade. Even though several vendors are producing great products and making huge profits, there are some problems to be resolved to make ERP applications a continuous success in the next decades. Current ERP applications have the low reusability and interchangeability of various modules among different vendors' packages. One of the main reasons for these shortfalls is a tight coupling of ERP domain knowledge with the particular implementation tools. Also, efforts in establishing and using the standards in specifications of ERP applications have been inconsequential. In this article, strategic steps to wield a dominant power in the future ERP market are discussed. These steps are as follows: 1. Knowledge Modeling: Abstraction of Domain Knowledge from Tools; 2. Componentization of Domain Knowledge; 3. Implementation of Componentized Domain Knowledge; 4. Marketing Strategies for Domain Knowledge Components.

INTRODUCTION

Since the early 1990s, a notion of business reengineering has been very popular in many companies, especially in the USA. One of the contributions of business reengineering is that corporate information systems should be viewed as an enabler to transform the business processes and consequently organizational struc-

Previously published in *Challenges of Information Technology Management in the 21ˢᵗ Century*, edited by Mehdi Khosrow-Pour. Copyright © 2000, Idea Group Publishing.

tures. To fulfill the mission of an enabler of business transformation, corporate executives found that corporate information systems should be planned, designed and implemented from an enterprise-wide perspective. A collection of islands of software located in various divisions of an organization could not satisfy the new needs of large corporations.

To deliver an integrated set of software systems for various functions of a company, including accounting, manufacturing, logistics and others. Recently, ERP vendors such as SAP, Baan, PeopleSoft, Oracle and J. D. Edwards have seen their sales growing exponentially. Behind the successful stories of ERP, however, there are several issues to be dealt with in order to adapt to the ever-changing computing environment and maintain the competitive advantages.

Borrowing the idea from the industrial manufacturing, software components built based on standard specifications can be a building block for resolving the current problems in designing ERP applications. To build software components, however, we need to have a set of specifications at the knowledge level. In this article, knowledge modeling abstracted from the implementation tools is discussed as a precursor for building the components for ERP applications after the problems of current ERP applications are discussed and core competencies of ERP vendors are reviewed from a perspective of overall computing architectures.

PROBLEMS OF CURRENT ERP DESIGN

Currently, each ERP vendor has been developing its own proprietary systems in various domain areas. Since ERP customers prefer the seamless systems across their business functions, ERP vendors are continuously expanding into new domain areas. However, one vendor does not necessarily produce superior ERP packages across all business functions. Each vendor maintains superiority in some functional domains, e.g., PeopleSoft for human resource management.

From a perspective of ERP customers, they have to opt for using all ERP applications primarily from one vendor or selecting many packages from different vendors. If customers can choose the best from different ERP vendors without worrying about the compatibility among different vendors' ERP packages, they can maximize the productivity gains by installing the best ERP applications in their organization. From an ERP vendor's perspective, it is very difficult to specialize in any particular domain functions (e.g., manufacturing, financials, etc.) because many customers want a smorgasbord of ERP packages from one vendor. If ERP packages from different vendors are interchangeable or compatible, some problems aforementioned can be somewhat resolved.

There have been overlaps in efforts developing virtually the same type of applications (e.g., accounting packages) by many different vendors. Reinventing a wheel is a last thing we need to do. Current ERP designs in industry lack the reusability and interchangeability of domain application components. To develop a successful and dominant company in the ERP market, a strategic move to a component-based ERP design and marketing will be required. ERP vendors should be in a business of specifying the ERP components as well as building them. Once the design of specifications for ERP components is produced, manufacturing of each component can be outsourced to third-party developers.

CORE COMPETENCIES OF ERP VENDORS

Currently, ERP vendors' core competency appears to reside in its conceptualizations of application domain knowledge in financials, manufacturing, distribution and others rather than the application development tools (e.g., OneWorld from J. D. Edwards). Even though they are making profits by selling the ERP software on different machines, there will be even more profitable and huge markets for specifying and producing various components of each application. Readers are reminded that automobile companies make huge profits specifying and selling the automobile parts (or components). For example, GM controls an automobile business by specifying how the third-party manufacturers produce the parts for GM cars and trucks. Controlling the standards for specifications of parts endows an intrinsic dominant power to GM. GM does not produce all the parts. GM basically controls the specifications of parts.

By breaking down a huge complex application package into many independently packaged components, we can sell each component to all types of customers. Customers of ERP products do not have to be a mid-sized company wishing to have the financial applications installed. We can expand the market to software developers and end-users as well as our traditional mid- to large-sized companies. For example, if we package the accounts receivable application as a separate independent product using DCOM (Distributed Component Object Model) standard in Microsoft Windows 98/NT environment, potential profits could be immense.

COMPONENT-BASED ERP DESIGN

What is important is that we need to rethink how we develop the applications. Software design should be more or less like designing and manufacturing automobiles. GM and Ford make money by specifying components and assembling cars as well as by manufacturing parts. ERP vendors should be prepared to design and sell components of applications as well as the final whole ERP solution. Packaging of each component needs to be done using the industry standards. Once we conceptualize and build each component, we can package it using Microsoft DCOM, OMG's (Object Management Group) CORBA (Common Object Request Broker Architecture), SUN's JavaBeans or whatever. ERP vendors are not in a business of setting the standards for packaging. Their strength should be in conceptualization and specification of components and packaging them in various forms.

Currently, most of conceptualizations of knowledge in application domains are already available in the forms of computer code and some high level designs. Unfortunately, however, they are frequently hidden and dormant. They are tightly coupled with the tools (e.g., OneWorld). What we need to do is to abstract the knowledge from the tools and specify each knowledge component independently of any tools. Then, each knowledge component can be manufactured using whatever tools in a massively distributed environment. Thereby, we can give a new profitable life to this latent asset of ERP vendors. We need to recreate and re-package the knowledge. For effective packaging and distribution, it is very important to adopt a distributed object-oriented approach in software development and to normalize the database systems.

More specifically, the following needs to be done:

1. Knowledge Modeling: Abstraction of Domain Knowledge from Tools:

When designing software systems, we need to think about what is constantly changing and what is not. Invariant parts of the system should be separated from the variant parts in order to make a whole system adaptable to a new environment. In the ERP market, the domain knowledge in accounting or manufacturing does not change much over time while implementation tools are almost constantly changing. When there are new implementation tools available, the domain knowledge should be easily ported to a new tool environment.

Figure 1: Multiple Levels of ERP

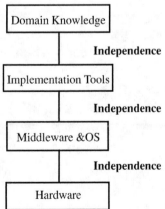

As shown in Figure 1, knowledge models in various domains should be independent of any lower-level abstractions, including implementation tools, middleware and others. Knowledge modeling has been a research topic in artificial intelligence for a long time and there are many models available now. For the ERP knowledge, however, two modeling tools can be most effective: i.e., object-oriented modeling for business activities and entity-relationship modeling for persistent data. These object models and entity-relationship models should be independent of any particular tools or technical environment. Depending on a market situation, we should be able to implement the knowledge models in almost any programming language and hardware environment.

2. Componentization of Domain Knowledge

One of the most important characteristics of components is the separation of "what" from "how". Each component should have a clearly defined interface specifying "what" it does while hiding "how" it does. Using this interface, each component can communicate with other components. A collection of objects will constitute a various grain size of knowledge in each domain application as patterns or frameworks of objects. IBM's San Francisco project can provide a good reference model. For more details, visit the following Web site: http://www.ibm.com/Java/Sanfrancisco/.

3. Implementation of Componentized Domain Knowledge

As we have seen over many years, technical environments are changing at a very fast speed. ERP vendors should not be in the component packaging business. Currently, there are several packaging standards available, including Microsoft's DCOM (Distributed Component Object Model), OMG's (Object Management Group) CORBA (Common Object Request Broker Architecture) or SUN's JavaBeans. Knowledge components specified should be packaged using whatever standards popular. If we design and specify the domain knowledge independently of any particular packaging standard, we should be able to repackage the domain knowledge components as dictated by the market.

4. Marketing Strategies for Domain Knowledge Components

To become and stay a dominant power in the ERP market, an ERP vendor needs to control and own the standards for ERP components and allow others to manufacture the approved components. Open Applications Group's work can be a good place to see what is going on in the area of open standards. For more details, readers are referred to the following Web site: http://www.openapplications.org/. Microsoft practically controls the microcomputer market by owning a standard in the operating systems while many other companies build software based on Microsoft's standard. Each ERP vendor does not have to manufacture all the components.

Once an ERP vendor possesses the standards, it should be an owner of components catalogue. The catalogue of ERP components should be a market place where software builders can shop to build or customize their own applications. it should be more than just a component builder. We should create and control the market for ERP components. Readers are reminded that NYSE (New York Stock Exchange) has become a very profitable venture by creating a market for stock exchanges and by controlling how stocks should be exchanged. We should be able to set the rules for building and exchanging components in the ERP market. Thereby, we can dominate the ERP market for a long time.

CONCLUDING REMARKS

As in the industrial sectors of the USA economy, there will be more profits in specifying and designing software packages rather than just manufacturing them even in the software business in the near future. These days, manufacturing of software can be achieved less costly by exporting it to countries like India. In the ERP market, we need to think more like Nike. Designing Nike shoes is a lot more profitable than just manufacturing them. Activities involved in designing the specifications for the ERP components are quite distinct from manufacturing them. Once an ERP vendor controls the knowledge component specifications for the ERP domains, it can be in a strategic position to dominate the ERP market with an absolute competitive advantage in the 21st century.

Chapter 16

Knowledge and Object-Oriented Approach for Interoperability of Heterogeneous Information Management Systems

Chin-Wan Chung and Chang-Ryong Kim
Korea Advanced Institute of Science and Technology, Korea

Son Dao
Hughes Research Laboratories, USA

For the interoperability of heterogeneous information management systems, schema mapping approaches have been used to build a unified view. The schema mapping approach offers full transparencies and is very powerful from the user's point of view. However, the traditional mapping approach needs to be strengthened for information management systems that have non-traditional data types, no schema, or incompatible schemas. We have incorporated numerous concepts and constructs associated with the knowledge and object-oriented paradigm such as abstract views with a set of procedures, encapsulation, inheritance and class composition hierarchies to resolve the above problem. This extension also accommodates the ability to determine and explicitly represent the semantics in the schema. Additionally, we have outlined a query processing method using the unified view. We are currently developing a prototype to support seamless access to structured data and unstructured data managed by different information management systems.

Previously published in the *Journal of Database Management*, *vol.10*, *no.3*, Copyright © 1999, Idea Group Publishing.

The information of a large organization is distributed across diverse information management systems. The diversity is mainly caused by the difference of requirements of applications, the advances in information management technologies, the ad hoc historical development of systems, and evolution of systems in organizations. Therefore, it is unlikely that the diversity will diminish. The interoperability of heterogeneous information management systems is necessary to provide the sharing of an organization's information.

In past years, several projects have been developed to address the interoperability. Their approaches, federated or schema mapping approach, centered around the ability to define a unified view and to support translation to/from local schemas (Chung, 1990; Dao et al., 1987; Garcia-Solaco et al., 1995; Thomas, 1990). The schema integration process for building this unified view is a very critical process in the federated approach.

The federated approach using the relational data model as a common data model offers full data distribution transparency and is very powerful from the user's point of view. But this approach is limited with respect to information management systems that have no schema or incompatible schema models (e.g., file systems, text, spatial, geographical information systems).

In the federated approach, a common data model is needed to represent the unified view. Several research projects suggest the use of relational, semantic, entity-relationship (ER)/extended ER, and object-oriented data models, etc, for the common data model.

Databases offer facilities for managing large amounts of data, but are limited in their expression and structuring facilities; while object-oriented programming languages provide features for expressing and structuring complex entities (through data abstraction, encapsulation, and inheritance). The object-oriented data model incorporates ideas from the semantic data model and the object-oriented programming language. Semantic data modeling offers richer types of relationships (i.e. aggregation and groupings), whereas the object-oriented language encapsulates behavioral aspects of objects. The object-oriented data model is currently implemented in several object-oriented database management systems (OODBMS) (Butterworth, 1991; Deux, 1991; Kim et al., 1990; Lamb et al., 1991; Soloviev, 1992).

Our approach is to use advanced modeling concepts (i.e. a semantic data model, knowledge representation) in an object-oriented paradigm to form a common data model. The goal of the model is to provide flexible features to resolve data structure incompatibilities of underlying data models, interrelationships of objects at different locations during schema integration, and the semantics required by different applications.

Using the common model, a unified view can be built from local schemas through schema integration. Once a unified view is provided, users can develop applications which access data objects in the unified view. This access will be translated to an access to local data.

The use of object-oriented techniques has already been presented in other papers (Ahmed et al., 1991; Bertino et al., 1989). While we use a federated approach, (Ahmed et al., 1991; Bertino et al., 1989) used a multidatabase approach. In a multidatabase approach, a common data model is selected, then local schemas for local databases are imported to the location(s) which uses the common data model. The imported schemas are translated to schemas in the common data model to provide a uniform interface; however, the schemas are not integrated. Therefore, the multidatabase approach does not require a unified view. On the other hand, the approach does not support the data distribution transparency. The approach in (Bertino et al., 1989) is based on the operational mapping which consists of defining the correspondence between operations at different levels. Our approach is based mainly on the structural mapping and somewhat on the operational mapping. The formation of a query utilizes the structure and the message sending to an object utilizes the operation.

Non-object-oriented approaches (traditional approaches) use data models other than the OO data model as a common data model. As mentioned earlier, the object-oriented data model combines the features of the semantic data model and the object-oriented programming language. The OO data model is a superset of other data models. Therefore, other data models cannot effectively represent some of the features of the OO data model such as multimedia data types and methods. Consequently, it is difficult to interface the OODBMS using a non-object-oriented approach. We use a federated and object-oriented approach to support the transparency of the locations of diverse databases including object-oriented databases.

From the above discussions, we observe that there are needs for a new approach for an effective interoperability, and they are the motivations of our research as follows:

- It is necessary to provide the interoperability among information management systems that have non-traditional data types or incompatible schemas.
- In any case, the users should not be responsible for finding the locations of necessary data. The system should support the data distribution transparency.
- In the past, only the feasibility of the interoperability was considered. However, an environment to achieve interoperability without much difficulty must be provided.

The initial local DBMSs to be interfaced are the relational DBMS, the object-oriented DBMS, and the hierarchical DBMS. Recently, use of the relational DBMS has been wide-spread, while the object-oriented DBMS is suitable for engineering and manufacturing applications. An interface to the hierarchical DBMS IMS in a heterogeneous database environment is important because IMS has been the most heavily used mainframe DBMS in large organizations. The interoperability of these three major types of DBMSs covers many important issues and it will be the basis for future expansion.

The remainder of this paper is organized as follows: The common data model is presented in the next section. The following section describes the interface between the object-oriented database and the relational database, and the subsequent section briefly explains the interface to the hierarchical database. The architecture of a prototype is described in the following section. A comprehensive example is given in the next section.

INTEGRATED KNOWLEDGE-OBJECT-ORIENTED DATA MODEL

A common data model is required to support the integration of multiple databases. Extensibility and flexibility features are the major advantages of the OO data model as a common data model compared with other data models. Although the OO data model provides basic features for general requirements, specific features need to be added to effectively support different areas of applications. In particular, since we are concerned with the integration of heterogeneous databases, our approach is to consider the structures and representations of objects tightly coupled with the operations that one may want to use on them. Thus, we propose to start with the OO data model to support general concepts. We then extend the concepts to support more specific issues such as query decomposition, data distribution, and translation of queries and responses. The result is a model that merges OO concepts with special extensions to access heterogeneous databases. This model is called an Integrated Knowledge-Object-Oriented Data Model (IKOODM) and it can be implemented using an OODBMS.

In other words, IKOODM is an extension of the OO data model, and it provides constructs necessary to build a unified view, using basic features of the OO data model. The point is that by including frequently used features in IKOODM, the features are supported in the system level rather than the application level. Thus, many users can share available IKOODM features without having to redundantly develop the same features using OODBMS features directly.

IKOODM Core Modeling Elements

The core model consists of objects, classes and relationships.

(1) Object

Objects represent instances of entities modeled in a database, or real world concepts perceived by applications. The uniform treatment of instances of any real world entity as an object simplifies the user's view of the real world. Objects can be created, updated and deleted dynamically. Moreover, the interaction between objects is supported through message passing.

(2) Class

The class is a major data abstraction in IKOODM. Instances of classes are objects. Objects with similar attributes and event structures are grouped into a class. A class definition is also stored as an object, called a class-object. In IKOODM, there are two types of classes: base class and abstract class. A base class has the same meaning as a class in the object-oriented paradigm; therefore, it has stored instances.

A base class is used to represent a local data object (e.g., a relation in a relational database) and the data access path created during schema integration. The access path represents the relationship between the instances of two entities. The relationship enables the access to instances of one entity from instances of the other entity. For instance, there is an access path between the department entity and the employee entity because each employee is a member of a department. (See the next section for further discussions and an example.)

An abstract class is used to represent a high level abstraction to describe the unified view during schema integration. An abstract class is derived based upon the methods supported by the system or the applications. The system-methods include semantic model concepts such as generalization and specialization. An abstract class is analogous to a view. A relational view (currently, a view is well-defined in a relational database) is limited to the expressiveness of the query language SQL. Meanwhile, the term abstract class is used to emphasize that the methods used to derive an abstract class can be expressed in any declarative or procedural languages and that an abstract class can contain methods and information for using the class.

The class is defined as follows:

DEFINE CLASS <class name>

Internal Structure:

 <attribute 1>, <attribute 2>, ...,<attribute n>

Semantic Link:

 To-class:

Declaration methods:
 <generalization, specialization, binary
   association or user-defined methods>
 Derivation Structure:
 Constraints:
 Data distribution:
 Manipulation methods:

Internal Structure describes the property of a class. Semantic Link represents the semantic relationship from this class to other classes. To-class specifies one or a list of destination classes. Declaration methods are used to create the class and its relationships to other classes during schema integration. Derivation Structure provides information necessary to use this class during query processing. Manipulation methods are used to process queries referencing the class.

The role of Declaration methods is to represent the relationship between a class and other classes, whereas Manipulation methods are the main features to capture and specify behavior of a class in the model. Whenever a class is referenced in a query, Manipulation methods in the class make necessary transformations of the query.

Example: Suppose a student class is a generalization of undergrad-student and grad-student relations which are stored at different locations.
DEFINE CLASS student
Internal Structure:
 <name>, ...
 Semantic Link:
 To-class: grad-student, undergrad-student
 Declaration method: Generalization (grad-
     student, undergrad-student)
 Derivation Structure:
 Manipulation method:
  Generalization-Decomposition (student)
 Data distribution: {grad-student is
    fragmented at Site 1 in DBMS x,
    undergrad-student is fragmented at
    Site 2 in DBMS y}

(3) Relationship

Semantic links are used to describe relationships among classes. We have extended the basic generalization abstraction used in conventional OO paradigm to support data distribution relationships (e.g., horizontal and vertical fragmentations). In addition to conventional OO methods for generalization, specific methods will be provided to support the definition of a unified view and the access to multiple databases. For each type of relationship, a pair of methods is required: declaration methods and manipulation methods.

Any types of relationships can be specified by providing appropriate declaration methods. A manipulation method associated with a relationship defines steps to simplify a query using the relationship. These methods are stored in a high-level class and inherited to appropriate classes in IKOODM. Therefore, once the methods are defined, they are supported by the model. These methods are class methods which operate on class-objects in contrast to instance methods which operate on objects. For instance, in the above example, Manipulation method Generalization-Decomposition takes the query referencing the student class and decomposes the query into two subqueries, one referencing the grad-student class and the other the undergrad-student class. The method does not operate on a specific student object.

The declaration and manipulation methods are similar to the data definition language and the data manipulation language in the conventional DBMS. The difference is that the methods can be expressed either declaratively or procedurally. In addition, since codes defined as methods in classes are used by the system or applications, modularization and reusability of codes are promoted.

We describe a few relationships that are very useful and powerful for integrating multiple databases. The generalization and the specialization can be used to represent horizontal and vertical fragmentations. These relationships induce the inheritance property. That is, the inheritance (ISA relationship) describes the relationship between a class and the class generalized (or specialized) from it. The binary association describes the accessibility relationship between two classes.

Generalization

Generalization allows the creation of abstract classes through the projection and union of existing base or abstract classes.

Declaration Methods:

GC = Generalization [C1, C2, ..., Cn]: the new class GC consists of instances that are in C1, C2, ..., or Cn. That is, generalization is the union of disjoint classes, e.g., student = Generalization [grad-student, undergrad-student]. The new class GC inherits the common attributes of C1, C2, ..., and Cn.

Manipulation Methods:

Q = Generalization-Decomposition [GC]: Q is a set of subqueries, of a query referencing GC, returned by the decomposition of the generalization class GC.

Horizontal Fragmentation:

Besides creating a high level of abstraction corresponding to the real world concept, generalization is used to represent the horizontal fragmentation in a distributed database environment. For example, grad-student is physically stored in a database at a location different from undergrad-student. In this case, generalization is used to provide data distribution transparency.

Specialization

Declaration Methods:

SC = Single-specialization [C1, <restricted attributes>,<predicate>]: the new class SC contains restricted attributes of C1, and SC consists of instances that satisfy the predicate on some of the restricted attributes. For example, grad-compsc-resume = Single-specialization [grad-student, <name, grade, dept, experience>, <grad-student (dept = 'computer science')>]. SC2 = Group-specialization [C1, C2, ..., Cn, <common restricted attributes>,<predicate>]: the new class SC2 contains common restricted attributes and it consists of instances that satisfy the predicate on some of the restricted attributes. For example, work-study = Group-specialization [employee, student, <name, ID, status>, <employee (status = 2) and student (status = 2)>].

Manipulation Methods:

Q = Specialization-Decomposition [SC or SC2]: Q is a set of subqueries, of a query referencing SC or SC2, returned by the decomposition of SC or SC2.

Vertical Fragmentation:

Single-specialization and Group-specialization can be used to represent a unified view to represent the vertical fragmentation of different base classes that have common attributes and that are physically distributed in different locations.

Binary Association

This relationship describes the access path between two classes.

Declaration Methods:

Association [C1, C2]: C1 and C2 are the two classes that will be associated with each other iff there is an access path between C1 and C2. The identification and modeling of the access path is explained in the next section.

Manipulation Methods:

Q = Association-Decomposition [C1, C2]: if C1 and C2 are at different locations or under different DBMSs, Q is a set of two subqueries, of a query referencing C1 and C2, one referencing C1 and the other C2.

IKOODM Structure

For resolving semantic heterogeneities and supporting access to disparate data sources, we extend the core model into a multi-layered model that supports different levels of abstractions: enterprise semantics, data structures, and object storage. This is illustrated in Figure 4.

(1) Object Storage Layer

The base class can be stored and managed by a relational, object-oriented, hierarchical, image database system or file system. The object storage layer is composed of different classes, one for each type of DBMS, and their subclasses, one for each DBMS. Each class provides the necessary methods to transform between different structure representations, and to interface with the underlying systems. The methods will be transferred permanently and executed at the appropriate local site.

For example, a relational class is composed of a set of common methods that are used to transform a query to a relational query in SQL, and its subclass is composed of a set of specialized methods for interfacing a different DBMS (e.g., Sybase, Oracle, DB2, Ingres). In this example, the set of common methods for the relational class can be reused to interface any relational DBMS which uses SQL. The set of common methods consists of programs which translate queries in an OO query language into queries in a standard SQL such as ANSI SQL2. SQL2 has large intersections with SQL variants used by popular relational DBMSs. The methods in a subclass of the relational class (a subclass for a specific relational DBMS) translate the features of the standard SQL into those of the variant of SQL used by the relational DBMS.

(2) Data Structure Layer

This layer is composed of all the base classes that are supported in the unified view. The mapping information and methods that resolve the data access path from one base class to another are captured in this layer. Class objects in this layer send a request to an appropriate class in the object storage layer to receive the data content. This layer provides the data management system independent capabilities for a wide variety of systems supported by the object storage layer.

(3) Enterprise Semantic Layer

This level of abstraction captures the semantic relationship of different applications/users' views of the underlying data. The enterprise semantic layer consists of abstract classes which are derived from the base classes in the data structure layer or from the abstract classes in this layer. The semantics are derived based on the interrelationships among the underlying schemas coupled with the integrity constraints of an enterprise that the users are trying to model. The enterprise semantics are built during schema integration. The declaration and manipulation methods described previously are used to create and manipulate the unified views and their relationships. Moreover, the users can specify other model concepts required by their applications and provide their own methods. In general, this layer allows us to express such knowledge declaratively instead of embedding it in procedural codes.

In general, the use of the class hierarchy and the method to support IKOODM layer structure will greatly enhance the modularity and reusability of the software as shown in the example in *(1) Object Storage Layer* of this subsection. The reusability here only refers to sharing the source code of the method because the object code will be different for different types of computers on which the method is to be reused. The source code in a language can be reused when compilers for the language are available on different computers. For example, C++ language programs are widely used on different computers. The parts of a program related to I/O require modifications. However, there are many routines in distributed database software that contain little or no I/O related parts, such as routines for distributed query decomposition and query translation. Once the method is compiled for a target computer, it is possible to invoke the compiled method that are not linked with the main process using dynamic loading and linking techniques supported by some operating systems such as UNIX.

The Advantages of IKOODM

In this subsection, we summarize the advantages of IKOODM compared with existing approaches.

(1) The interoperability is extended to diverse information management systems by taking an object-oriented approach.

Previously, the relational data model has been successfully used as a common data model to integrate traditional information management systems such as relational database systems, network database systems, and hierarchical database systems. However, a relational approach is not appropriate for incorporating information management systems that have non-traditional data types (e.g., image, video, text) or incompatible schemas.

The OO data model provides multimedia data types; therefore, images or videos in local information systems can be modeled using corresponding multimedia data types in the common OO data model. Furthermore, the methods associated with multimedia data types can be used for the presentation of the multimedia data transferred from local information systems. This is an important aspect because the user interacts only with the global user interface and the common schema in a heterogeneous information management system environment.

While the traditional data models are compatible enough to be mapped to the relational data model, the OO data model is incompatible with the traditional data models because the OO data model captures the behavior in addition to the structure. Since the information content of the OO data model is a superset of the relational model, the relational approach cannot provide the interoperability when an OO database system is included.

(2) The data distribution transparency is supported by using a federated approach.

The past researches that proposed an object-oriented approach used a multidatabase approach. Although the local schemas are translated to schemas in the common data model, they are not integrated in multidatabase approach (Litwin et al., 1990). Consequently, the multidatabase approach does not support the data distribution transparency.

(3) An environment which reduces the difficulty of achieving interoperability is provided by extending the OO data model.

IKOODM is structured in three layers, and incorporates specific methods in the classes in the layers in order to facilitate efficient development of system software for managing heterogeneous databases as well as construction of a unified view.

The system software can be well modularized and structured. As shown in Figure 4, a method in a class in the enterprise layer decomposes a query referencing the class into queries referencing classes in the data structure layer. Then, a method in a class in the data structure layer further decomposes subqueries by locations. Finally, methods in the object storage layer translate a subquery in two steps; the first step translates the subquery into a query language of the target data model, and the second step adds specifics of the target DBMS.

The unified view can be constructed utilizing the methods for schema integration such as generalization and specialization. In addition, the knowledge in the enterprise semantic layer can be used for the construction and the update of the unified view. The knowledge includes the integrity constraint, attribute relationships, and schema interrelationships, and it can be expressed declaratively.

INTERFACE BETWEEN OBJECT-ORIENTED DATABASES AND RELATIONAL DATABASES

A unified view of the databases needs to be provided to users and applications to support a location and structure transparent access to distributed object-oriented (OO) databases and relational databases. We use IKOODM to provide a unified view of OO databases and relational databases. In fact, there are OO data model primitives which can be used as IKOODM features for constructing the data structure layer in a unified view.

Since the schema translation and integration are essential processes for providing a unified view of heterogeneous databases, we will focus on the schema translation and integration. A major ingredient of the schema integration is the modeling of access paths. An access from instances of an entity to instances of another entity can be made when there is a relationship between instances of the two entities.

In the OO data model, the class composition hierarchy (or part-of hierarchy) (Kim et al., 1990) is used when the domain of an attribute in a class is another user-defined class. Such an attribute is called a composite attribute. For example, suppose an EMPLOYEE class includes attributes DEPT and AGE with domain classes DEPARTMENT and INTEGER, respectively. The domain of AGE is a system-defined class INTEGER consisting of a set of integers, whereas the domain of DEPT is a user-defined class DEPART-MENT consisting of a set of department objects. In this case, DEPT is a composite attribute and there is a class composition hierarchy, between EMPLOYEE and DEPARTMENT, which specifies an assignment relation-ship between employee objects and department objects. Therefore, the class composition hierarchy (CC-hierarchy) represents the relationship between the instances (i.e., objects) of two classes. Depending on the numbers of objects of one class related to objects of the other class, the relationship between the classes may be one-to-one, one-to-many, or many-to-many. We use the CC-hierarchy to model the access path.

While the CC-hierarchy is an explicit structure, the access path can also be modeled using a behavior of an object that returns objects of a different class. However, in order to implement the behavior of an object to access other objects, the access request must be known prior to the submission of the request. For complex requests, it is difficult to expect all possible requests. Our goal is to support arbitrary queries which are non-procedural and formulated dynamically. We use the CC-hierarchy because the explicit structure in a unified view helps the formulation of a complex query navigat-ing through several classes. The CC-hierarchy corresponds to the binary association in IKOODM. The class and object, which are the IKOODM core elements, are also OO data model primitives.

In the relational data model, the relationship between two relations is represented by the joining attributes which are the common attributes of the two relations. The access paths among the relations can be found by identi-fying joining attributes.

In order to provide a unified view of OO databases and relational databases in terms of OO data model primitives, the relational data definition must be translated to an equivalent OO data definition. In addition, the definitions of the OO databases which have relationships to relational databases need to be modified to include access paths to the relational databases.

A relation R with attributes will be translated to a base class C with the same attributes. Since R is a relation in at least first normal form, C does not contain any composite attributes. Obviously, C does not include any methods either. A class translated from a relation is not in a class hierarchy with any class in an OO database or classes translated from other relations. Initially, the translated class becomes a subclass of the system-defined root class (or any class which has the characteristics of the root class).

The sets of classes in local OO databases are linked by class hierarchies (or ISA hierarchy) and CC-hierarchies. These class structures become a part of the integrated schema. All the methods in the local classes are included. At this point, the integrated schema consists of class structures from local OO databases and standalone classes from local relational databases. The integrated schema is completed by adding CC-hierarchies to represent access paths.

Consider the access path between two classes C(R) and C(S) translated from relations R and S, respectively. The access path in the relational database is via joining attributes. In creating a CC-hierarchy between C(R) and C(S), we have to decide the direction of the CC-hierarchy. The value of a composite attribute can be a set of object identifiers (OIDs) of the class which is the domain of the composite attribute. Therefore, if there is a one-to-many relationship from R to S, the direction of the CC-hierarchy becomes C(R) to C(S). This is accomplished by adding a composite attribute to C(R). The domain of the composite attribute is the set of C(S).

If the relationship between R and S is one-to-one or many-to-many, the direction of the CC-hierarchy is arbitrary. Suppose the direction of the CC-hierarchy is C(R) to C(S). If the relationship between R and S is one-to-one, the domain of the composite attribute is C(S). If the relationship is many-to-many, the domain is the set of C(S).

When a global query references both a relational database and an OO database, a translator must generate a relational query to access the relational database. The relational query retrieves the values of attributes from the relational database. Therefore, the access path between a relation and a class exists only if there is a common attribute in the relation and the class. Thus, the access path between a relation and a class can be handled in the same way as the modeling of the access path between two relations.

Consider an access path between two classes in different local OO databases. This type of access path is not different from the access path in the local OO database design. However, there is one important difference in terms of actual data storage. The local OO database is populated according to the local OO data definition. The values of composite attributes in a local OO data definition are stored in the local OO database. On the other hand, the composite attributes added in the global view merely specify the access paths.

Suppose there is a common attribute between the two classes. An effective way to handle the values of the added composite attribute is to compute the values during the query execution time by using the values of the common attribute. For this reason, we only consider the access path between classes in different local OO databases when there is a common attribute in the classes. Therefore, the method for creating a CC-hierarchy can be applied to model all possible types of access paths: between relations, between a relation and a class, and between classes.

Since the issue of handling OIDs in the unified view requires more research, we outline our approach. An OID in the unified view consists of the OID of a local object and the site of the object. Using the site information, a message sent to an OID in the unified view can be routed to the local object. In case the local object is a tuple in a relation, the primary key value of the tuple takes the role of the OID. A message to a tuple is only to retrieve the value of an attribute corresponding to the message name. Therefore, a message using the primary key value is translated to an SQL query which contains the primary key value in the WHERE clause.

The following example illustrates the creation of access paths and an integrated schema. Consider a relational database at Location 1 consisting of a relation DESIGN (DS#, DESIGNER, MANUFAC_COST) and an OO database at Location 2 with two classes DRAWING (DR#, CAD_SYSTEM, DS#, PICTURE (DOMAIN_IS IMAGE)) and IMAGE (). We only specified the domain of a composite attribute which represents a CC-hierarchy. The two local databases are depicted in Figure 1. A single-arrow on a CC-hierarchy indicates the direction of an one-to-one relationship.

There is a common attribute DS# between the relation DESIGN and the class DRAWING. We assume that a design consists of many drawings. Since the relationship between DESIGN and DRAWING is one-to-many, a CC-hierarchy is created from C(DESIGN) to C(DRAWING) by adding a composite attribute DRG whose domain is a set of C(DRAWING). The three translated classes are given below.

Figure 1: Local Data Definitions

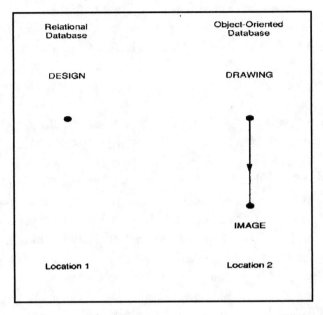

Figure 2: An Integrated Schema

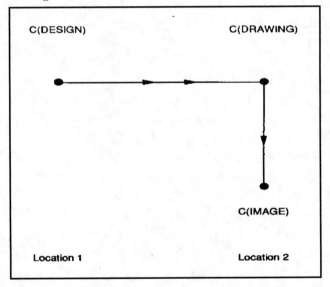

C(DESIGN) (DS#, DESIGNER,
  MANUFAC_COST, DRG (DOMAIN_IS
  SET OF C(DRAWING)))
C(DRAWING) (DR#, CAD_SYSTEM, DS#,
  PICTURE (DOMAIN_IS C(IMAGE)))
C(IMAGE) ()

Figure 2 shows the integrated schema in the OO data definition. It is straightforward to represent the integrated schema using IKOODM, which will be shown two sections after. A double arrow on a CC-hierarchy indicates the direction of an one-to-many relationship. The processing of a query referencing the integrated schema is being investigated. A query processing method is outlined using an example two sections after.

INTERFACE TO HIERARCHICAL DATABASES

Currently, the interface between the OO database and the hierarchical database is made in two steps: the OO database to/from the relational database and the relational database to/from the hierarchical database (the actual transformation is not between databases but between data models). The interface between the OO database and the relational database was discussed in the previous section.

For the interface between the relational database and the hierarchical database, we specifically investigate the relational query language SQL interface to the hierarchical DBMS IMS. IMS is based on a hierarchical data model and uses DL/1 as a data manipulation language. Two major issues of the interface are (1) the translation of hierarchical data definition to an equivalent relational data definition and (2) the translation of an SQL statement to an equivalent program processable by IMS. Another important issue is the automatic selection of IMS secondary indexes. The secondary index is an integral part of data management. The secondary index management of IMS is quite different from that of the relational DBMS. An SQL interface to IMS has been implemented and the performance of he interface has been tested using various IMS databases (Chung et al., 1993).

PROTOTYPE ARCHITECTURE

In this section, we describe the architecture of a prototype, Federated Information Management System (FIMS). In our prototype, data are stored in relational, object-oriented, and hierarchical DBMSs.

FIMS Architecture

FIMS provides the users with an illusion of a globally integrated system using either a single OO query language or a graphical interface. FIMS architecture is shown in Figure 3. Major components of FIMS are: Query Browser and Editor (QuBE), Distributed Information Manager (DIM), Local Information Manager (LIM), and Knowledge-Based Manager (KBM). We use IKOODM as the common data model to represent the unified view.

Figure 3: FIMS Architecture

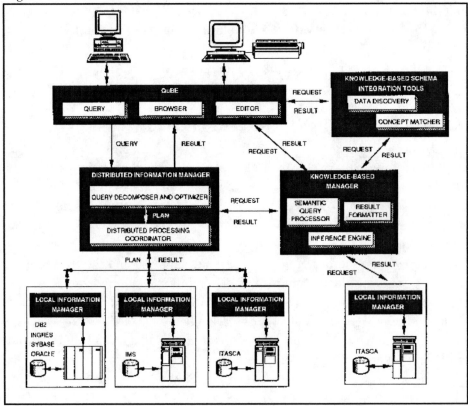

(1) Query Browser and Editor (QuBE)

QuBE supports a uniform and seamless interface for querying, browsing, and editing data and metadata. Users can browse, edit, and query through all IKOODM classes using a directed graph metaphor. Each node in the graph represents a class and each link represents a relationship between classes. The editing mechanism is used by the DBA or the Knowledge-Based Schema Integration Tools (KBSIT, see the next subsection) to generate and update IKOODM classes. The query mechanism supports both OO queries, and class requests which are transformed to an internal language (OO query language). QuBE is developed using the C++/Interviews object-oriented graphics which is built on top of X-windows. (see (Williamson et al., 1990) for more details).

(2) Distributed Information Manager (DIM)

DIM decomposes the query sent by QuBE. DIM interfaces with KBM to extract information in the data structure and the enterprise semantic classes for query decomposition. The Query Decomposer And Optimizer decomposes the query into a set of subqueries expressed in an OO query language. The Distributed Processing Coordinator sends the subqueries to LIMs.

(3) Local Information Manager (LIM)

LIM executes a local query autonomously and interfaces with a local DBMS. During local query processing, LIM may need to communicate with other LIMs to receive or send the data. Each LIM has its own controller to coordinate the query processing. LIM also translates a subquery expressed in the OO query language into a query or a program in a data manipulation language used by the local DBMS.

(4) Knowledge Based Manager (KBM)

As discussed before, we used IKOODM to represent classes in the unified view, the relationships among the classes, and the data distribution. The information is itself another database. Therefore, a database management system is required to store and manage the information. We choose an OODBMS as the underlying DBMS because the OO data model provides a better fit to our IKOODM. We have chosen ITASCA OODBMS in our prototype; however, any OODBMS with comparable functionality can be used. KBM provides a common interface to ITASCA to support requests from other modules: DIM, QuBE, and KBSIT. It also supports integrity constraints during update of IKOODM. The semantic query processor in KBM provides query formulation capability when requested through the graphical interface. Based on the intent of the user's request, it automatically traverses though IKOODM classes to build a query and sends it to DIM.

There are two types of requests: retrieval and update. DIM sends a request to KBM to retrieve information about IKOODM classes for query decomposition and optimization. The browser mechanism in QuBE interfaces with KBM to traverse through IKOODM classes for displaying purpose. KBSIT sends both retrieval and update requests to KBM during schema integration.

Semantics Issues in Schema Integration

In this subsection, we describe our basic approach to handling semantics in schema. There are several major semantics problems with the schema integration process (Larson et al., 1989):

Schema Semantics

The knowledge about the semantic relationships of local information management systems is usually represented implicitly or explicitly in the data model and in the applications. Four major input sources that can be used for acquiring the relationships are the users, the database administrator (DBA), the database schema and the data. It is not feasible in practice to gather all DBAs, the original designers, and the users from different organizations together at a particular time and place. In addition, documentation of the database specifications is missing most of the time. The lack of knowledge of the underlying local information systems makes the integration process difficult.

Schema Incompatibilities

Another problem with schema integration is that each local schema is designed independently and tailored for its own domain. For example, two different data structure might represent the same data; the same field names might represent different data; there may be different unit representation of the same data, etc. Advanced data modeling techniques and transformation algorithms need to be designed to integrate the structure.

Automatic Tools

Manually integrating the separated schemas is an error prone process and because of its complexity, it is not practical to keep track of the relationships, the data structure, and different rules or special cases employed during the schema integration process.

Research progress in (Garcia-Solaco et al., 1995; Larson et al., 1989; Yu et al., 1990) points out that success in schema integration depends on understanding the semantics of the schema components (e.g., attributes, relations, entity sets, relationship sets), and the ability to capture and reason with the semantics. Our approach is to determine and explicitly represent attribute relationships and schema interrelationships in IKOODM. Concepts in the object-oriented approach such as complex objects, methods, and inheritance provide better features for representing the relationships than other approaches. Moreover, the ability to use either declarative or procedural languages as appropriate is helpful to solve semantic and structural incompatibilities. Case-based reasoning techniques are being explored to partially automate the schema integration process.

The solution to the schema integration problem cannot and will not be solved by one algorithm or some representation scheme. Rather, a system approach that uses a set of tools to assist the database administrator/user in building and managing the information is the best solution. We are currently defining and prototyping Knowledge-Based Schema Integration Tools which is a set of tools that are required for the schema integration process. In our approach, schema integration is composed of three major phases as follows:

(1) Schema Definition Phase

All local data objects (i.e., relation or segment) and methods that are used to interface with the underlying DBMSs are defined in the object storage layer of IKOODM.

(2) Data Discovery Phase

In a database environment, the data, the queries, the schemas, the users, and the DBA's knowledge are the major resources which can be used to identify the semantics of an attribute in a class. The goal of this phase is to first identify the semantics of an attribute and its relationship with other attributes. Second, a representation schema is needed to represent this semantics. The first goal can be achieved manually using the above resources. Our research focuses on partially automating this process. Common concepts, concept hierarchies, and aggregate concept hierarchies are used to achieve the second goal (Yu et al., 1990). The hierarchies will clarify the meaning of an attribute that is usually expressed more syntactically in the database. This phase will give us a richer semantic view associated with each schema attribute. The hierarchies are currently not expressed in IKOODM. The relationships between classes are expressed using the data structure layer.

(3) Schema Reclassification Phase

Concept hierarchies produced by the second phase may be reclassified when integrating new schema objects to form a unified view (enterprise layer). The reclassification depends upon the results from identifying the similarities and differences of schema attributes. A similarity function algorithm is currently under development for this purpose (Yu et al., 1990).

In addition, we are using the case-based reasoning provided by our Modular Knowledge Acquisition Tools (M-KAT) (Dolan, 1989) to capture the schema integration problems and solutions. M-KAT is a set of automated knowledge acquisition tools for capturing problem-solving expertise. Each example of a schema integration problem-solving is a case. The schema integration process involves taking a concept hierarchy acquired from the data discovery phase and encoding them as input specifications. Transformation heuristics for schema reclassification such as generalization and specialization are encoded as rules, and are attached with the concept hierarchies. Output specification is the suggested enterprise class. As schema integration proceeds, more and more problem-solving cases are acquired and stored in the M-KAT knowledge-base when approved by the DBA. Each case can be used to help in the integration of other similar schemas. By applying the learning techniques, we want to achieve two goals: (1) to partially automate certain kinds of reclassification and (2) to have the system learn more knowledge about the concept hierarchies from various schema integration cases. We are currently in the process of identifying different sets of tools to partially automate the processing steps for the above three phases.

AN EXAMPLE

We present an example which illustrates the IKOODM modeling and the interface to heterogeneous databases in an OO paradigm. In particular, we will show the retrieval of non-conventional data which is difficult without using an OO approach. This example also shows the object identifier (OID) based retrieval which is different from the conventional value-based retrieval. Since the OO query language is not standardized, we will describe the query processing informally using an SQL-like OO query syntax.

Suppose CAR_BODY_DESIGN is a relation stored under a relational DBMS at Site 1, TRUCK_BODY_DESIGN is a root segment under IMS at Site 2, and DRAWING and IMAGE are classes under an OODBMS at Site 3 with the following definitions:

    CAR_BODY_DESIGN (DS#, DESIGNER,
      MANUFAC_COST, DS_DATE)
    TRUCK_BODY_DESIGN (DS#, DESIGNER,
      MANUFAC_COST, DS_DATE)
    DRAWING (DR#, ENGINEER,
      CAD_SYSTEM, PANEL_NAME, DS#,
      PICTURE (DOMAIN_IS IMAGE))
    IMAGE ()

Using the method described three sections before, the above local data definitions are translated to the base class definitions as follows:

    C(CAR_BODY_DESIGN) (DS#, DESIGNER,
      MANUFAC_COST, DS_DATE, DRG
      (DOMAIN_IS SET OF C(DRAWING)))
    C(TRUCK_BODY_DESIGN) (DS#,
      DESIGNER, MANUFAC_COST,
      DS_DATE, DRG (DOMAIN_IS SET
      OF C(DRAWING)))
    C(DRAWING) (DR#, ENGINEER,
      CAD_SYSTEM, PANEL_NAME, DS#,
      PICTURE (DOMAIN_IS C(IMAGE)))
    C(IMAGE) ()

As a representative of defining a class, the creation of an abstract class VEHICLE_BODY_DESIGN from the base classes C(CAR_BODY_DESIGN) and C(TRUCK_BODY_DESIGN) is described below.

    DEFINE CLASS
    VEHICLE_BODY_DESIGN
    Internal Structure:
    <DS# int>, <DESIGNER char 25>,
    <MANUFAC_COST float>,
    <DS_DATE date>,
    <DRG set of C(DRAWING)>
    Semantic Link:

To-classes: C(CAR_BODY_DESIGN),
  C(TRUCK_BODY_DESIGN),
  C(DRAWING)>
Declaration method: Generalization
  (C(CAR_BODY_DESIGN),
  C(TRUCK_BODY_DESIGN))
  Association
  (VEHICLE_BODY_DESIGN,
  C(DRAWING))
Derivation Structure:
Manipulation method:
  Generalization-Decomposition
  (VEHICLE_BODY_DESIGN)
  Association-Decomposition
  (VEHICLE_BODY_DESIGN,
  C(DRAWING))
Data distribution:
  {C(CAR_BODY_DESIGN)
  fragmented at S1 in RDBMS x,
  C(TRUCK_BODY_DESIGN)
  fragmented at S2 in IMS}

The classes in the IKOODM layers are shown in Figure 4. Consider a user request to find OID's of the DRAWING such that the name of the panel is a quarter panel and the manufacturing cost of the vehicle body which contains the panel is over 150. An SQL-like OO query of the request is as follows:

VEHICLE_DRAWING_OID =
  SELECT OID
  FROM C(DRAWING)
  WHERE PANEL_NAME =
    'quarter panel' AND
  (VEHICLE_BODY_DESIGN.DRG
  MANUFAC_COST > 150)

where, VEHICLE_BODY_DESIGN.DRG is a composite attribute representing a CC-hierarchy between VEHICLE_BODY_DESIGN and C(DRAWING).

QuBE sends this query to DIM. Since VEHICLE_BODY_DESIGN has two subclasses C(CAR_BODY_DESIGN) and C(TRUCK_BODY_DESIGN) which correspond to base classes, the Query Decomposer And Optimizer in DIM decomposes the query to the following subqueries using the Manipulation method Generalization-Decomposition:

Q1: CAR_DRAWING_OID =

Figure 4: A Unified View in IKOODM

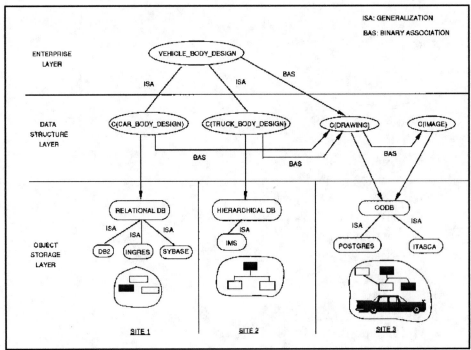

```
    SELECT OID
    FROM  C(DRAWING)
    WHERE PANEL_NAME =
     'quarter panel' AND
    (C(CAR_BODY_DESIGN).DRG
     MANUFAC_COST > 150)
Q2: TRUCK_DRAWING_OID =
    SELECT OID
    FROM  C(DRAWING)
    WHERE PANEL_NAME =
     'quarter panel' AND
    (C(TRUCK_BODY_DESIGN).DRG
     MANUFAC_COST > 150)
```

At this time, the Query Decomposer And Optimizer establishes the following merging relationship:

```
    VEHICLE_DRAWING_OID =
    CAR_DRAWING_OID U
    TRUCK_DRAWING_OID
```

where U is the set union operator.

The subqueries Q1 and Q2 are further decomposed by locations, using the Manipulation method Association-Decomposition in C(CAR_BODY_DESIGN) and C(TRUCK_BODY_DESIGN), as follows where Qij is the subquery of Qi at Site j:

Q11: DS#_SITE1 =
   SELECT DS#
   FROM C(CAR_BODY_DESIGN)
   WHERE MANUFAC_COST >
      150

Q13: CAR_DRAWING_OID =
   SELECT OID
   FROM C(DRAWING)
   WHERE PANEL_NAME =
   'quarter panel' AND
    DS# IN DS#_SITE1

where IN is an operator testing the membership. DS# IN DS#_SITE1 implies that a semijoin can be used to process Q1 and that qualified DS# from Site 1 is transferred to Site 3. Similarly,

Q22: DS#_SITE2 =
   SELECT DS#
   FROM (TRUCK_BODY_DESIGN)
   WHERE MANUFAC_COST >
      150

Q23: TRUCK_DRAWING_OID =
   SELECT OID
   FROM C(DRAWING)
   WHERE PANEL_NAME =
   'quarter panel' AND
    DS# IN DS#_SITE2

The Distributed Processing Coordinator in DIM sends the subqueries to LIMs. Each LIM translates the subqueries to queries in the query languages used by local DBMSs. Q11 is already in SQL. The only translation is the change of the global definition C(CAR_BODY_DESIGN) to the local definition CAR_BODY_DESIGN. As explained previously, Q22 is first translated to a relational query, which Q22 already is. Then, using the procedure described in (Chung et al., 1993), the relational query is translated to a DL/1 program, which is submitted to IMS. Since Q13 and Q23 are OO queries submitted to an OODBMS, the only translation is the change from C(DRAWING) to DRAWING. LIM also provides an interface to a local DBMS.

The variable VEHICLE_DRAWING_OID contains the OID's of the drawing requested by the user. Suppose VIEWER is the OID (that is, the OID is in the variable VIEWER) of an object whose class defines a method PRESENT which contains an image preview program. For any OID X from VEHICLE_DRAWING_OID, the following message displays the picture of a selected panel:

PRESENT VIEWER (PICTURE X)

In this case, the method PRESENT performs the following: (1) create a temporary bit map file from an object whose OID is X.PICTURE, (2) invoke an image preview program with the temporary file as an input, (3) determine the location and size of an window using data in an object whose OID is VIEWER, and (4) delete the temporary file. As shown above in (PICTURE X), messages are also supported to retrieve the value of each attribute of an object.

This example shows how a user can identify and view the pictures of particular panels of certain vehicles using data distributed in heterogeneous databases.

CONCLUSIONS

A model and methods were developed using an object-oriented paradigm for interoperability of diverse information management systems. An integrated knowledge-object-oriented data model was established to provide a uniform view of heterogeneous databases which represents both structure and behavior. The model synthesizes concepts from knowledge representation, object-oriented programming, and semantic data models. The methods were derived for translating data definitions and queries between object-oriented databases and relational databases and between relational databases and hierarchical databases. Consequently, users and applications can access the three types of databases through a unified view and using a standard query language.

An object-oriented approach allows us to handle traditional data and non-traditional data such as images in a uniform way as well as to identify and explicitly represent the semantics in the schema. In addition, the encapsulation and the IKOODM layer structure that uses the class hierarchy promote the code reusability. Therefore, the ability to describe both structure and behavior in a unified view not only accommodates the access to heterogeneous databases but also facilitates the development of a heterogeneous database management system in the software engineering point of view. However, the features of the object- oriented data model and language are still being developed, thus the lack of the standard of the model and language is currently a problem. The architecture of a prototype was established and the prototype interfacing the relational database, object-oriented database and the hierarchical database is being developed.

The research in the following areas is necessary in the future in order to provide interoperability more effectively and to a wider range of information management systems:

- Since the object-relational database system(ORDB) attracts a considerably attention recently, it is desirable to interface ORDB.
- The distributed update problem has not been completely solved when it is coupled with recovery in a multi-user environment.
- A knowledge-based approach is promising to develop a tool for automating the schema integration process as much as possible.

ACKNOWLEDGMENTS

The authors wish to thank the editor, an associate editor, and a reviewer for helpful comments and suggestions. This research was supported in part by the grant from the Korea Science and Engineering Foundation with the grant number KOSEF 95-0100-23-04-3.

REFERENCES

Ahmed R. (1991). The Pegasus heterogeneous multidatabase system. *IEEE Computer*, 24(12), 19-27.

Bertino, E., Negri, M., Pelagatti, G. and Sbattela, L. (1989). Integration of heterogeneous applications through an object-oriented interface. *Information Systems*, 14(5), 407-420.

Bukhres, O. (1993). InterBase: An execution environment for heterogeneous software systems. *IEEE Computer*, 26(8), 57-69.

Butterworth, P., Otis, A. and Stein, J. (1991). The gemstone object database System. *Communications of the ACM*, 34(10), 64-77.

Chung, C. (1990). DATAPLEX: An access to heterogeneous distributed databases. *Communications of the ACM*, 33(1), 70-80. (corrigendum, 33(4), 459, 1990.)

Chung, C. and McCloskey, K. (1993). Access to indexed hierarchical databases using a relational query language. *IEEE Transactions on Knowledge and Data Engineering*, 5(1), 155-161.

Dao, S. and Templeton, M. (1987). Strategies for accessing distributed data. *Minnowbrook workshop on database machines and AI*. New York.

Deux, O. (1991). The O2 system. *Communications of the ACM*, 34(10), 34-48.

Dolan, C., Cuda, T., Goldman, S. and Keisey, D. (1989). Automatic knowledge acquisition using case-based reasoning tools. *Hughes Research Lab. Technical Report*.

Garcia-Solaco, M., Saltor, F. and Castellanos, M. (1995). A structure based schema integration methodology. *Proceedings of 11th International Conference on Data Engineering*, 505-512.

Hurson, A., Pakzad, S. and Cheng, J. (1993). Object-oriented database management systems: evolution and performance issues. *IEEE Computer*, 26(2), 48-60.

Kaufman, K., Michalski, R. and Kerschberg, L. (1991). Mining for knowledge in databases, goals and general descriptions of the INLEN system. *Knowledge Discovery in Databases*, 449-462. Cambridge, MA: MIT.

Kim, W. (1990). Architecture of the ORION next-generation database system. *IEEE Transactions on Knowledge and Data Engineering*, 2(1), 109-124.

Lamb, C., Landis, G., Orenstein, J. A. and Weinreb, D. (1991). The objectstore system. *Communications of the ACM*, 34(10), 50-63.

Larson, J., Navathe, S. and Elmasri, R. (1989). A theory of attribute equivalence in databases with applications to schema integration. *IEEE Transactions on Software Engineering*, 15(4), 449-463.

Litwin, W., Mark, L. and Roussopoulos, N. (1990). Interoperability of multiple autonomous databases. *ACM Computing Surveys*, 22(3), 267-293.

Qian, X. (1995). Query interoperation among object-oriented and relational databases. *Proceedings of 11th International Conference on Data Engineering*, 271-278.

Reddy, M. P., Reddy, P. G. and Gupta, A. (1994). A methodology for integration of heterogeneous databases. *IEEE Transactions on Knowledge and Data Engineering*, 6(6), 920-933.

Soloviev, V. (1992). An overview of three commercial object-oriented database management systems: ONTOS, objectstore, and O2. *ACM SIGMOD Record*, 21(1), 93-104.

Thomas, G. (1990). Heterogeneous distributed database systems for production use. *ACM Computing Surveys*, 22(3), 237-266.

Williamson, R., Goldman, S. and Dao, S. (1990). Query browser and editor design document. *Hughes Research Lab., Technical Report*.

Yu, C., Sun, W., Dao, S. and Keirsey, D. (1990). Determining relationships among attributes for interoperability of multidatabase systems. *Workshop on Multidatabases and Semantic Interoperability*, 10-15. Tulsa, OK. November 2-4.

Chapter 17

A Recursive Approach to Software Development

Shirley A. Becker
Florida Institute of Technology, USA

Alan A. Jorgensen
Advanced Engineering Technology, Melbourne, FL, USA

Researchers and practitioners alike agree that the waterfall approach to software development results in poor quality software systems. Unfortunately, the waterfall approach is inherently used in almost all of today's development efforts resulting in system failures. The problem lies in the forward, linear development effort that produces inconsistent and incorrect specifications, designs, and code artifacts. It is proposed in this paper that a recursive software development process be used as a means of managing the complexity of today's software systems. The recursive approach has the flexibility needed to perform development activities in any order to ensure that system requirements are met.

INTRODUCTION

Since the recognition that a "coding and debugging" process doesn't produce defect-free software systems, software development process models have continued to evolve. The models range from a simplistic, sequential set of work activities as defined in the waterfall approach to more sophisticated cyclic work activities as provided by the incremental and spiral models. These software process models include a set of development phases that are typically performed in a predefined order based on top-down decomposition.

Previously published in *Challenges of Information Technology Management in the 21ˢᵗ Century*, edited by Mehdi Khosrow-Pour. Copyright © 2000, Idea Group Publishing.

Figure 1: Waterfall Model

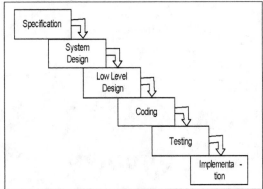

Figure 2: Incremental Development Model

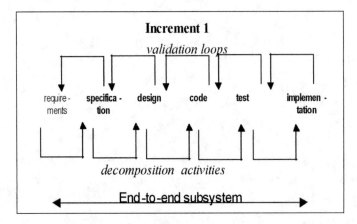

The waterfall software development process model was the first attempt at formalizing the development process by identifying an ordered set of work phases (Royce, 1970). The sequential nature of performing these phases, as shown in Figure 1, resulted in missed requirements, incorrect and incomplete designs, and various defects uncovered late in the development process, among other problems. As a result, the waterfall approach is now considered an unacceptable if not an obsolete approach to software development because of its missing feedback loops. However, it laid the groundwork for developing more rigorous process models for software development.

The incremental development process model supposedly addressed the weaknesses of the waterfall model by decomposing a system into increments each of which is completed using a set of development activities. Each increment, as shown in Figure 2, may be viewed as a fully functional "end-to-end" component that can be readily integrated into previous increments. A major drawback to this approach is that the decomposition of a system into increments may not be a straightforward process as it may be difficult to identify and prioritize "self-contained" subsystems (Sorensen, 1995).

The spiral process model of software development made risk an inherent component of an iterative development process through the introduction of prototyping (Boehm, 1988). Prototyping is used to minimize the risk of misunderstood or missing requirements and to gain insight into the technical aspects of the system under development. Too often the prototype, developed using a waterfall approach, is implemented even though there are missing, incomplete, or incorrect parts.

Though industry has advanced from adhoc development practices to more rigorous software development process models, there is still room for improvement. The incremental and spiral approaches helped us recognize the need for structured yet flexible process models for software development. Unfortunately, these models still fall short of providing the means for developing high-quality software systems.

In this chapter, we describe a software process model that addresses several weaknesses inherent in the popular software process models. Section 2 describes a shift in the way that we view software development. To support this enhanced view of software development, a recursive software process model is described in Section 3. The chapter concludes with future research directions.

CHANGING OUR MENTAL MODEL

Top-down decomposition, which is inherent in all the popular development process models, has established the paradigm for intellectually managing the requirements. Unfortunately, when top-down decomposition is used as a basis for development work, there is a tendency to develop "isolated" lower level designs

Figure 3: Part of a Function Hierarchy

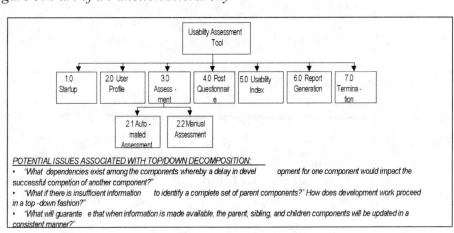

Figure 4: "Dependent Composition" of System (S)

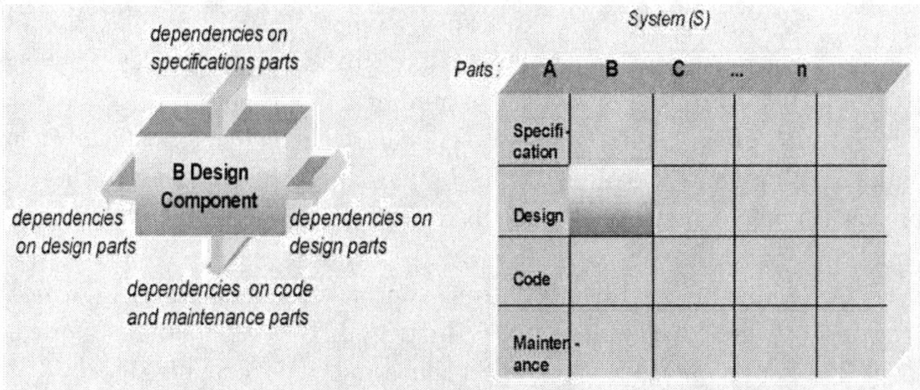

- System S is a composition of all of its parts including their dependencies on one another.
- Design part B cannot exist independe   ntly of any other part.
- System requirements are not met until all parts are successfully developed.

as newly discovered design components or modifications to existing ones are not reflected in parent and sibling components. This mental model of software decomposition suffers from the waterfall approach of forward, linear development with little or no modifications to previous work. This may be the result of project pressures, poor or missing information management, lack of an enforced process, or the result of other organizational impediments. Figure 3 shows a function hierarchy representation of top-down decomposition with a list of potential problems.

There is a natural order to development work that should be driven by a common understanding of system requirements in conjunction with development goals. This natural order is based on a mutual dependence that exists among all software parts such that there can be no "whole" software system when components are missing, incomplete, or incorrect. In addition, each part is a system in itself comprised of other parts that are mutually dependent and make up a whole. No system part can be viewed in isolation of other parts, as it does not exist independently of them. This concept of "dependent composition" is shown in Figure 4 where dependencies among parts are multidimensional (though shown here in a three dimensional form for illustrative purposes).

This inherent complexity requires a mental shift in the way that the software development process is viewed. What is needed is a more effective approach to understanding software behavior than is traditionally offered by a hierarchical decomposition of separate software parts. A recursive expansion process is proposed that is based on creativity and critical thinking given what is known about the system at any given point in time.

Figure 5: The Recursive Software Development Process

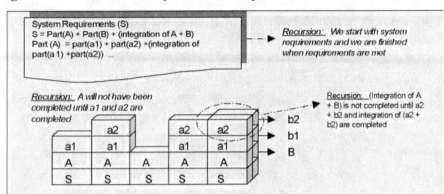

Figure 6: An Illustration of a Missing Constraint

The design for a running sales average is presented in Mills, et al., (1986, p. 11) in box structure notation whereby a set of inputs results in a predictable output. In theory, the correctness of the design holds. In a real-world environment, the design will fail because constraints on the application are not part of the design.

The running average is computed by: $R(i) = \dfrac{S(i) + S(i-1) + \ldots + S(i-11)}{12}$

Where: S represents an input (called a stimulus), R the output (called a response), and i, the index representing the order of arrival of the inputs.

When this program is implemented, the storage set aside for the running sum will overflow when submitted two or more inputs that, when added together, are larger than the maximum allowed integer. A constraints is needed as part of the design: (if $S(i-k) > MaxSum - R(i)$ then *error*.) To make this design complete, MaxSum becomes part of the input history, and an error message becomes part of the output set.

RECURSIVE SOFTWARE PROCESS MODEL

Recursion is the method in which a problem is solved by reducing it to smaller (simpler) cases of the same problem (Kruse & Ryba, 1999; Rogers, 1967, p.6).

A software process model is described that focuses on recursive expansion of specification, design, code and other components driven by clearly defined development goals (e.g., time-to-market, number of defects). The recursive approach is a mental shift from the way other software process models define the development process. In this approach, development work starts with the whole system in terms of system requirements, and finishes with the implemented system, as system requirements are met.

The recursive development process, illustrated in Figure 5, shows the complexity of software development as each part is not complete until its requirements are met, and requirements may change as dependencies on other parts are discovered. In this figure, it is shown that the system requirements are formalized in specifications and designs (parts A and B), which in turn will be expanded into more granular specification, design, and code artifacts (a_1, a_2, ..., a_n and b_1, b_2, ..., b_n). A recursive process effectively manages this complexity because of its flexibility in performing specification, design, code, maintenance, and other activities not in a pre-defined order but intuitively as system requirements become known.

It is important to note that this conceptualization requires a new way of thinking about completion criteria for a particular development activity. Often times, completion criteria are used to determine when a specification, design, code or other artifact is completed. A false sense of closure may be promoted because "completed" artifacts are stored and seldom updated when missing, incorrect, or incomplete requirements are discovered at a later date. The waterfall approach is implicitly being followed to develop these software systems.

It is inherent in the recursive software process that each part is complete and correct when the whole system is complete and correct. Completion criteria are useful in providing insight into missing or incorrect system behavior but must be viewed as feedback tools and not closure mechanisms. Given the number of dependencies that exist among the system parts, it is virtually impossible to conclude that work on any "one part" is finished until the system as a whole is implemented.

What is needed is a set of "readiness criteria" driven by the development goals in order to determine when to move on to the next development activity. Readiness criteria may include traditional completion and correctness checks, but the emphasis shifts from a sense of closure with this phase of work to one of expanding upon it. This approach provides a conducive environment for discovering gaps in our specifications, designs, and code that need to be filled in before the system is implemented.

Table 1: An Extraction of Quality Goals for Software Development IEEE Standard 830-1993

Goal:	Description
Correct	All artifacts produced are correct in terms of capturing the "true" requirements of the user.
Precise & Unambiguous	Each artifact can be directly expanded into granular details without interpretation.
Complete	Each artifact captures the necessary and sufficient behavior.
Consistent	Each artifact captures the same behavior as its abstracted counter parts. There is no conflicting terms or contradictory behavior.
Modifiable & Maintainable	Each artifact is supported by dictionary definitions, search mechanisms, and naming conventions.
Holistic	Each artifact encompasses the whole system in terms of its relationships with other components (e.g., interfaces).
Tolerant	Each artifact must be tolerant of mistakes made (e.g., incomplete, inconsistent) due to the size and complexity of the application under development.
Understand-able	All parties using the artifact can understand it or have supporting artifacts to assist in understanding it (e.g., repository).

Readiness Criteria

In order to understand what readiness criteria means for a development activity, we need to understand what drives the development process. Most everyone would agree that high quality is an aspiration for all software projects yet few of us would agree on what "quality" really means. Though quality is typically inferred to mean "zero-defect", there may be other goals that are as important as or may take precedence. Time-to-market, for example, may have a higher priority than zero-defects in order to maintain a competitive advantage. Quality may also translate into customer satisfaction, usability, and understandability, among other goals (refer to Table 1 for a comprehensive list of development goals).

Readiness criteria associated with the *modifiable and maintainable* goal, for example, might mean that a checklist is used during a team review (along with other readiness criteria) to determine whether a particular artifact has followed naming conventions, maintained version control, and is readily accessible in the database along with all supporting artifacts (links to parent, child, sibling parts), among others.

Time-to-market goals, for example, may dictate that after a certain amount of functionality has specified, the design and coding activities are initiated. The time-to-market readiness criteria may be based on a schedule of work with tollgate or milestone dates that specify when work activities are initiated, expanded or stopped.

Representation of Software Complexity

A readiness criterion for determining whether system requirements are met is the inclusion of all inputs, outputs, computation, and real-world constraints. Many common software problems arise when system constraints have not been included in the software system (refer to Whittaker & Jorgensen (1999) for a discussion on software failures). A software part and its dependencies on other parts can only be fully understood in terms of its inputs, outputs, computations, and constraints.

Four types of constraints have been identified by Jorgensen (1999) that are integral in the completion of the system as a whole and in terms of each specification, design, and code component. The four constraints are:

- *Input Constraint* – Each input that is received by the system is constrained by a range of valid data that would result in a correct (or predictable) output. A designed input constraint, for example, would check parameter data to ensure that it falls within an acceptable range.
- *Output Constraints* – Each output generated by the system is bound by the constraints on the receiving media, such as field width, and required output precision and range, among others. These constraints need to be taken into consideration in order to ensure that valid output is presented to the user (e.g., display data is not truncated) or is passed to a calling routine.

- *Computation Constraints* – Computation constraints ensure that the inputs and new data are properly constrained in order to produce valid computational results. Without such constraints, the stored data may become corrupted and/or unpredictable outputs generated resulting in system failure or inaccurate results.
- *Data Constraints* - Data constraints validate the consistency of new data with system requirements and system constraints as well as check for corrupted data from previous computations.

Figure 6, for example, shows the computation of a running average design that fails due to a missing computation constraint. Without such constraints, a system part is guaranteed to be incomplete producing a range of unpredictable failures upon implementation.

There are many specification, design, and coding techniques that provide a notation for inputs, outputs, and functionality. But what these software techniques are missing is explicit representation of system constraints on inputs, outputs, data, and computation. The inclusion of these constraints in software development artifacts is essential in ensuring system requirements are met. Thus, constraint specification and design become an integral part of the recursive development process.

CONCLUSION AND FUTURE RESEARCH

The recursive approach to software development holds great promise as a means of developing high-quality software systems. This approach focuses on recursive development such that a system and its parts are completed when system requirements have been met. This requires a mental model of software as a sum of its parts and their dependencies with other parts. None of the other software development process models provide the flexibility needed to support this system view.

Our research efforts are focused on the use of this approach for more complex software systems with an emphasis on developing tools to support its use. The Goal, Question, Metrics (GQM) is being studied as a viable tool for establishing goals and readiness criteria to manage work. Self-validating code is being studied as another tool for ensuring that system constraints are inherently part of the code artifacts.

REFERENCES

Boehm, B. (1988). A spiral model of software development and enhancement. *IEEE Computer*, May, 61-72.

IEEE Standard 830-1993. (1994). Recommended Practice for Software Requirements Specification. *Standards Collection on Software Engineering*, New York: IEEE Press.

Jorgensen, A. (1999). Software design based on operational modes. *Dissertation*, Computer Science, Florida Institute of Technology.

Kruse, R. and Ryba, A. (1999). *Data Structures and Program Design in C++*. Upper Saddle River, NJ: Prentice Hall.

Mills, H., Linger, R. and Hevner, A. (1986). *Principles of Information Systems Analysis and Design*. New York: Academic Press, Inc.

Rogers, Jr., H. (1967). *Theory of Recursive Functions and Effective Computability*. New York: McGraw-Hill.

Royce, W. (1970). Managing the development of large software systems: Concepts and techniques. *WESCON*, August; reprinted in *Ninth International Conference on Software Engineering*, 328-338. IEEE Computer Society Press 1987.

Sorensen, R. (1995). A comparison of software development methodologies. *CrossTalk,* January, 12-18.

Whittaker, J. and Jorgenson, A. (1999). Why software fails. *ACM Software Engineering Notes.*

Chapter 18

Adding Alternative Access Paths to Abstract Data Types

Xavier Franch and Jordi Marco
Universitat Politècnica de Catalunya, Spain

We present in this paper a proposal for developing efficient programs in the abstract data type (ADT) programming framework, keeping the modular structure of programs and without violating the information hiding principle. The proposal focuses in the concept of "shortcut" as an efficient way of accessing to data, alternative to the access by means of the primitive operations of the ADT. We develop our approach in a particular ADT, a store of items. We define shortcuts in a formal manner, using algebraic specifications interpreted with initial semantics, and so the result has a well-defined meaning and fits in the ADT framework. Efficiency is assured with an adequate representation of the type, which provides O(1) access to items in the store without penalising the primitive operations of the ADT.

INTRODUCTION

Modular programming with abstract data types (ADT) (Liskov & Guttag, 1986) is a widespread methodology for programming in the large. In this field, it is crucial the distinction between the specification and the implementation of ADTs, which results in the existence of different modules for them and which can be summarised with the information hiding principle: an ADT must be used just regarding the properties stated in the specification, without any knowledge of the characteristics of its implementation, which remains hidden. This principle simplifies the relationships between modules and supports the development of programs, because it is easier to code them, to test them, to reuse them and to maintain them.

However, the information hiding principle collides, often dramatically, with a very usual requirement on programs: their efficiency, mainly characterised by their execution time. The reason is that the access to a data structure implementing an

Previously published in *Challenges of Information Technology Management in the 21ˢᵗ Century*, edited by Mehdi Khosrow-Pour. Copyright © 2000, Idea Group Publishing.

ADT must follow the properties that define it, which were stated in an abstract manner without taking into account the problems related to its subsequent implementation (as it must be). In case of a context using ADTs with strong efficiency requirements (for instance, program analysis tools construction, system programming, geometric computing and combinatorial computing), their full reusability can become impossible and it may be necessary to carry out many modifications to fit it to this context; even more, such modifications can be so important to decide throwing away the implementation and developing a new one.

This conflict between efficiency and modularity is a well known problem in the ADT framework, recognised as such in the most important textbooks on data types and data structures (Aho, Hopcroft & Ullman, 1983; Horowitz & Sahni, 1994; Cormen, Leiserson & Rivest, 1990), and solved in many cases sacrificing modularity to achieve efficiency. Fortunately, there are many widespread ADT-libraries that have coped the problem by incorporating the notion of *location* (i.e., a cursor —an integer referring to an array position— or a pointer) in ADT interfaces. This is the case for instance of STL (Musser & Saini, 1996) and LEDA (Mehlhorn & Naher, 1999), both of them providing a similar solution to the problem: when a new element is stored in the data structure, its location is returned as part of the result, being later usable as parameter in other operations (removal, lookup and modification). Unfortunately, these libraries present some drawbacks due to the fact that they are designed with the concept of location incorporated in the component from the very beginning. Therefore, the implementations that can be used for the ADT are often restricted to a fixed set (which makes these libraries not flexible enough), the behaviour is less clear (locations and elements appear at the same level) and some classical low-level problems appear (for instance, meaningless uses of cursors and pointers).

Our goal in this paper is to define a general framework to reconcile both criteria, efficiency and modularity, obtaining thus efficient programs reusing existing implementations of ADTs without any modification, and following the information hiding principle. The proposal is based on the definition of an alternative way to access data, that we call *shortcuts*. Shortcuts are added to existing ADTs in a systematic manner, obtaining new ADTs (compatible with the previous ones) that incorporate these alternative access paths. Then, the users of the new ADT will be able to access the data therein not only by means of the operations introduced in the original specification (that are the ones defining the underlying mathematical model), but also using other new ones which follow these alternative paths, when the use of the former operations is considered unacceptably expensive. We are going to develop the proposal on a particular ADT, a *STORE* of items, although the conclusions of our work can be applied to any other container-like ADT, i.e. those ones arranging collections of items with an arbitrary (but completely defined) policy. More details can be found at (Marco & Franch, 1997).

The ADT *STORE* is presented in sections 2 and 3, without and with short-cuts, respectively. Section 4 proposes the model of stores with shortcuts, while section 5 shows the implementation. Finally, section 6 gives the conclusions and some future work.

THE ABSTRACT DATA TYPE *STORE*

From now on, we focus on the study of a particular ADT (however, it should remain clear that the results are valid any other container-like ADT, see for instance [Marco & Franch, 1997]), the ADT *STORE*, defined as a collection of items, with operations of insertion, removal and retrieval of items. Just to fix a particular definition of stores, we use a short version of the one defined by Booch in (Booch, 1987), although this selection is arbitrary. Items are pairs <key, value>, and so the removal and the retrieval are key-based; keys must provide a comparison operation, *eq*. As stated in Booch (1997), it is an error trying to remove or to retrieve items using undefined keys, and also trying to insert a pair with a key that is already therein.

We use in the paper an algebraic specification language with conditional equations, interpreted with initial semantics (Ehrig & Mahr, 1985), close to OBJ-3 [GW88] but with many simplifications to make it more readable (see Franch & Marco [2000] for a complete OBJ-3 specification of the *STORE* with shortcuts). To simplify matters, we manage errors as in Goguen, Thatcher & Wagner (1978),

Figure 1: An ADT for a store of items

---

specification STORE **imports** KEY+VALUE+BOOL
  sort store
  operations create: $\rightarrow$ store
         insert: store key value $\rightarrow$ store
         remove: store key $\rightarrow$ store
         retrieve: store key $\rightarrow$ value
         defined?: store key $\rightarrow$ bool
  errors insert(insert(A, k, v), k, v'); remove(create, k); retrieve(create, k)
  equations
    [eq(k, k') = false] => insert(insert(A, k, v), k', v') =
               = insert(insert(A, k', v'), k, v)
    remove(insert(A, k, v), k) = A
    [eq(k, k') = false] => remove(insert(A, k, v), k') =
               = insert(remove(A, k'), k, v)
    retrieve(insert(A, k, v), k) = v
    [eq(k, k') = false] => retrieve(insert(A, k, v), k') = retrieve(A, k')
    defined?(create, k) = false
    defined?(insert(A, k, v), k') = eq(k, k') or defined?(A, k')
end STORE

---

grouping all the error expressions in a separated area and assuming implicit error propagation. For simplicity purposes too, we define the ADT as a non-parameterised one, obtaining thus classes of (total and heterogeneous) algebras as models, instead of functors. The specification of the type is straightforward (see Figure 1).

We fix the model of the ADT *STORE* interpreting the equations with initial semantics. Given the properties stated on *insert* (see first equation) we can say that the model (with respect to the carrier set of the *store* sort) is the set of partial functions $K \to V$, being K and V the carrier sets of the sorts *key* and *value*, respectively. The operations of the model are the intuitive interpretation of the ADT operations over these functions; for instance, *create* is interpreted as the function g satisfying $\text{dom}(g) = \emptyset$.

Implementations for the ADT will make use of hashing, AVL trees and so on. Every implementation has a different behaviour with respect to execution time, and it can be the case of implementations with a non-constant access time to items, even linear time (e.g., unordered arrays). In this paper, we focus on implementations in main memory (and so we measure efficiency with the asymptotic big-Oh notation [Knuth, 1976; Brassard, 1985]).

THE ABSTRACT DATA TYPE *STORE* WITH SHORTCUTS

The goal of this section is to extend the ADT *STORE* by adding shortcuts to access directly the items contained in stores. As a design requirement, we want a specification not only correct but also useful. This means mainly two things. First, the new ADT must be compatible with the former one, in the sense that the old operations must be preserved with the same signature and with the same behaviour as before, when shortcuts are not taken into account. On the other hand, the specification must allow feasible implementations; the main consequence of this is recycling of free shortcuts, although this is not necessary from the specification point of view.

We begin by introducing a new sort *shortcut*. The values of this sort are generated using two operations *first_sc:* $\to$ *shortcut* and *next_sc: shortcut* $\to$ *shortcut*, which are declared as private to avoid out-of-control creation of shortcuts by *STORE* users; shortcut creation is restricted to *STORE*. We provide also with a (public) operation of shortcut comparison, *eq_sc*.

Shortcut creation takes place when adding new pairs to the store. So, we add a new operation *last_sc: store* $\to$ *shortcut*, which return the *shortcut* to be used to access the last pair <key, value> inserted into the *store*. Typically, this operation should be called once a new pair enters the store. The obtained shortcut can be stored in other data structures, and then coupling of ADTs (for building

Figure 2: Public signature of an ADT for stores with shortcuts

---

sorts store, shortcut
operations   create, insert, remove, retrieve and defined? as in
fig. 1
            last_sc: store → shortcut
            remove_sc: store shortcut → store
            retrieve_sc: store shortcut → value
            defined_sc?: store shortcut → bool
            modify_sc: store shortcut value → store
            key_for_sc: store shortcut → key
            sc_for_key: store key → shortcut
            eq_sc: shortcut shortcut → bool

---

new data structures) can be carried out both in an efficient and modular way. In addition to this, the ADT provides a new operation, *sc_for_key*, to obtain the shortcut bound to a pair at any moment.

Last, we add operations to access the store by means of shortcuts: removal (*remove_sc*), retrieval (*retrieve_sc*) and modification (*modify_sc*). Furthermore, we introduce an operation to find out if a given shortcut is defined (*defined_sc?*), because we consider an error to access the structure using an undefined shortcut; in fact, as we have mentioned earlier, this kind of control is one of advantages with respect the usual notion of pointer.

We address now to the specification of the type, focusing just on its most interesting parts (see Franch et al. [2000] for a full version in OBJ-3). To simplify the final product, we introduce a new private operation to add pairs <key, value> with its shortcut, *insert_sc: store key value shortcut → store*. We need two error expressions (see fig. 3, expressions 1 and 2), to avoid key or shortcut repetition (the first error coming from Booch's definition, the second one coming from our approach). Note the absence of the commutative equation over *insert* that appeared in the store without shortcuts (section 3). This is due to the fact that we need now to maintain the ordering of insertions to distinguish different shortcuts; in other case the following property would hold:

last_sc(insert_sc(insert_sc(A, k, v, q), k', v', q') = last_sc(insert_sc(insert_sc(A, k', v', q'), k, v, q)

which is obviously wrong.

In order to obtain shortcuts for the store, we introduce another private operation *new_sc: store → shortcut* which is the one responsible to associate a shortcut to a new pair entering in the store. Then, we can bound the public *insert* operation with the private *insert_sc* one:

(E1) insert(A, k, v) = insert_sc(A', k, v, new_sc(A))

where *A'* will be defined later.

A point is worth to be mentioned: as far as *insert_sc* is not commutative, *insert* is not commutative also. This is really a difference in the underlying model, but in fact it does not impact on the practical use of the type. Changing to another type of semantics, as we mention in the future work (section 7) would solve this problem.

The simplest policy to generate new shortcuts would consist in obtaining the shortcut successor of the last generated one. However, this criteria works not well when removals are taken into account, because removals set free previously generated shortcuts. Although from the specification point of view we could reject the possibility of reusing these shortcuts, we decide not to do that, because feasible implementations of the ADT will need to reassign released shortcuts in further insertions (to avoid holes in the underlying data structure). The specification of *new_sc* results in (see Figure 3, equations from 3 to 5): if there are no shortcuts to reassign, the new shortcut is the next of the last generated one; if there is at least one shortcut to reassign, it is the last released one.

We should mention that reassignment conveys a danger: it is impossible to be sure that all the users of a store having copies of the reassigned shortcut are aware that the pair bound to the shortcut has changed; it could be the case of accessing the store by means of a copy of the shortcut created before its last assignment. In fact, it would be not difficult to take care of this, adding new operations on the ADT to create and destroy copies of shortcuts in a controlled way; however, we have decided not to do that because the same problem arises when considering keys instead of shortcuts, and usually this situation is not explicitly handled in usual container-like ADTs.

To specify the auxiliary operations appearing in these two equations, we need to keep track of released shortcuts, with the help of a new operation *mark_sc: store shortcut → store*. Marks appear when items are removed (either by key or by shortcut) and disappear only when the shortcut is assigned again, by means of an *unmark_sc: store shortcut → store* operation. These operations are specified in Figure 3, equations from 6 to 15.

The *unmark* operation plays an important role also when considering insertions. In equation (E1), the store A' should eliminate any remaining mark of the new shortcut, just in case it were a released shortcut. This is necessary to maintain the consistence of the store with respect to the state of shortcuts. So, equation (E1) takes as final form:

(E1) insert(A, k, v) = insert_sc(unmark_sc(A, new_sc(A)), k, v, new_sc(A))

The rest of the specification is straightforward.

SEMANTICS OF THE ABSTRACT DATA TYPE *STORE* WITH SHORTCUTS

As we already expected, the initial model of the ADT with shortcuts is different from the one without them. We are going to fix this model concerning the

Figure 3: An excerpt of the specification of an ADT for stores with shortcuts

---

1) **error** [defined?(A, k) = true] => insert_sc(A, k, v, q)
2) **error** [defined_sc?(A, q) = true] => insert_sc(A, k, v, q)

3) new_sc(create) = first_sc
4) [holes?(insert_sc(A, k, v, q)) = false] =>
$\qquad$ new_sc(insert_sc(A, k, v, q)) =
$\qquad\qquad$ = next_sc(last_sc_generated(insert_sc(A, k, v, q)))
5) [holes?(insert_sc(A, k, v, q)) = true] =>
$\quad$ new_sc(insert_sc(A, k, v, q)) =
$\qquad\qquad$ = last_sc_released(insert_sc(A, k, v, q))

6) remove_sc(insert_sc(A, k, v, q), q) = mark_sc(A, q)
7) remove(insert_sc(A, k, v, q), k) = mark_sc(A, q)
8) [eq(k, k') = false] => remove(insert_sc(A, k, v, q), k') =
$\qquad\qquad\qquad$ = insert_sc(remove(A, k'), k, v, q)
9) [eq_sc(q, q') = false] => remove_sc(insert_sc(A, k, v, q), q') =
$\qquad\qquad\qquad$ = insert_sc(remove_sc(A, q'), k, v, q)
10) [eq_sc(q', q) = false] => insert_sc(mark_sc(A, q'), k, v, q)
$\qquad\qquad\qquad$ = mark_sc(insert_sc(A, k, v, q), q')
11) **error** insert_sc(mark_sc(A, q), k, v, q)

12) unmark_sc(create, q) = create
13) unmark_sc(insert_sc(A, k, v, q'), q) =
$\qquad\qquad$ = insert_sc(unmark(A, q), k, v, q')
14) unmark_sc(mark_sc(A, q), q) = unmark_sc(A, q)
15) [eq_sc(q', q) = false] => unmark_sc(mark_sc(A, q'), q) =
$\qquad\qquad$ = mark_sc(unmark_sc(A, q), q')

---

algebras bound to the sorts of interest, *store* and *shortcut*. As far as we are working in the initial semantics framework, we are going to identify which are the terms representative of the classes in the quotient-term algebra (of the appropriate sorts), then we will formulate the model and we will establish the correspondence between the representative terms and the values of the model.

Model of *STORE* for the sort *store*

Given the equations of the type, the equivalence classes of the quotient term algebra will include combinations of the operations *insert_sc* and *mark_sc* over the empty store. Arbitrarily, we choose as representative of a class any of the terms with the marks appearing after insertions:

$\qquad$ t_{repr} ::= mark_sc(...(mark_sc(
$\qquad\qquad\qquad\qquad$ insert_sc(...(insert_sc(create, k_1, v_1, q_1), ..., k_n, v_n, q_n),
$\qquad\qquad\qquad$ q_{n+1}), ..., q_r)

such that: i, j: $1 <= i, j <= n$: $(i <> j => \text{not eq}(k_i, k_j)) \wedge$

i, j: $1 <= i, j <= r$: $(i <> j => \text{not eq\_sc}(q_i, q_j))$

The parameters k_i and v_i, $1 <= i <= n$, are the pairs <key, value> in the store, while $q_{n+1}, ..., q_r$ are all the released (and not reassigned) shortcuts.

It is clear that the model must include information about the correspondence between keys and values, and keys and shortcuts, and also the knowledge about which are the released shortcuts. So, we formulate as the carrier set corresponding to the sort *store*:

$\text{STORE}_{\text{store}} ::= (K \rightarrow V) \times (K \leftrightarrow A) \times A^*$ satisfying that

$(g, h, s) \in \text{STORE}_{\text{store}}$:

$\text{dom}(g) = \text{dom}(h) \wedge$

$s \cap \text{ran}(h) = \emptyset \wedge$

$s \cup \text{ran}(h) = [\text{first\_sc}, \text{next\_sc}^n(\text{first\_sc})]$

being $n = \| s \cup \text{ran}(h) \| - 1$, being $\text{next\_sc}^n(\text{first\_sc})$ the application n times of *next_sc* on *first_sc*, and being A, K and V the carrier sets of shortcuts, keys and values, respectively. We mix sequences and sets when using $\cup$ and $\cap$ with an intuitive meaning. The first function maps keys to values, the second one binds keys and shortcuts with a bijection (as required by the uniqueness property), while the sequence keeps track of released shortcuts. As the specification obliges shortcuts to be reassigned in reverse order of release, the sequence must be seen as a stack. We could think of not fixing which is the shortcut to reassign. However, in the initial semantics framework, we are obliged to determine the concrete reassignment policy to avoid inconsistences collapsing some of the carrier sets involved in the model (for instance, we could demonstrate the equality of two different values). In section 7, as future work, we mention the possibility of moving to other semantics providing a higher degree of flexibility.

The correspondence between the carrier set of $\text{STORE}_{\text{store}}$ and the representative term t_{repr} of the classes in the quotient-term algebra of *STORE* is established as:

$t_{\text{repr}} \leftrightarrow (g, h, s)$ such that: $s = q_r . q_{r-1} . ... . q_{n+1} . \lambda \wedge$

$\text{dom}(g) = \text{dom}(h) = \{k_1, ..., k_n\} \wedge$

i: $1 <= i <= n$: $(g(k_i) = v_i \wedge h(k_i) = q_i)$

The operations of the ADT can be defined in terms of this carrier set; for instance, the interpretation of *modify_sc(A, q, v)*, being (g, h, s) the model of A, requires $q \hat{\in} \text{ran}(h)$ and redefines the function g in the point $h^{-1}(q)$ such that $g(h^{-1}(q)) = v$.

Model of *STORE* for the Sort *shortcut*

On the other hand, the carrier set for the sort *shortcut* is any domain isomorphic to the quotient-term algebra for this sort. Given the absence of equations establishing relationships between the constructor operations for *shortcut*, the quotient-term algebra for the sort *shortcut* is characterised by having as carrier set the equivalence classes [*next_sc^n(first_sc)*], $n >= 0$. Among them, we remark the domain of natural numbers; in this case, the operations can be interpreted in the following way: 0, the interpretation of *first_sc*; +1, the interpretation of *next_sc*; and =, the interpretation of *eq_sc*. So, we can consider natural numbers as a valid model of shortcuts.

IMPLEMENTING THE ABSTRACT DATA TYPE *STORE* WITH SHORTCUTS

We focus in this section in the efficient implementation of stores with shortcuts. In fact, we are interested in determining the representation of the sorts, because the code for the operations can be derived automatically from it (we have done it [Marco & Franch, 1997]).

The essential point consists on adding a mapping from shortcuts to pairs <key, value> in the new ADT, while reusing the old ADT substituting values by the shortcut that identifies them. This is precisely a point worth mentioning that makes our approach different from other existing ones, as LEDA and STL: shortcuts can be added to any given implementation of the ADT, without any kind of restriction. In Franch et al. (2000) is presented an implementation in Ada 95 that takes profit of the generic mechanism to implement this idea.

Then, the representation of the store has three parts (see Figure 4). First, we consider the existence of an array *SC* of *N* positions to implement the mapping between shortcuts and pairs <key, value>. So, we implement shortcuts with natural numbers that indexing the array. The cells of *SC* will contain for the moment the pairs <key, value>.

On the other hand, the free positions of the array (those ones representing undefined shortcuts) will be managed as a stack. This stack has two parts: the upper one, containing the free shortcuts used before, in reverse order of release; and the lower one, containing shortcuts not used before, in increasing order of natural numbers. In fact, this kind of free space management is the usual one in chained data structures implemented with arrays (Aho et al., 1983; Horowitz et al., 1994), with an O(1) complexity.

Last, we reuse the given implementation of stores (hashing tables, AVL trees, etc.), passing the shortcuts as values bound to the keys. As a result, given a key, we obtain the shortcut with the efficiency of the former implementation and, if necessary, we can use it to recover the corresponding value in constant time. Therefore, the cost of all the previous operations is maintained. It is worth noting also that the data structure is robust with respect to movements of the keys in *M* (for instance, when deleting in an open addressing hashing table).

Figure 4: A valid state of the implementation for stores with shortcuts

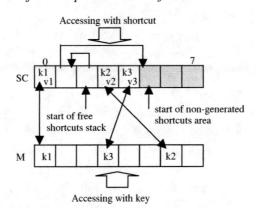

The operations accessing and not modifying the store by means of the shortcut are O(1), which was one of our goals. On the other hand, the operations accessing by key, or accessing by shortcut but modifying the store, have a complexity that depends on the underlying implementation of *M*; the important fact is that this complexity does not get worst with the addition of shortcuts. On the other hand, the representation needs *N**(space(shortcut)+space(key)) extra space. However, even this waste will generate a later saving of space, when shortcuts substitute keys (generally strings, which require most space than a shortcut).

Instead of the array *SC*, dynamic memory could have been used to store the pairs <key, value>. In this case, released shortcuts (i.e., pointers) would be managed directly by the memory allocator. The main consequence is that we can not assure that they are recycled with the chosen policy stated in the specification. A way to handle this problem would be to incorporate in the specification the memory allocator policy itself. In any case, this difference has not practical consequences.

CONCLUSIONS AND FUTURE WORK

We have presented a proposal aimed at reconciling two usually contradictory criteria in the ADTs framework: modularity and efficiency. To do this, we add a new type to implement the concept of shortcut as alternative path access to elements in the ADT, and we add many new operations to make proper use of shortcuts. Shortcuts are interesting because, besides of assuring O(1) access time to elements in the ADT, they present some nice properties: they are abstract (independent of the implementation of the ADT), persistent (movements inside the data structure do not affect them), secure (meaningless accesses are not possible) and they preserve behaviour (the new ADT behaves as the old one, and the efficiency of the former operations keep the same). These properties are the ones that distinguish clearly shortcuts from low-level concepts as pointers or cursors.

We have developed our work studying a concrete ADT, the store of items, writing down an algebraic specification for the type, identifying its mathematical model (which behaves in a predictable manner), and proposing an adequate (efficient) implementation for it. We would like to remark that most of our work can be applied to every other container-like ADT.

Concerning future work, there are two main lines of research. On the one hand, we are working on expressing our proposal in a generic manner (that is, suitable for a wide variety of ADTs with arbitrary implementations), with the same level of formalism as the one outlined here. To do this, we are defining a parameterised ADT which retains the most fundamental common properties of a wide variety of containers (in fact, the container itself acts as parameter), so that we can reformulate the methodology on it.

On the other hand, we want to study if other formal frameworks are more adequate than initial semantics. As it has been already pointed out, initial semantics forces us to determine in a precise manner which shortcuts are the ones assigned to new elements, and this is the reason why we have obtained a large specification which also suffers from implementation bias. For instance, the operation new_sc could be specified instead with the single equation $defined\_sc?(A, new\_sc(A)) \stackrel{e}{=} false$, which states that the shortcut assigned to a new pair must not be already assigned in the current store, but without fixing the assignment policy.

ACKNOWLEDGEMENTS

This work is partially supported by the spanish research programme CICYT under contract TIC97-1158.

REFERENCES

Aho, A., Hopcroft, J. and Ullman, J. (1983). *Data Structures and Algorithms*. Reading, MA: Addison-Wesley.

Booch, G. (1987). *Software Components with Ada (second edition)*. The Benjamin/Cummings Publishing Company Inc.

Brassard, G. (1985). Crusade for a better notation. *SIGACT News*, 16(4).

Cormen, T. H., Leiserson, C. E. and Rivest, R. L. (1990). *Introduction to Algorithms*. MIT Press.

Ehrig, H. and Mahr, B. (1985). *Fundamentals of Algebraic Specification*, 1. Springer-Verlag.

Franch, X. and Marco, J. (2000). Adding alternative access paths to abstract data types. *Technical Report LSI-00-1-R*, Universitat Politècnica de Catalunya.

Goguen, J., Thatcher, J. and Wagner, E. (1978). An initial algebra approach to the specification, correctness and implementation of abstract data types. In Yeh, R. (Ed.), *Current Trends in Programming Methodology*. Englewood Cliffs, NJ: Prentice-Hall.

Goguen, J. A. and Winkler, T. (1988). Introducing OBJ-3. *Technical Report SRI-CFL-88-9*, August.

Horowitz, E. and Sahni, S. (1994). *Fundamentals of Data Structures in Pascal (fourth edition)*. Computer Science Press.

Knuth, D. (1976). Big Omicron and big Omega and big Theta. *SIGACT News*, 8(2).

Knuth, D. E. (1998). *Sorting and Searching (second edition)*. Reading, MA: Addison-Wesley.

Liskov, B and Guttag, J. (1986). *Abstraction and Specification in Program Development*. MIT Press.

Marco, J. and Franch, X. (1997). Shortcuts: Abstract pointers. *Technical Report LSI-97-25-R*, Universitat Politècnica de Catalunya.

Marco, J. and Franch, X. (2000). Reengineering the Booch component library. In *Proceedings International Conference on Reliable Software Technologies - Ada Europe'00, LNCS 1845*, Postdam (Germany), June.

Mehlhorn, K. and Näher, S. (1999). *The LEDA Platform of Combinatorial and Geometric Computing*. Cambridge University Press.

Musser, D. R. and Saini, A. (1996). *STL Tutorial and Reference Guide*. Reading, MA: Addison-Wesley.

Chapter 19

Relational Data Modeling for Geographic Information Systems

Lawrence A. West, Jr.
University of Central Florida, USA

Brian E. Mennecke
East Carolina University, USA

This chapter addresses data modeling problems inherent in the use of geographic information systems (GIS) that are not adequately covered by traditional modeling techniques. GIS technology has only recently begun to be used for traditional system development by large numbers of organizations and there are few procedures for modeling GIS data and applications in a business context. This circumstance is partially a result of the fact that GIS developers have traditionally been knowledgeable end users or facilitators and they have generally been called on to build standalone systems, often for their own use. This paper discusses geographic systems and proposes relational modeling techniques that document organizational data integrity rules when systems that include spatial data are developed for more widespread use.

Data modeling is an effective design and communication tool associated with the development of relational databases and associated applications. A

Previously published in the *Journal of Database Management, vol.10, no.2,* Copyright © 1999, Idea Group Publishing.

fully developed data model includes a rich set of information on tables; fields; relationships, and, most importantly, the organization's business rules. Data models facilitate communication between developers and clients and, in modern development environments, CASE tools can be used to translate many model specifications directly into the physical database. Whether implemented in the physical database or enforced at the application level, the vision of the relationship between data and its uses that are expressed in the data model becomes a crucial contributor to the usability of the resulting database and suite of applications.

This paper addresses a data modeling problem inherent in the use of geographic information systems (GIS) which is not adequately covered by traditional modeling techniques. GIS are computer-based systems designed to capture, store, integrate, update, modify, create, display, and analyze geographic data. Though businesses and governments have used GIS technology for decades, it has only recently begun to be used for the development of databases and systems of the sort for which data modeling is appropriate. This situation is partially a result of the fact that GIS developers have traditionally been knowledgeable end users or facilitators who have been called on to build stand-alone systems for experienced end users, not "enterprise-wide systems" or systems for use by decision makers not familiar with GIS technology. Changes in these patterns have made the modeling issue much more important, yet we still lack standards for representing and communicating the use of and relationships between tables when one or more contain geographic coverages.

The goal of this paper is to suggest techniques for modeling relational databases that include a mix of both traditional tables and spatial coverages so that traditional business rules and data integrity rules can be documented for spatial databases. To accomplish this goal, the next section begins by defining several of the relevant terms used in the GIS field. Next, we discuss the important characteristics of spatial data and several of the modeling problems that are inherent in working with this data. After establishing the foundations for differences between spatial database systems and conventional relational systems, existing work in the field is discussed leading to the conclusion that there is no established modeling technique for GIS-based database systems. Following this discussion, two sections present a methodology for modeling spatial relationships as part of a comprehensive data model. The first of these sections addresses graphical representations of spatial entities and relationships, while the second covers modeling data integrity rules in spatial relationships. The paper concludes with a discussion of the implications of GIS technology in mainstream systems.

GIS TERMINOLOGY

Because some MIS researchers may be unfamiliar with GIS technology and the unique terminology used by its developers and users, this section includes several important terms and definitions.

GIS—Geographic Information System. Commonly used to mean the software that enables the display and manipulation of geographic data. Examples include ArcView, MapInfo, etc. This software is the counterpart to a database management system package prior to its application to a collection of data.

Geographic System (GS)—This term is introduced here to indicate a system; a collection of applications, data, procedures, personnel, etc.; which has a geographic component to it. This component would include, as a minimum, one or more data sets containing spatial data and a spatial database engine such as is found in GIS software. These systems could potentially have any of the attributes of any other computer-based information system plus the geographic component.

Coverage—A coverage in a GS is the counterpart to a table in a conventional database. Coverages are collections of records, with at least two parts having a 1:1 correspondence between records (Figure 1). One part is the description of an object's location in a coordinate system used by the GIS with typical coverage types including point (addresses and street lights), line (roads, streams, and utility lines), and polygon (political boundaries, sales territories). The second part is attribute data of the same type as is used in conventional DBMS. The attribute data is usually stored in a table having all of the properties of any 'traditional' table plus a key field linking each record in the attribute data to its appropriate spatial object.

Figure 1: Coverage Data

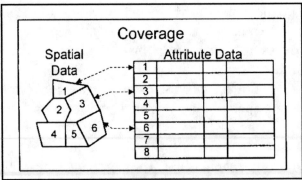

Good database design dictates that these attributes are about the objects represented in the coverage as would be accomplished by an appropriate level of normalization. Other terms for coverage include *layer* or *theme*.

Table—A GS can include both coverages and attribute data tables (tables not having corresponding spatial objects). In this paper 'table' will be used to mean a table not part of a coverage while a coverage table will refer to the attribute data of a coverage. This distinction will be important in later discussion.

Spatial Entity —Just as an entity is the modeling counterpart to a table, a spatial entity is the modeling counterpart to a coverage.

Data Model—The data model is all documentation pertaining to the database used by the system. It includes table and field specifications and all types of data integrity rules.

Graphical Data Model —The graphical data model (GDM) is a subset of the data model which graphically depicts entities and their relationships. Depending on model complexity and preferences the GDM may depict all fields in each table, just tables and primary and foreign keys, or just table names. Relationships may be shown with cardinality and descriptive text or just with depictions of their existence. At a minimum, the GDM will show each coverage, table, and relationship in the data model.

Object—In GIS an object is the counterpart of a record in a conventional RDBMS table. One object is one thing that has a spatial location and descriptive (attribute) data. When used in this context, 'object' is not to be confused with objects in object-oriented programming. However, some GIS do use an OOP approach and spatial records may also be objects from a programming sense.

WORKING WITH SPATIAL DATA

In traditional database designs, relationships are formed between entities when the primary key of one entity serves as a foreign key in another. Multi-table queries are almost always made along these paths using joins to select records in one table with key values matching selected records in another. These relationships are modeled using a number of techniques.

In a GIS, a new kind of join called the spatial join, is possible. The GIS engine is 'aware' of the area occupied by objects (records) in coverages and is able to tell when a record in one coverage overlaps the area occupied by a record in another. Furthermore, while joins in conventional systems typically test for equality of key values, spatial joins can be accomplished using a number of different criteria. Keywords in spatial joins include, "intersect," "are completely within," "completely contain," "have their center in," "nearest," "contain the center of," and "are within distance of" (Berry, 1993). Finally, GIS loaded with appropriate matchable street themes have the capability of estimating the x-y coordinates of a matchable object such as a street address.

With these capabilities, queries such as the following are possible:

- Select all customers whose addresses are within one mile of the store's location.
- Select the nearest store to a customer's location.
- Select the hospital emergency room which is closest to 123 Elm Street and which has a cardiac intensive care unit.
- Select all customers which live within 1/2 mile of any road of class 3 or above passing within 1/2 mile of the store's location.
- Select all employees whose zip codes fall within the service area of the XYZ HMO.

These capabilities highlight the modeling problem addressed by this paper. When there are two geographic coverages in a system, there is *automatically* a relationship between them. No matter where the coverages lie with respect to each other, a "Select the Nearest..." query will yield related records. When the coverages overlap spatially, then any of the spatial join types can be expected to yield related records. Furthermore, since the GIS engine is able to manage these relationships these systems do not provide relationship objects found in modern RDBMS. Instead, as Smith et al. write, "In a GIS, geometric and topological relations exist between the different geographic entities, be they points, lines or regions. There are so many potential relations that it is not possible to store them entirely explicitly within the system" (Smith et al., 1987).

Since any two coverages are automatically related, it is essential that the database designer distinguish between *accidental* relationships and those relationships having fundamental importance to the use of the system. Further, when spatial relationships are part of the system, rules for maintaining data integrity, especially rules enforcing standards for 'orphaned' records (insert and delete rules) must be established. Finally, the modeling technique must provide for the representation of 'traditional' data in the system. An overall approach for modeling data in a GS requires methods for:

- Representing spatial coverages
- Distinguishing between intended and incidental relationships between coverages
- Documenting the characteristics, including data integrity rules, of spatial relationships

- Documenting relationships between coverages and conventional (non-spatial) tables
- Documenting business rules pertaining to spatial locations

PREVIOUS WORK

The history of relational data modeling begins with Codd (1970) and Chen (1976) and is well known in the MIS field. While several refinements and alternative techniques have been suggested over the years, their details are incidental to the main point here and will not be discussed further. The graphical illustrations presented in this paper will use the modeling technique presented by Flemming and von Halle (1989) because its compact presentation better suits the limited space in a journal format. The same models could easily be constructed with the Chen technique.

Work specifically discussing the use of relational data models in GIS comes from the fields of computer science and can be generally characterized as being focused on the internal representation of the spatial data rather than on the relationships between coverages as discussed above. Each record or object in a spatial coverage consists of both attribute and spatial data (Figure 1). In the case of polyline or polygon coverages the spatial data is stored as either an ordered list of points defining the vertices of the objects (vector data) or as a collection of all the points making up the area of the object (raster data). These collections can themselves have attributes such as color, direction, or elevation and managing these 'sub-data' elements and their association with the record has been a matter of considerable interest.

An early paper by Freeman (1975) discusses relative locations of objects forming a picture and introduces a calculus using terms such as 'BELOW' or 'BETWEEN.' His discussion pertains to graphics in general, however, not just to geographic data and does not address the relationships between tables or even relational tables.

Several papers discuss the internal representation of spatial data. Worboys, Hearnshaw, and Maguire (1990) discuss an object-oriented model for representing both the internal elements of spatial data (coordinates of nodes, etc.), the relationship between coordinate data and the attribute data, and the relationship between what we are calling different spatial coverages. Van Roessel (1987) and van Roessel and Fosnight (1984) discuss the design of a relational data model for spatial data to facilitate the exchange of data between systems. As with Maguire's work, though, they focus on the relationships between elements of a spatial object and the object itself. That is, much of this work focuses on techniques for storing the attribute and spatial data in a unified system. Shekhar et al. developed an object oriented (from an OOP perspective) model for capturing a rich set of attributes about geographic data, including a rich capability for modeling time series data related to spatial objects.

Armstrong and Densham (1990) come closest to the theme of this paper in their analysis of database organizational strategies for spatial decision support systems. They develop a model of data representation that focuses on both the internal representation of spatial data and the relationship between spatial and non-spatial entities in a comprehensive model. Their conclusion, though, is that an extended network model is the most appropriate for creating systems of this type. Unfortunately, implementing their model requires that the database engine integrate the spatial data and additional data into one internal schema and is likely to create problems when attempting to link organizational data in an existing RDBMS.

Previous work suffers from one or both of two weaknesses with respect to the types of geographic systems proposed here. First, the work does not discuss the relationship of spatial data to non-spatial data in an enterprise-wide database. While many authors address the accuracy of geographic data and some address the accuracy of attribute data none discuss business rules of the sort commonly implemented in conventional database systems. Secondly, the work presumes the flexibility of designing customized data structures and a corresponding database engine to operate on the data. In an environment where business and government systems are developed using standard software packages and development languages, the system designer is more likely to be faced with an environment characterized by:

- Internal representation of the spatial data given by the selected GIS software package, and;
- Relational representations of attribute data due to the popularity of this data structure in both GIS software packages and for existing organizational DBMS.

It follows, then, that an approach that is familiar to developers and that is consistent with the capabilities of off-the-shelf GS development tools will be useful for production geographic systems in the foreseeable future. The next two sections present such an approach.

ILLUSTRATING SPATIAL DATA IN A GIS

This section covers techniques for illustrating spatial and non-spatial data in a graphical data model. The discussion includes techniques for illustrating and identifying spatial coverages and for illustrating and identifying spatial relationships.

Illustrating Spatial Coverages

When a system includes both conventional tables and spatial coverages, the illustration should clearly distinguish between these two data structures and it should allow the user to see the class of objects in each coverage. These goals may be accomplished by taking the following steps.

1. Use a large rectangle or other shape as a metaphor for the ground and place coverage entities inside this area. Entities shown outside this area will be implemented as conventional tables rather than coverages. In the case of complex or multi-page GDMs where all of the coverage shapes cannot reasonably be drawn in proximity to each other, the spatial indication boundary can be repeated in multiple parts of the GDM. It would be understood that each of these individual areas is actually representing the entire spatial area of interest.

2. Annotate each spatial entity with a symbol to indicate the type of objects it contains. Symbols should be easy to construct with any graphics program capable of creating the basic symbology of the GDM itself and should bear some resemblance to the type of object being represented. Table 1 contains proposed symbology for representing coverage types. Figure 2 illustrates the application of these principles in a simple GDM

Table 1: GDM Coverage Type Symbology

Symbol	Meaning	Examples
◇	Polygon	Political boundary, service area, property boundaries, zoning designations
◇◇	Complex Polygon	Polygons with multiple areas constituting the same logical object, donut-shaped objects, etc.
N	Line or Polyline	Roads, power lines, rivers
$x, y\, N$	Matchable address layer	A coverage which contains street networks along with the information which will enable the system to determine the approximate x, y coordinate of an address.
123Ø•	Address Table	A point coverage which has been produced from conventional records which have been converted to a coverage using a matchable address layer
•	Point	Street address, telephone pole, accident site, fire hydrant
$x, y\, ,Ø$•	Event Table	A conventional table in which one attribute contains the x coordinate address of a point in the GIS's coordinate system and another attribute contains the y coordinate. Such tables can be converted to coverages by many GIS.

Figure 2: Spatial Entities in a GDM

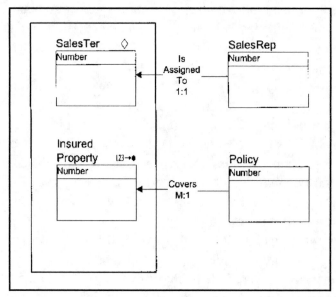

for a property insurance company and Appendix A includes more of the symbology in a more comprehensive GDM. The relationship between the sales representatives and sales territories is shown in the traditional manner but no relationships, other than the collective identification as spatial coverages, have yet been illustrated between the coverage entities. These relationships will be discussed and modeled next. Each sales representative is assigned exclusive rights to one sales territory and so sells all policies insuring property falling within his/her territory. Sales territories are represented as polygon coverages and insured property is shown as an address table for which spatial coordinates were derived from street addresses and a matchable address coverage.

Illustrating Spatial Relationships

As discussed previously, the inclusion of spatial coverages in a bounding box illustrates the natural spatial relationships that exist between records in any two coverages sharing a common coordinate system. It is likely, however, that referential business rules similar to those applied to relationships between conventional tables may apply to relationships between geographic coverages as well. A method must be adopted to distinguish between the 'accidental' relationships that exist between all spatial coverages and intended relationships that implement some business rule of the organization.

For example, if it is company policy that each covered address be

Figure 3: Spatial Relationships in a GDM

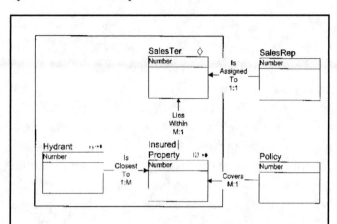

serviced by the sales representative for the territory in which the property lies this rule may be illustrated by specifying the relationship explicitly in the data model. This rule corresponds to a traditional one-to-many relationship between tables except that there is no explicit primary key-foreign key link to establish the relationship. In another case, rates for fire policies may be based on the distance from the insured property to the closest fire hydrant.

Illustrating intentional relationships between coverages in a geographic system can be accomplished by connecting each coverage in the relationship with a line. Annotate the line with a short descriptive name and the cardinality of the relationship. Alternatively, the relationship could include the relationship set diamond symbol from Chen (1976). Figure 3 shows an extension of the GDM with intended geographic relationships illustrated. Note that the hydrant coverages is shown as an event theme. The data may be obtained from utility companies that often survey hydrant, utility pole, manhole, and other locations with global positioning systems (GPS) that record latitude and longitude measures for object locations.

DOCUMENTING SPATIAL DATA INTEGRITY RULES

This section covers the enforcement of data integrity rules as they pertain to spatial coverages. While many of these rules are similar to those found in conventional database design the spatial aspects of the data present some additional challenges to the designer. These challenges are in the area of enforcing existential integrity, referential integrity, and triggering operations and occur because, unlike conventional database systems, there are, as yet, few provisions for enforcing data integrity rules in GIS. The specific problems and suggested approaches are presented below.

Documenting Existential Integrity Rules

Existential integrity in conventional systems requires that each record be unique. This requirement is enforced by guaranteeing the uniqueness of the primary and alternate keys of each record in a table and the existence of values in each field of a primary key (nulls are not allowed). Spatial coverages may have the same rules for their attribute data, but must also consider the spatial uniqueness and completeness of each record. Since the enforcement of rules in these areas will vary within the application, or even between coverages in the same database, these rules must be specified at design time and enforced within the database or the using application.

Spatial uniqueness determines whether a record in a coverage is allowed to overlap the area occupied by another record in the same coverage. For example, in a polygon database containing the legal descriptions of property records, it is not legal for the area of one parcel of land to overlap the area of another. Each area of land must be within a unique parcel and each parcel must have an ownership status. On the other hand, a polyline coverage mapping bus lines in a city may have different routes intersecting or occupying the same streets on portions of their routes.

Spatial completeness determines whether or not records in a polygon coverage must completely fill the bounding area of the coverage. In the property records mentioned above, it would make no sense to have an area of land not belonging to a legally described parcel. Such an area would be ownerless; therefore, the system must enforce the completeness of the coverage. On the other hand, it would be acceptable for a coverage of city boundaries to have gaps in it representing unincorporated areas of a county.

Because coverages may only have one spatial attribute, uniqueness and completeness applies to the coverage as a whole and may be specified in the coverage description area of the coverage's entry in the data dictionary. It

Figure 4: Documenting Spatial Uniqueness & Completeness

Coverage:	SalesTer
Type:	Polygon
Description:	Each record describes one sales territory in which a single sales representative can issue policies.
Unique?:	Yes
Complete?:	No

would be unlikely that point or line coverages would require complete coverage but all coverage types could potentially require unique (no overlap) coverage. Figure 4 illustrates an example page header for a coverage's entry in the data dictionary.

Documenting Referential Integrity

It is also necessary to document the nature of each intended spatial relationship in the data dictionary. This documentation should include conventional referential integrity rules for the relationship (insert and delete rules) as well as any spatial restrictions on the nature of the relationship. These spatial restrictions may be thought of as rules that must be enforced by the GIS engine.

These rules must be derived from the spatial selection capabilities of the GIS engine as it is the engine that must perform validity checking on the spatial objects. For example, according to the example business rules given earlier the relationship between SalesTer and Insured Property in Figure 3 would be a "Lies Within" relationship. All Insured Property locations must lie within an existing company sales territory. On the other hand, the company may have a rule that says that new customers are automatically assigned to the closest sales representative as determined by their sales territories. With this rule, customers will automatically be assigned to the appropriate sales representative if they happen to live within an established sales territory, but will be assigned to the closest representative if no territory contains their address. Figure 5 illustrates the relationship documentation for the relationship between the SalesTer and District entities.

Figure 5: Sample Documentation for a Spatial Relationship

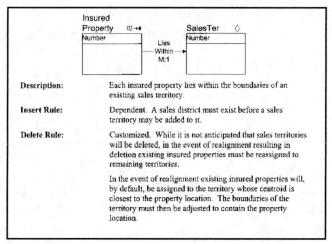

Figure 6: Documenting Triggering Operations

User Rule:	Policy rates will be calculated based, in part, on the distance of the proposed insured property from an existing fire hydrant and from an existing fire station.
Event:	Insert, Update
Entity:	Policy
Attribute:	Policy*Rate
Condition:	[Exact calculation is omitted]
Action:	Update the policy rate

Documenting Triggering Operations

Triggering operations (or triggers) are data integrity rules that may not be specified using the earlier methods. Triggers frequently require calculations, reference to additional fields (other than primary or foreign keys), or summaries of values in multiple records for determining the validity of a proposed action.

Actions requiring integrity enforcement through triggering operations are common when dealing with geographic records. One example of a trigger could be created by an ordnance that prohibits certain land use (e.g., liquor stores) within a specified radius of property designated for a different use (e.g., schools). While it is simple to detect whether or not an object exists within this radius, reference must be made to additional information to determine the two types of objects to enable detection of a violation of the trigger condition.

Documentation for triggering operations on spatial data will resemble the documentation for conventional data and may be specified with a number of formats. The operation illustrated in Figure 6 uses the Rule-Event-Condition-Action format presented by Flemming and von Halle (1989, Chap. 9).

IMPLICATIONS FOR SYSTEM DEVELOPMENT

The focus of this paper has been on identifying and documenting spatial data integrity issues involved with geographic systems. The technical (and therefore, practical) issues associated with implementing these rules is well beyond the scope of this paper but there are some important ramifications to the issues raised here. Foremost among these ramifications is the fact that working with spatial data requires more computational power than traditional database structures. As geographic systems are implemented in support of applications (as opposed to standalone information systems) response time issues will become more and more important.

Designers will need to be acutely aware of which transactions against the system will invoke a spatial integrity check and will need to focus their attention on those high frequency, important transactions made against large spatial data sets. As with conventional systems, designers will need to consider methods for enhancing performance. Indexing spatial coverages is one method of speeding performance that is supported by many GIS. Other techniques, such as dividing coverages into tiles or batch processing, may be suitable.

A final consideration may involve redundant relationships between tables and coverages. That is, relationships that may be implicit in existing relationships may be duplicated by new relationships in order to avoid spatial joins in high volume transactions. The relationship between SalesRep and Policy illustrated in Figure A1 (Appendix A) is not needed as this relationship can be traced through the SalesTer coverage and Insured Property. However, some transactions may be faster by avoiding the spatial join. This technique would only be practical with stable spatial selection criteria and relatively stable data, but it would remove day-to-day processing from the GIS engine.

Finally, certain integrity rules may have implications for hardware and software selection. If the system requires that spatial completeness be enforced, for example, it will be necessary to ensure that the underlying GIS software supports snap-to-object drawing and the detection of unassigned areas and their conversion to objects.

CONCLUSIONS

GIS are becoming more popular for transaction processing, management support, and decision support systems. As they become integrated with other organizational systems, their design must reflect the same considerations for data integrity protection found in other systems. This paper has presented a methodology for identifying and documenting data integrity considerations for geographic systems. The methodology is an extension of techniques already in use and can be implemented with tools likely to be found in any programming shop.

APPENDIX A: LOGICAL DATA MODEL

The graphical data model depicted in Figure A1 is a simple illustration of many of the graphical techniques suggested in this paper. Examples of data integrity rules illustrated in the paper were also drawn from this model. The model is far from complete and is presented for illustration purposes only. As with any data modeling effort, as all business rules are explored and incorporated the model becomes more complicated.

Figure A1: Graphical Data Model

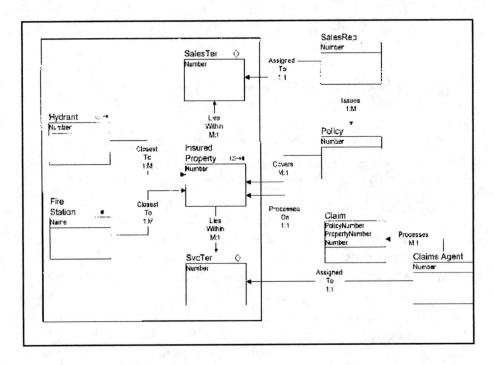

A few brief notes about the model are presented below.

1. Note that relationships exist between SalesRep and Policy and between Claims Agent and Claim, even though these relationships can be traced through the spatial relationships. These relationships may be added for two reasons:

   a. Changes over time may require that the agent who sold a policy or processed a claim be linked to the claim or policy while the relationship established through the spatial relationship establishes which agent processes new policies and claims.

   b. The 'conventional' foreign key relationship is faster for the system to process. If transaction analysis determines that linking from SalesRep to Policy is a frequent or important join, then the redundant relationship may be established.

2. Insured Property is shown as an address table. This table is a conventional relational table that has had spatial coordinates added by looking up addresses in a matchable street coverage. This street table is an important part of the system's operation, but is not shown as part of the GDM as it is a utility coverage and the company does not use this table's data directly.

3. Note that there is no explicit relationship between many of the GIS coverages even though they lie in the same area of interest. Again, the modeling technique suggested here clearly distinguishes those spatial relationships that are of interest from those that are not.

4. As models become more complete, and therefore more complex, it is likely that they will span many pages or that it will be difficult to represent all of the spatial entities in proximity to each other. As suggested in the text, it may be necessary to break the spatial area of the GDM into multiple sections in order to effectively illustrate all of the relationships. This technique is not shown here.

REFERENCES

Berry, J. K. (1993). *Beyond Mapping: Concepts, Algorithms, and Issues in GIS*. Ft. Collins, CO: GIS World Books.

Chen, P. P. S. (1976). The entity-relationship model: Toward a unified view of data. *ACM Transactions on Database Systems*, 1(1), 9-36.

Codd, E. F. (1970). A relational model of data for large shared data banks. *Communications of the ACM* 13(6), 377-387.

Flemming, C. and von Halle, B. (1989). *Handbook of Relational Database Design*. Reading, MA: Addison-Wesley.

Freeman, J. (1975). The modeling of spatial relations. *Computer graphics and image processing* 4, 156-171.

Shekhar, S., Coyle, M., Goyal, B., Liu, D. and Sarkar, S. (1997). Data models in geographic information systems. *Communications of the ACM*, 40(4), 103-111.

Smith, T. R., Menon, S., Star, J. L. and Estes, J. E. (1987). Requirements and principles for the implementation and construction of large-scale geographic information systems. *International Journal of Geographical Information Systems*, 1(1), 13-31.

van Roessel, J. W. (1987). Design of a spatial data structure using the relational normal forms. *International Journal of Geographical Information Systems*, 1(1), 33-50.

van Roessel, J. W. and Fosnight, E. A. (1984). A relational approach to vector data structure conversion. *Proceedings, First International Symposium on Spatial Data Handling*. Geographical Institute, University of Zurich, Zurich.

Worboys, M. F., Hearnshaw, H. M. and Maguire, D. J. (1990). Object-oriented data modeling for spatial databases. *International Journal of Geographical Information Systems*, 4(4), 369-383.

Chapter 20

Software Process Models are Software Too: A Domain Class Model for Software Process Models[1]

Daniel Turk
Colorado State University, USA

Vijay Vaishnavi
Georgia State University, USA

A software process model describes a set of partially-ordered sequences of activities that are carried out in order to accomplish certain goals. While numerous process modeling approaches have been proposed over the years, it seems that none of them have yet addressed the full range of concepts described in this definition. Most focus on activities and activity ordering; few, if any, focus on representing organizational goals and process improvement. Most provide concrete implementation approaches; few, if any, describe the general model(s) upon which these implementations are built. This paper suggests a new approach for developing software process modeling systems.

If "Software Processes are Software Too," as suggested by Osterweil (1987), then so are software process models, and hence there may be processes and models that are used in regular software development that may be useful in the process modeling domain as well. The paper focuses on the domain class model as an example of one type of model that might be produced if an approach such as the Unified Process were used in the process modeling

Previously published in *Challenges of Information Technology Management in the 21st Century*, edited by Mehdi Khosrow-Pour. Copyright © 2000, Idea Group Publishing.

domain. Such a process, and the set of models produced by it, if used, may be helpful in moving the process modeling field forward. While identifying the conceptual needs of process modeling systems, these models leave totally open the choice of how to formalize and implement actual solutions. A domain class model for process models is developed as an example of one of these models.

INTRODUCTION

A software process model describes a set of *partially-ordered* sequences of *activities* that are carried out in order to accomplish certain *goals* (Curtis, Kellner, & Over, 1992; Feiler & Humphrey, 1993). While numerous process modeling approaches have been proposed over the years (Arbaoui & Oquendo, 1994; Barghouti & Kaiser, 1992; Conradi et al., 1992; Curtis, Kellner, & Over, 1992; Dowson, 1987, 1993; Engels & Groenewegen, 1994; Finkelstein, 1989; Humphrey, 1989; Humphrey, 1995; Jarke et al., 1998; Kellner, Briand, & Over, 1996; Lehman, 1997; Paulk et al.,1995; Roland et al., 1995; Starke, 1994; Sutton & Osterweil, 1997; Workflow Management Coalition, 1994), it seems that none of them have yet addressed the full range of concepts described in this definition. Most focus on activities and their ordering; few, if any, focus on representing organizational goals and process improvement. Most provide concrete implementation approaches; few, if any, describe the general models upon which these implementations are built. This paper suggests a new approach for developing software process modeling systems.

In his landmark paper, Leon Osterweil (1987) stated that "software processes are software too." Thus was launched more than a decade of work whereby software processes have been modeled as computer programs. The focus has been on using computer languages, developing new ones or extending old ones, to model software processes in an executable manner. This dynamic approach is believed to allow better modeling of software development processes than more static approaches can provide.

However, it seems that an important implication of Osterweil's assertion has gone largely unnoticed: *If software processes are software too, and thus are modeled by computer programs, then so are software process models, and hence the processes used to develop regular software might be valuable to use in developing process modeling software as well.*

The Unified Process (Booch, Rumbaugh, & Jacobson, 1999; Rumbaugh, Jacobson, & Booch, 1999; Jacobson, Booch, & Rumbaugh, 1999), and most other approaches, suggest that in software development a number of models are useful: domain, application, test, etc. The domain model describes in a system-independent way 1) the requirements that a user will want the system to be able to do for them, and 2) the general conceptual ideas or constructs in the domain of interest and the interrelationships between these constructs. These two aspects of the domain model, usually known as the requirements and class models, provide a strong basis for building and maintaining correct, robust, and flexible systems. The application model builds on the domain model and describes a specific solution approach or design for a given application. If "process models are software too," then they should benefit from following a similar process and from the development of such models for the process modeling domain.

This paper describes a domain class[+] model for software process models that was developed following such a process. Use cases were developed describing requirements for process modelers. The domain class model was built based on these requirements and a study of the process modeling literature, and a formal process modeling language was specified and a prototype process modeling system was built to demonstrate the feasibility, and to test the validity, of some of the model's key ideas.

In this paper we focus on the domain class model as an example of one type of model that might be produced if an approach such as the Unified Process were used in the process modeling domain. We believe such an approach, and the set of models produced by it, if used, may be helpful in moving the field of process modeling forward. While identifying the high-level concepts and interrelationships of the process modeling domain, this domain class model leaves totally open the choice of how to *formalize* and *implement* actual solutions. Other parts of our research project focus on the requirements and application models, and on building executable process modeling systems.

A DOMAIN CLASS MODEL

A domain class model describes the key concepts in the domain of interest - the constructs, their relationships, interactions, and behavior. In our case, the domain of interest is software development process modeling. This paper develops such a domain model, and, in so doing, documents a conceptual PML (process modeling language).

As identified above, numerous people have worked on process modeling and have identified many concepts that need to be represented in PMLs. These concepts might be organized into the following areas: 1) Core PM issues, 2) Constraint-oriented issues, 3) Goal-oriented issues, 4) Process Improvement issues, 5) Enactment issues, and a number of 6) Miscellaneous issues that do not warrant separate areas at this time.

We now develop our domain model one area at a time, with each area being identified by a different graphical notation in Figure 1. For instance, the core process modeling concepts are boxed with solid lines, while the constraint-oriented constructs are boxed with dotted lines. Each of the five areas is similarly identified.

Core Process Modeling Constructs

As identified by Curtis, Kellner, & Over (1992) and almost all others working on process modeling, activities and deliverables are the most commonly-identified core process modeling issues. Activity-sequencing is also a central concern, but since there are so many questions and issues associated with activity sequencing it is frequently addressed separately and we have chosen to consider it separately.

An activity is a task or operation performed in order to reach a goal (WfMC, 1994). An activity can be fundamental, and therefore indivisible (atomic), or it can be high-level and composed of sub-activities (WfMC, 1994).

Activities generally produce or depend on deliverables. An activity that depends on, or uses, a deliverable requires that deliverable as input. An activity may optionally produce one or more deliverables as output. These core process modeling constructs are illustrated in Figure 1 as classes outlined with solid lines.

Constraint-Oriented Constructs

The second most frequently-identified issues in process modeling involve the sequencing of activities and the specification of constraints on activities and deliverables. What is the order in which a specified set of activities should be performed? In what ways is the performance of these activities constrained? What are the rules that define if or when an activity may be performed? What assertions must be true before, during, or after an activity is performed? What activities produce a deliverable? What deliverables must be available before an activity can proceed? While these are fundamental process modeling questions, they may be some of the hardest to answer. Constraint-oriented constructs are used to model these issues and are illustrated in Figure 1 as classes outlined with dotted borders.

A "normal sequence" may specify the order in which activities typically occur, repetition (iteration), selection, and whether the activities occur in parallel or not. Normal sequencing of activities, such as the ordering specified in the waterfall model, could be viewed as activity1→activity→ dependencies. In other words, a succeeding activity is dependent on a preceding activity in order to be initiated. There are actually quite a variety of software development process dependencies that can exist, or that might need to be modeled, when documenting a process model. In addition to activity1→activity2 dependencies, there may be activity→deliverable, deliverable→activity, and deliverable1→deliverable2 dependencies.

Activity→deliverable dependencies are where activities produce deliverables, or conversely, where deliverables depend on activities in order to be produced.

Figure 1: Process Modeling Domain Class Model

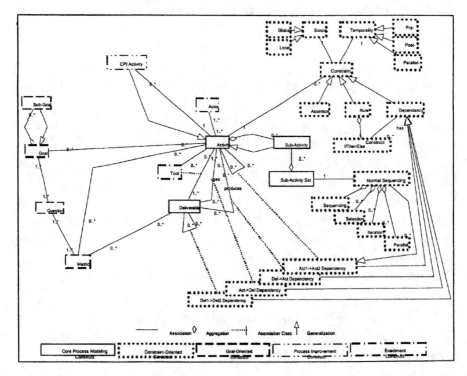

Deliverable→activity dependencies are the complement of activity→deliverable dependencies. In this type of dependency, an activity is dependent on a deliverable; in other words, the activity requires the deliverable (of yet another activity) as input so that it can carry out its task. Finally, a deliverable1→deliverable2 dependency is where a second deliverable requires the existence of the first in order for the second one to be created.

Besides "normal sequencing" and dependencies, two other types of constraints may exist: rules and assertions. A rule is a condition-action pair where, if the condition is true then the action will be performed. Rules are basically if-then-else statements with several additional constructs attached. Some rules will be local in scope to certain activities; they will be relevant only while these activities are running. Other rules may be global in nature; they are applicable throughout the process model. Rules may be active before, at the same time as, or after activities run.

Sometimes it is necessary to specify that certain statements of fact be true at various points in a process. Assertions represent these statements of fact. Assertions are simply conditions, just like the conditions in Rules. However, Assertions have no Actions associated with them — an Assertion's condition must simply be true, locally or globally, and before, during, or after whatever activities it is associated with.

From the discussion above we can see that all Constraints are global or local, and may be temporally active before (pre), while (parallel to), or after (post) their associated Activities are executing. From this, we can then see that Dependencies are specific types of constraints. For instance, an activity→deliverable dependency can be seen as a post-constraint: namely, the deliverable will be completed after the activity is carried out - the deliverable will be produced as a result of the activity. Alternatively, we could see an activity→deliverable dependency as a pre-constraint: the activity must be carried out before the deliverable can exist. Constraint-oriented constructs are indicated in Figure 1 as classes with dotted borders.

Goal-Oriented Constructs

For those who must perform them, activities, their sequencing and constraints, and associated deliverables (inputs and outputs) are of prime concern. However, for those who are charged with managing the organization, the activities are simply the means to reaching the organization's goals. In fact, totally different sets of activities, constraints, etc. might conceivably accomplish the same set of goals. Or, conversely, different goals might be met by the same set of activities.

In order for management to assess how well activities accomplish goals, there must be some relationship between the two. The GQM (Goal-Question-Metric) paradigm Basili (1992) provides a framework for relating goals to activities and for assessing how well goals are met. As originally defined in the GQM paradigm, *goals* are things an organization wants to accomplish, sets of *questions* are asked to determine if the goals are being met, and *metrics* are used to collect data to provide answers to questions.

While not originally applied to SWD processes, GQM can be useful in this area as well. Organizations identify goals, and questions are asked and data is collected via various metrics to assess how well these activities are meeting the goals. The classes in Figure 1 with a dashed border illustrate how GQM is tied with the activities and deliverables of a process model.

Process Improvement Constructs

As soon as goals are included in our model, process improvement becomes an interest. Software process improvement (SPI) and continuous process improvement (CPI) refer to the idea that an organization continually attempts to improve the processes it uses for producing software. Thus we include a process improvement area in our model.

CPI is realized through activities, whose sole purpose is to improve the SWD process, which are carried out in parallel with (or before or after) SWD activities. While it would be possible to model CPI activities as regular SWD activities, we have chosen to include explicit CPI constructs because of their unique importance in the SWD process. While CPI activities have all the features of regular SWD activities, they may also be local or global, and may carried out before, after, or in parallel with the SWD activities with which they are associated. In Figure 1, the classes with a dashed and double-dotted border identify the process improvement area.

Enactment Constructs

Finally, we are interested in who performs various activities and in documenting tools that can be used to fully or partially automate certain tasks. In the model these aspects are specified with actor and tool constructs, which indicate how the process is enacted.

Each activity may be performed by one or more actors. For any deliverable produced by or used in an activity, one or more tools may be used to help automate the deliverable's production or maintenance. If an activity is carried out solely by an actor with no help from a tool, the activity is considered manual. If a tool fully carries out an activity, the activity is considered automated. Tool-assisted activities are carried out by actors with the help of tools. The classes in Figure 1 with a dashed and dotted border identify the enactment area's constructs.

SUMMARY

This paper has suggested that if "software processes are software too," then so are software process *models*, and hence software process modeling systems might benefit from following similar approaches as those recommended for software development in general. Currently, approaches such as the Unified Process recommend the construction of a variety of models – such as a domain class model – during software development. In this paper we presented a process modeling domain class model that documents key constructs that are important in process modeling, organized into five fundamental areas. By focusing on this larger perspective, by formally documenting this model, and by including a broader range of constructs than are usually included in current process modeling systems, this paper is intended to be a stimulus in designing better and more useful process modeling systems.

ENDNOTES

1   With due respect to Osterweil (1987), "Software Processes are Software Too."
2   Many people use the terms *object* and *class* interchangeably; however, the Unified Process and the UML (Unified Modeling Language) distinguish between the two. A class model describes general categories, while an object

model describes specific instances. Class diagrams have been a part of the OO (Object-Oriented) design culture for quite some time, and are a central part of the UML as defined by Booch, Rumbaugh, and Jacobson (1999).

REFERENCES

Arbaoui, S. and Oquendo, F. (1994). Goal oriented vs. activity oriented process modelling and enactment: Issues and perspectives. *3rd European Workshop on Software Process Technology (EWSPT'94)*, Feb 7-9, 1994, Villard de Lans, France.

Barghouti, N. S. and Kaiser, G. E. (1992). Scaling up rule-based software development environments. *International Journal of Software Engineering and Knowledge Engineering,* 2(1), 59-78.

Basili, V. R. (1992). Software modeling and measurement: The goal/question/ metric paradigm. *Computer Science Technical Report Series CS-TR-2956, UMIACS-TR-92-96*, September. College Park, MD: University of Maryland.

Booch, G., Rumbaugh, J. and Jacobson, I. (1999). *The Unified Modeling Language User Guide*. Reading, MA: Addison-Wesley.

Conradi, R., Fernstrom, C., Fuggetta, A. and Snowdon, R. (1992). Towards a reference framework for process concepts. *2nd European Workshop on Software Process Technology (EWSPT'92)*, Sep 7-8, 1992, Trondheim, Norway.

Curtis, B., Kellner, M. I. and Over, J. (1992). Process modeling. *Communications of the ACM*, 35(9), 75-90.

Dowson, M. (1987). Iteration in the software process: Review of the 3rd international software process workshop. *Proceedings of the 9th International Conference on Software Engineering (ICSE'87)*.

Dowson, M. (1993). Software process themes and issues. *2nd International Conference on the Software Process (ICSP'93/ICSP2)*, Feb 25-26, Berlin, Germany.

Engels, G. and Groenewegen, L. (1994). SOCCA: Specifications of coordinated and cooperative activities. In Finkelstein, A., Kramer, J. and Nuseibeh, B. (Eds.), *Software Process Modelling and Technology*, 71-102. New York: John Wiley & Sons.

Feiler, P. H. and Humphrey, W. S. (1993). Software process development and enactment: Concepts and definitions. *Proceedings of the Second International Conference on the Software Process: Continuous Software Process Improvement*, Feb 25-26, Berlin, Germany.

Finkelstein, A. (1989). Not waving but drowning: Representation schemes for modelling software development. *11th International Conference on Software Engineering (ICSE'89)*, May 15-18, Pittsburgh, PA, USA.

Humphrey, W. S. (1989). *Managing the Software Process*. Reading, MA: Addison-Wesley.

Humphrey, W. S. (1995). *A Discipline for Software Engineering*. Reading, MA: Addison-Wesley.

Jacobson, I., Booch, G. and Rumbaugh, J. (1999). *The Unified Software Development Process*. Reading, MA: Addison-Wesley.

Jarke, M., Jeusfeld, M. A., Quix, C. and Vassiliadis, P. (1998). Architecture and quality in data warehouses. *Proceedings of the 10th International Conference on Advanced Information Systems Engineering (CAiSE'98)*, June 8-12, Pisa, Italy.

Kellner, M. I., Briand, L. and Over, J. W. (1996). A method for designing, defining, and evolving software processes. *Fourth International Conference on the Software Process (ICSP'96/ICSP4)*, Dec 2-6, Brighton, UK.

Lehman, M. M. (1997). Process modelling–Where next? *19th International Conference on Software Engineering (ICSE'97)*, May 17-23, Boston, MA.

Osterweil, L. J. (1987). Software processes are software too. *9th International Conference on Software Engineering (ICSE'87)*, April 1987.

Paulk, M., Weber, C., Curtis, B. and Chrissis, M. B. (Eds.). (1995). *The Capability Maturity Model: Guidelines for Improving the Software Process*. Reading, MA: Addison-Wesley.

Rolland, C., Souveyet, C. and Moreno, M. (1995). An approach for defining ways-of-working. *Information Systems*, 20(4), 337-359.

Rumbaugh, J., Jacobson, I. and Booch, G. (1999). *The Unified Modeling Language Reference Manual*. Reading, MA: Addison-Wesley.

Starke, G. (1994). Why is process modelling so difficult? *3rd European Workshop on Software Process Technology (EWSPT'94)*, Feb 7-9, Villard de Lans, France.

Sutton, Jr., S. M. and Osterweil, L. J. (1997). The design of a next-generation process language. *Proceedings of the 6th European Software Engineering Conference (ESEC'97); 5th ACM SIGSOFT Symposium on the Foundations of Software Engineering (FSE'97)*, September, Zurich, Switzerland, 142-158.

Workflow Management Coalition. (1994). *WfMC Workflow Reference Model*. Downloaded version 1.1, dated 29-Nov-94, from www.aiim.org/wfmc October 1997.

Chapter 21

A Process Model for Certification of Product and Process

Hareton Leung and Vincent Li
Hong Kong Polytechnic University, Hong Kong

Software certification has become more and more popular, especially for software developers, as it can provide confidence to customers that the product is of acceptable quality. Software certification can be done at two levels: the development process and the software product itself. There are many different certification schemes, such as ISO 9001 and CMM for development process, and Y2K compliance for software product. This chapter first identifies two process models, one for process certification and another for product certification. We then propose a certification process for Commercial off-The-Shelf (COTS) product and its development process. Finally a generalized model of certification process (GCM) for both product certification and development process certification is developed. Example certification schemes are then mapped to this model to illustrate its validity. The evaluation shows that the popular certification schemes fit well into GCM. GCM may be used as a basis to develop a certification scheme for particular application domains or to validate a particular certification process.

INTRODUCTION

In recent years, *certification* has gained prominence in the standards world. In fact, it has its origins in the very foundation of standardization. Certification is the procedure by which a third party gives written assurance that a product, process or service conforms to specified characteristics. Certification involves an assessment process, which compares the actual measurements of the characteristics of interest with the specifications of those characteristics.

Previously published in *Challenges of Information Technology Management in the 21st Century*, edited by Mehdi Khosrow-Pour. Copyright © 2000, Idea Group Publishing.

Figure 1: Use of Certification

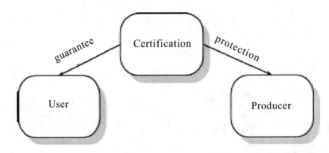

Both ISO and IEEE define certification similarly. According to ISO, conformity certification is "the action of certifying by means of a certificate of conformity that a product or service is in conformity with specific standards or technical specifications" (Geneva, 1980). IEEE defines conformity certification as "the process of confirming that a system, software subsystem, or computer program is capable of satisfying its specified requirements in an operational environment" (Neumann, 1989).

Historically, software certification is an extension of system certification. In most systems, software is only one of the components. As shown in Figure 1, certification can serve as:

- a guarantee to the customer that the software product possesses a certain set of well defined attributes that makes it suitable for its intended use, and
- a protection for the producer against costly legal suits by the customer, when the customer is not satisfied with the product.

Software certification can be done at two levels: *process certification* and *product certification*. Historically, as software was perceived as intangible, a common way to certify software was to rely on the thoroughness of its development methodology. This led to the certification of process. The basic assumption is that the development process can assure that the developed product complies with its specifications.

Recently, developing software systems from Commercial Off-The-Shelf (COTS) components has received great attention, as it promises a more cost-effective way for software development (Voas, 1999; Voas, 1998; Software Engineering Institute, 1995). However, there is often difficulty in selecting the right COTS and gaining confidence that the COTS will function as advertised. An objective of this study is to develop a certification model for COTS products, to ensure the quality and functionality of the COTS products, as well as to give confidence to the customers of COTS products. Also, a general certification model is needed to act as a basis to develop a certification scheme for particular application domains and to validate a particular certification process.

Section 2 discusses process certification and product certification. Some examples of each type of certification will be given. Section 3 first outlines the Process Certification (PCC) model and Product Certification (PDC) model, and then compares these certification models. Also, certification processes for COTS product and its development process are discussed in this section. Section 4 proposes a generic certification model, which encapsulates both the PCC and PDC models. Section 5 provides the conclusion.

CERTIFICATION

Process Certification

A commonly used definition of software quality is "the totality of features and characteristics of a product or service that bear on its ability to satisfy stated or implied needs" (Neumann, 1989). Given this definition there would appear to be no such thing as process quality. However, by implication a quality process is one which leads to the production of a quality product.

One approach to achieving high quality is to use an effective and defined production process. There is, however, no general agreement on the exact nature of such a process. Quality Management Standard (QMS) such as ISO 9001 and maturity model provides a baseline for an adequate production process by constraining the process to fulfil certain key requirements. It is hoped that companies, which follow the QMS, will have the capability and commitment to produce quality products. Two examples of process certification are described as follows.

ISO9001 Quality Management

A popular leading international QMS adopted for software development is ISO 9001. In applying ISO 9001 to software it has to be recognized that software differs in a number of ways from other industrial products, and that the processes used to produce software are not typical industrial processes. ISO 9000-3 helps to address some of these differences with reference to the software lifecycle and supporting activities. ISO 9001 certification assessment is divided into three steps: exchange information and prepare for the assessment, perform an on-site assessment and evaluate the result, and renewal audit on a regular interval.

Bootstrap Assessment Method

BOOTSTRAP is an European method for software process assessment and improvement (Card, 1993). It enhanced and refined the Capability Maturity Model (CMM) developed at the Software Engineering Institute (SEI) for software process assessment (Humphrey, 1995), and adapted it to the European software industry. Bootstrap designed a very detailed process quality attribute hierarchy and enhanced the SEI Questionnaire by taking into account the ISO 9000-3 guidelines for software quality and the European Space Agency (ESA) PSS-05 software engineering standards. In addition, it refined the SEI maturity level algorithm to calculate a maturity level for each of the individual process quality attributes. Thus, the result of the assessment is a process quality profile, which clearly identifies strengths and weaknesses of the process. This quality profile serves as a quantitative basis for making decisions on process improvement. BOOTSTRAP can also be used as a preparation for the ISO 9001 certification.

Bootstrap assessment consists of three steps: briefing section, assessment preparation, and on-site assessment visit.

Product Certification

Another level of software certification is the product certification. Product certification involves directly assessing the equivalence of key attributes of software at the level of its specifications, as well as behaviour. The notion of software product quality can be decomposed into a number of characteristics (McCall, Richards & Walters, 1977; Boehm et al., 1978; Hausen; Ross, 1989). Such characteristics typically include: reliability, usability, functionality, maintainability, correctness, portability and testability.

The first definition of the characteristics of software product quality appears in the Factor-Criteria-Metric model of McCall (1977). This model assumes that there are a number of high-level quality factors (e.g., usability) and that these factors may be defined in terms of some criteria (e.g., modularity). The lowest level is the metrics, which measure the criteria. Other well-known quality models include Gilb's method of designing by objectives (Gilb, 1987).

The ISO/IEC 9126 also defines a set of software product quality characteristics, which is a useful baseline for product assessment activities (ISO/IEC 9126, 1991). The ISO/IEC 9126 quality model is given in Figure 2.

Two examples of product certification are described as followed.

Figure 2: ISO/IEC 9126 Quality Model

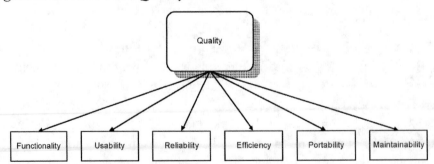

Department of Defense Y2K Certification Process

The Department of Defense Y2K certification process is a structured process that is used to validate the effectiveness of the Y2K renovation solutions through a combination of test data review and independent test of the solution in an operationally representative environment (DoD Y2K Certification Process). The process provides the quantitative evidence that expected diligence was employed during the renovation effort and that the renovated system is ready for deployment. The Y2K certification process consists of 3 main stages: preparation, assessment and evaluation.

Hong Kong Article Numbering Association's Software Certification Program

The Hong Kong Article Numbering Association (HKANA) Software Certification Program (SCP) is a software testing service offered by the HKANA (1987). It aims to check the compliance of a software application to the European Article Numbering Association International Electronic Data Interchange (EDI) standard (EANCOM). Under the SCP, a set of pre-defined testing material will be provided to the SCP Executor to test the software developer's application. The testing material focuses on the conformance of local EANCOM standard and the capability of the software application in translating information into EDI EANCOM standard documents and to communicate with selected networks and HKANA's EZ*Trade service. The SCP certification process is divided into 4 stages: application, software developer internal quality check, external on-site audit, and certification.

CERTIFICATION MODELS

This section will first present two certification models, one for process certification and another for product certification. We then adopt these models to the certification for COTS product and the certification of development process of COTS product respectively. Note that there are two key participants of the certification process: the certification body and certificate applicant (or the software developer). They play different roles in the process.

For the presentation of the certification process, we have adopted the IDEF0 notation (Klinger). Boxes within the figure depict the sub-activities of the activity named by the figure. Arrows between boxes depict availability of work products to activities. Arrows entering the left side of a box are inputs to the activity. Arrows exiting the right side of a box are outputs from the activity. Arrows entering the top of a box are controls that regulate the activity, and those entering the bottom are mechanisms that support the activity. A sequential ordering of boxes does not necessarily imply a sequential flow of control between activities.

Figure 3: PCC Model

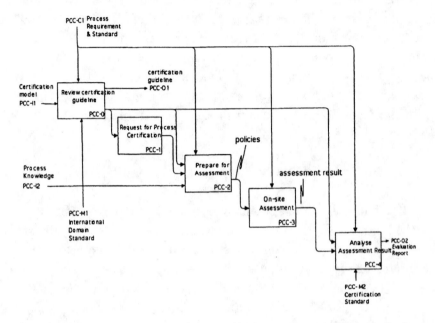

ProCess Certification (PCC)

Figure 3 shows the model of Process Certification (PCC). There are five major stages.

PCC-0: Review certification guideline

The certification body will study the process requirement, analyse the relationship between the process requirement and the certification model, and identify some important requirements. It will then issue and publish the certification guidelines. An applicant will study the certification model and process requirement, and gather some important information for process implementation. It then implements the certification requirement into the production process before the process assessment.

PCC-1: Request for process certification

After the implementation of the certification requirement in its production process, the applicant will apply for certifying the production process and submit an application form to the certification body. The certification body will process the certification request and generate an application number to identify each certification.

PCC-2: Prepare for assessment

The certification body will prepare the assessment guidelines and certification requirements to assess the production process of the applicant. It may provide a pre-assessment service and audit training to the applicant. The applicant should ensure that the production processes fulfil the requirement of certification. The applicant then requests for certifying the process.

PCC-3: On-site audit

The certification body will send assessors to the applicant's development site. Assessors will follow the assessment and certification guidelines to collect the process information and assess the applicant's production process. The applicant should provide the necessary information to help assessors to assess the production process. Finally, the assessors should produce an assessment report.

PCC-4: Analyse assessment result

The certification body will evaluate the assessment result to determine whether the production process passes the assessment. It will send the final result back to the applicant. The applicant should analyse the assessment result to identify areas for improvement. Generally, the certification body should evaluate its certification guideline after each certification to ensure that it keeps pace with the environmental and technological changes.

Certification for Development Process of COTS(CDPCC)

Next we illustrate a potential use of PCC by adopting it to certifying the development process of COTS. We will assume that a slightly modified waterfall model will be used for the development of COTS. The only difference between the traditional development and COTS component development is the scope of the development. Traditional development may develop a large system which contains many features, such as database, accounting, security, etc. A COTS component will mainly focus on one specific feature. The development process for COTS is largely the same as the traditional development. Thus, we can apply the PCC model in certifying the development process of COTS. But some points should be noted during process assessment of COTS.

1. In the COTS development, the most important part of the product is the interface that is used to connect to the main system. In the process assessment phase, the assessor should pay more attention on how the interface is designed and the interface documentation.
2. Another concern is the testing stage. As the buyers of the COTS product will not receive its source code, the only testing they can do is black-box testing. The assessor should pay special attention to the testing process.

Figure 4. PDC Model

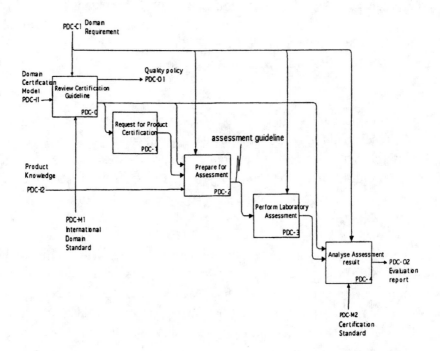

ProDuct Certification (PDC)

Figure 4 shows the process flow of the Product Certification (PDC) model. Like the PCC model, PDC also consists of five major stages.

PDC-0: Review certification guideline

The certification body will study the domain requirement, analyse the relationship between the domain requirement and the domain certification model, and identify some important criteria. It will issue and publish the certification guidelines. An applicant will study the certification model and domain requirement, and gather some important information for product implementation. The applicant then implements the certification requirement into the product before any product assessment.

PDC-1: Request for product certification

After the implementation of the certification requirement in its product, the applicant will apply for certifying the product and submit an application form to the certification body. The certification body will process the certification request and generate an application number to identify each certification.

PDC-2: Prepare for assessment

The certification body will prepare the assessment schedule and assessment material (e.g., test case) to assess the product of the applicant. It may provide some pre-assessment material to the applicant's staffs to familiarize them with the certification process. The applicant should do the pre-assessment to ensure the product can fulfill the requirement of the certification. The applicant then requests for certifying the product when it is ready.

PDC-3: Perform laboratory assessment

The assessors of the certification body will follow the assessment and certification guidelines to assess the applicant's product in the laboratory. The applicant should provide all documentation of product to the assessors. Finally, the assessors should produce an assessment report.

PDC-4: Analyse assessment result

The certification body will evaluate the assessment result to determine whether the product passes the assessment. The certification body may provide detail assessment information to the applicant if the certification failed. The applicant should analyse the assessment result to identify areas for improvement.

Figure 5. CCPD Model

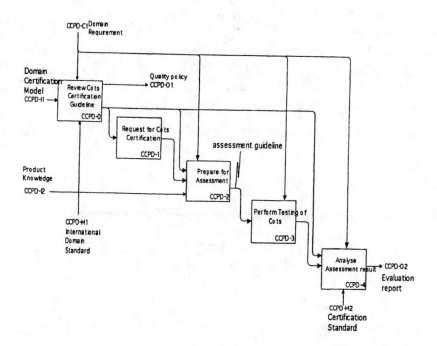

Certification for COTS ProDucts(CCPD)

Figure 5 shows the process flow of the Certification for COTS (CCPD) model. Like the PDC, CCPD also consists of five major stages. Some stages are very similar with the PDC stages. Only CCPD-0 and CCPD-2 are different with PDC-0 and PDC-2 respectively.

CCPD-0: Review COTS certification guideline

The certification body will study the COTS domain requirement, and identify some important criteria. Then it will issue and publish a certification guideline. An applicant will study the certification guideline and domain requirement, and gather some important information for COTS implementation. The applicant then implements the certification requirement into the COTS. For example in the E-commerce area, the producer of COTS for security should study the certification guideline and domain requirement in internet security, and identify the type of security product, such as secure storage, secure web transactions, and secure payment. If the COTS is classified as the secure web transactions, then it may need to be implemented with some of the following approaches, such as Secure Socket Layer (SSL), Secure Hypertext Transfer Protocol (S-HTTP), Private Communication Technology (PCT), and Web Security through the use of Generic Security Service Application Program Interface (GSSAPI).

CCPD-2: Prepare for assessment

The certification body will gather the domain requirement, certification guideline and COTS requirement to prepare the assessment schedule and assessment material to assess the COTS. As the interface of the COTS component is more important than traditional products, the certification body may specially prepare the interface assessment for each COTS component. As the buyers of COTS will not receive its source code, the assessor may decide to use some white-box test cases to evaluate its behaviour. The certification body may also spend more time in designing the system connection to the COTS component. Thus, the prepara-

Table 1: 4-point Similarly Scale

Similarity scale	Degree of similarity
Slightly similar	Less than 25%
Partially similar	26% ~ 50%
Largely similar	51% ~ 75%
Mostly similar	More than 75%

Table 2: Models Comparison

PCC	PDC	Similarity
PCC-0	PDC-0	Mostly similar.
PCC-1	PDC-1	Mostly similar.
PCC-2	PDC-2	Partially similar. PCC-2 needs to generate the assessment guideline for assessing the process, while PDC-2 needs to prepare the assessment material (test case) to assess the product.
PCC-3	PDC-3	Largely similar. Criteria are different. PCC uses subjective criteria, as different assessors may have different interpretation of the assessment guideline. PDC often uses objective criteria based on the test execution result. The locations where the assessment takes place are different.
PCC-4	PDC-4	Mostly similar.

Figure 6: GCM

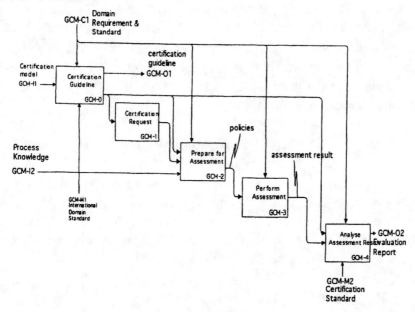

tion for assessment of COTS component may require more effort than that of traditional products. The applicant should do a pre-assessment to ensure the COTS can fulfil the requirement of the certification. The applicant then requests for certifying the COTS when it is ready.

Models Comparison

This section compares the PCC model with PDC model. The focus of the comparison includes the action, input, control, support and output of the process. Table 1 shows the relationship between the scale and degree of similarity.

Table 2 compares PCC to PDC. Both certification models have the same number of stages and are very similar. Most of the procedures of both models have the same purposes and provide similar functions, although they differ in some fine details. For example, PCC-0, PCC-1, and PCC-4 are mostly similar to PDC-0, PDC-1, and PDC-4 respectively. The key difference is that the objective of PCC is on the production process, while that of PDC is on the software product itself.

The other two stages also show a high degree of similarity. For example, the Prepare for Assessment stage of PCC (PCC-2) needs to prepare the assessment guideline to assess the process while the corresponding stage of PDC only needs to prepare the assessment material to assess the product.

For PCC-3 and PDC-3, the major difference is the assessment criteria. PCC involves some degree of subjectiveness, as the assessment is partly dependent on the assessors, while the PDC often uses objective criteria based on the test execution result. Also, in product assessment, PDC will assess the product in a special laboratory which is usually not the applicant's own development site. But the process certification will definitely assess the process at the development site, as the assessors need to appraise the staff's working procedures and the production methodologies.

A Generic Certification Model (GCM)

As discussed in Section 3.3, the main difference between PCC and PDC is the assessment stage. Thus, a Generic Certification Model (GCM) for both certification processes is suggested in Figure 6. The GCM is a natural and obvious adaptation of both PCC and PDC. Its model description is given in Table 3. GCM consists of five stages: certification guideline, certification request, prepare for assessment, perform assessment, and analyze assessment result.

MODEL EVALUATION

This section evaluates the validity of GCM by comparing it to the example certification schemes presented earlier in Section 0. Table 4 summarizes the findings. All four schemes can be easily mapped to the five stages of GCM. Note that although the DoD certification process starts from the assessment and does not formally include the first two stages of GCM, it nevertheless needs to provide the certification guideline to the applicant. It also needs to collect some data before the certification. Therefore the first two stages of GCM are implicitly done.

CONCLUSION

Software certification is an appealing trend as it can greatly improve the overall quality level of software and helps to control the cost of development. This paper

Table 3: GCM Description

		Certification body	Applicant
GCM-0 : *Certification guideline*		Gather the certification model information to issue, update and maintain certification guidelines.	Study the entire domain or process requirement, and domain or process certification model.
	Input:	Certification model	Certification model
	Control:	Domain or process requirement & standard	Domain or process requirement & standard
	Support:	International domain standard	International domain standard
	Output:	Certification guideline	Certification guideline
GCM -1: *Certification request*		Process the application	Send an application to the certification body to request for certification.
	Input:	Domain or process certification model, Certification guideline	Application form, Quality policy
	Control:	Nil	Nil
	Support:	Nil	Nil
	Output:	Application category	Application no., Certification process request
GCM -2: *Prepare for Assessment*		Help the applicant to produce documentation to pass the assessment	Prepare and implement the certification criteria to the whole company, pre-assess it before real assessment.
	Input:	Certification guideline, process knowledge, application category	Certification guideline / memo
	Control:	Domain or process requirement & standard	Domain or process requirement & standard
	Support:	Nil	Nil
	Output:	Assessment material, schedule, certification guideline and documentation	Assessment schedule, quality policy and documentation
GCM -3: *Perform assessment*		Do the assessment	Cooperate with the assessors during the assessment and provide the necessary information.
	Input:	Assessment material and certification guideline	Company policies, process or product information
	Control:	Domain or process requirement & standard	Domain or process requirement & standard
	Support:	Nil	Nil
	Output:	Assessment result	Assessment information
GCM -4: *Analyse assessment result*		Evaluate the assessment result to see if there is something that fail the assessment	Analyse the assessment result and identify improvement if some components fail the assessment
	Input:	Assessment result	Assessment results and its own process or product
	Control:	Domain or process requirement	Domain or process requirement
	Support:	Certification standard	Nil
	Output:	Evaluation result	Improvement list

Table 4: Evaluation of GCM

GCM	ISO9000	Bootstrap	DoD Y2K	HKANA - SCP
GCM -0	Mostly similar.	Mostly similar.	Mostly similar.	Mostly similar.
GCM -1	Mostly similar.	Mostly similar. Although the model does not mention any certification application, it should receive an application before any certification.	Mostly similar. As DoD department needs to ensure all the system in other departments pass the Y2k test. Thus, applicants are invited.	Mostly similar. The applicant needs to apply for the certification and pays the fee.
GCM -2	Mostly similar. The certification body will prepare the assessment guideline & help the applicant to improve the process by meeting the certification requirement. The applicant follows the assessment guideline to improve the process.	Largely similar. During the initial phase, a pre-assessment questionnaire is distributed in order to prepare and collect information. The applicant fills in the questionnaire.	Mostly similar. Before the assessment phase, the applicant needs to collect the test data and generate the test case.	Mostly similar. Before the assessment phase, the certification body prepares the test data and generates the test case.
GCM -3	Mostly similar. Assessors assess the production process in the development site.	Mostly similar. Between 110 & 150 questions are discussed during the on-site visit, which covers all key aspects of the software development process.	Mostly similar. Assessment is done in the laboratory by following the assessment guideline.	Mostly similar. An on-site assessment will be carried out by executing the prepared test cases.
GCM -4	Mostly similar.	Mostly similar. Improvement action planning starts immediately after the on-site visit.	Mostly similar. The applicant provides the evidence that the system is ready to be certified and deployed.	Mostly similar. The applicant verifies the completeness of the report and to clarify any queries that may arise.

proposes a general certification process model which includes both process certification and product certification. We believe that GCM captures the essence of most certification schemes. It can be used as a basis to develop various kinds of process and product certification method. As the GCM components are reusable, they can increase the efficiency and effectiveness to develop a new certification method. GCM can also provide a basis to check whether a certification method has all the key elements required for effective certification.

We also illustrate the model by adopting it to the certification of COTS products. The certification for the development process of COTS is very similar to the process certification model, except that some special attention should be paid to the assessment method. We also believe that these certification guidelines can help to assess and certify the COTS product.

GCM is evaluated by matching it against several process certification and product certification schemes. The result is very encouraging as these schemes fit well into GCM. We will analyse additional certification schemes to further verify the model. We also plan to study the assessment stage in greater details, as it is the most critical part of the certification process. Our aim is to develop an objective method to automate this stage.

REFERENCE

APICS Certification. http://www.apics.org/Certification/cert2top.htm.

Boehm, B. W., Brown, J. R., Lipow, M., MacCleod, G. L. and Merrit, M. J. (1978). *Characteristics of Software Quality*. North-Holland, Amsterdam.

Card, D. (1993). Bootstrap team, "Bootstrap: Europe's assessment method." *IEEE Software*, May, 93-95.

DoD Y2k certification process. http://www.army.mil/army-y2k/ CertificationProcess.htm.

Geneva, *Certification: principles and practice*, International Certification body for Standardization, 1980.

Gilb, T. 'Design by Objective' North-Holland, Amsterdam, 1987.

Guides to Software Evaluation. http://www.scope.gmd.de/documents/EvalGuide/

Hausen, H., *Yet Another Modelling of Software Quality and Productivity*, GMD, Germany.

Hong Kong Article Numbering Association Software Certification Program Information Kit, Document No.: IK980713, Information Technology Division Hong Kong Productivity Council, 1987.

Humphrey, W. S. *The Capability Maturity Model: Guidelines for Improving the Software Process*, Softtware Engineering Institute, Addison Wesley, 1995.

ISO/IEC 9126. (1991). Information technology → Software product evaluation → quality characteristics and guides for their use.

ISO9000 certification process. http://www.qrccentral.com/timeline.htm.

Klingler, C. D. A Practical Approach to Process definition. http://www.asset.com/stars/lm-tds/Papers/ProcessDDPapers.html.

Logica Consultancy Ltd. (1988). *Quality Management Standards for Software*. Logica Consultancy Ltd., London, April.

McCall, J. A., Richards, P. K. and Walters, G. F. (1977). *Factors in Software Quality*, vols. I-III. NTIS AD/A-049-014/015/055, Rome Air Development Center, NY, USA, November.

Neumann, B. D. (1989) *Software Certification*. London; New York: Elsevier Applied Science.

Rae, A. K., Hausen, H. L. and Robert, P. (1995). *Software Evaluation for Certification: Principles, Practice and Legal Liability*. London; New York: McGraw-Hill.

Ross, N. (1989). Version 2.0 high-level data model design. *ESPRIT REQUEST Project*.

Software Engineering Institute. (1995). A commercial/business perspective. *Proceedings of the SEI/MCC Symposium on the Use of COTS in System Architecture and COTS Integration, Special Report CMU/SEI-95-SR-007*, 24, June.

Voas J. (1999). Certification: Reducing the hidden costs of poor quality. *IEEE Software*, July/August, 22-25.

Voas J. (1998). Certifying off-the-shelf software components. *IEEE Software*, June, 53-59.

About the Editor

Salvatore (Sal) Valenti received his degree in Electronic Engineering from the University of Ancona in 1983. Since 1990, he has performed research at the Istituto di Informatica of the University of Ancona. He has tutored a number of Master Thesis students in the fields of Software Engineering and Computer Based Assessment. He has been a member of several research projects funded by the Ministry of University and of Scientific and Technological Research (MURST), by the National Research Council (CNR) and by the European Community. His research activities are in the fields of Software Engineering, mainly in the elicitation of functional specifications in the area of Requirements Engineering, and on Computer Based Assessment. He is the senior assistant professor in Computer Science at the University of Ancona. He has been on the editorial board for the *Journal of Information Technology Education* since 2001. He has reviewed articles in the *Interactive Learning Environments Journal*, *Educational Technology & Society*, *Campus Wide Information Systems Journal*, *Journal of International Forum of Education Technology & Society* and *IEEE Learning Technology Task Force*, and Arizona State University/College of Education's journal, *Current Issues in Education*. For the International Conference of the Information Resources Management Association (IRMA), he was the track chair for "Computer Aided Software Engineering" in 2000 and "Software Engineering" in 2001, and is the track chair for "Virtual Universities" for the 2002 conference. He was on the "Web-based Teaching" panel at the 31st Annual Meeting of the Decision Sciences Institute (DSI 2000), on the "Web-based Education: Changing the Equilibrium?" panel at the 2001 IRMA International Conference, and on the "Web-based Education and Diffusion" panel at the 9th European Conference on Information Systems (ECIS 2001). He has also served on the International Program Committee for several international conferences from 1997 to the present.

Index

W